Winnefred & Agnes

The true story of two women
by Agnes Lottering

KWELA BOOKS

Cover design and typography by Nazli Jacobs
Set in 10 On 12.5pt Sabon
Printed and bound by Paarl Print,
Oosterland Street, Paarl, South Africa
First edition, first printing 2002
Second (revised) printing 2002

ISBN 0-7957-0156-X

I dedicate this book to my children Rhonda, Beryl, Llewelyn, Paul Johnathan and Iris; to Mytell, my son-in-law Kevin, Jessica, Irene, Ivy, my sister, and to Sylvia Osborn, who was my inspiration whilst the work was still in its infancy.

Also to my grandchildren – I love you all equally: Carmel and Gillian Pretorius; Reagan, Rodney-Grant, Michelle and Michael Matthews; Brendon, Leight and Garrad Stoffels; Cassandra Andrea, Alfonso and Ricardo Lottering.

And to my great-grandchildren Zoe and Robin Meintjies Pretorius, Tyrell Matthews Kok and Ronaldo Pretorius Mei.

For Robert Papini: *Umadlathudlathu, umahamba ethapuza ezinqolobaneni zezwe. Thatha mfo kaPapini, thatha*!

For Annari van der Merwe: *Ntombi yokheto! Ecaphuna emthonjeni wengqondo iphuzise inhliziyo, hamba ntombazane hamba*! You go, girl!

Agnes Rorke/Lottering

Agnes Lottering

Author's Introduction

I AM A COLOURED: designated by the apartheid regime an 'Other Coloured'. For I am a true half-and-half mixture of black and white, of Zulu and Irish to be precise – and extremely proud of that.

My father was a Rorke, a descendant of the Rorke who established Rorke's Drift. Three Rorkes – two brothers and a cousin – had come out from County Dublin in Ireland to settle in the Cape of Good Hope in the early nineteenth century. The son of one of these, who was to be known as 'Jim' Rorke, was my great-grandfather. He joined the army in the Cape, then moved to the north and became a First Lieutenant in the Buffalo Border Guard. It was he who established the trading store at what became known as Rorke's Drift, near Isandhlwana. He was also Clerk of the Court in Pietermaritzburg and Government Border Agent in Northern Natal.

His son James Michael Rorke, my grandfather, fought in the Zulu Wars at Isandhlwana and Rorke's Drift, and was apparently not only a gallant soldier but a gallant Casanova too. For he had a roving eye and a restless heart that was never satisfied with one woman. Neither were the women always his own colour. In fact, James Michael Rorke was regarded as something of a Great Chief among the Zulus, noted not only for his gallant deeds but also for having many Zulu wives – and many children. In this he was not alone among the early pioneers – one need only think of John Dunn, who in this regard outdid all the others.

How do we explain this urge, which all the early pioneers seem to have felt? I believe it was related to the fact that they looked at this land and liked what they saw. Imagine what it was like, or what it must have been like in their eyes. It must indeed have seemed a Garden of Eden. The intertwining pathways formed a tapestry of breathtaking beauty; you saw only what the Creator himself had created. It's easy to imagine that the sensational rare beauty of savage Chaka Land could cause a total delirium. My feeling is that nothing could dampen the pioneers' insatiable appetite to conquer that which is rare and primitive.

This was a paradise, indeed a land of milk and honey, a land free for everyone to roam and cultivate at pleasure and leisure. There were no roads, no bridges, no railways and no towns. There was simply no one to harass them for any kind of market or industry. They were therefore independent, self-contained, self-supporting, and very resourceful. The openness and freedom of choice must have overwhelmed them with a kind of frenzy. Sometimes I think of it in the form of a dream – vivid, grotesque, and yet real. An epic in which people and terrain are indistinguishable.

Even the mystic dongas, wearing their ancient blood-stained cloaks – showing a deeper dent here, and an even deeper gash there, as though a sword had left a gaping wound to bleed forever – never bothered the pioneers. Terrifying ravines, with their broken teeth and stubble beards of coarse briars and thistles, and stagey old parched river beds seemed to whisper in a hoarse thirsty undertone to the mountains who bore such strong, unshakeable granite necks. And they all seemed to turn around and utter a croaking sound: 'Hey there, brother – give a man a handshake.'

These pioneers were like knights – not in shining armour – in tattered and torn old battered ten-gallon hats, galloping with the wind, leaving a trail of male essence. In stinking riding breeches and far more stinking long-johns, concealed by old soldiers' uniforms, and smelling worse than their horses' perspiration, they headed, headstrong beyond all measure, straight down the Tugela, down the Ulundi Valley, across the Black and White Umfolozi, down to Pongola and into the waiting arms of Swaziland where some of them found peace and solace at last.

One interesting story about my grandfather, James Michael Rorke, tells how the Great Chief Myeni of Ubombo got to know about this noble white man and summoned him to go to the rescue of his eldest son, who was being held to ransom in a war in Swaziland. Chief Myeni, who inspired fierce respect among his subjects, summoned his trusted indunas to travel to Ngome where the young James Michael lived with his first Zulu wife, who already had a few children, to ask him this great favour. Would he dare to go to the rescue of the Chief's son in Swaziland? This was a risky task, but the brave soldier could not refuse the Chief.

The journey to Swaziland took three days on horseback and somehow James Michael succeeded in the rescue. He had to tie the Chief's son to his stirrup, allowing his weight to hang and float in the Pongola River which was swollen in flood. The safe return home of his son caused great excitement at the Chief's sprawling kraal. It was something unheard of: the whole area was shouting and chanting warrior songs of praise to this gallant white man who had done such a brave deed.

The white soldier had to go back home once the feasting was over, but first the Chief called up the indunas to discuss what reward would be suitable. They gathered in the cattle kraal, as was customary in the Zulu nation – for that is where all big indabas were finalised with the headmen. The Chief asked for order, and while everyone was all ears announced that he would give the white man his daughter in marriage, for that was the dearest and most valuable gift a man could have – a gift to make a man of a man!

James Michael could not refuse. It would have been discourteous and disrespectful not to accept such a gift from the Chief. Of course many cattle were also given to him together with the bride.

Carried by the young virgins of the tribe on a special embroidered grass mat, she was brought to the kraal, where the white man had to thank the Chief by dancing and throwing up a spear, then kneeling down in front of the bride and offering himself to her and praising the ancestors of the Myeni tribe for such a beautiful princess. He had to promise the Great Chief that he would look after her until she grew old.

Then he rode back home to prepare for the wedding feast, which would be held in three weeks' time, because the great trek from Ubombo to Ngome took a week on foot. He had to prepare plenty of Zulu beer, and oxen to be slaughtered. All the village had to be told and friends invited.

With the white man gone, the bride found herself astonished at her father's decision. It is said she cried and asked her father: 'Hawu, Baba wami – why do you give me to a white spook? How will he plough?

How will he make my hut? A man who has no colour – what kind of a man is that? What kind of children will I have? Oh, my great father, you have shamed me! From this day my ancestors have disowned me and I am banished from my people forever, to go and live in a strange country with an even stranger man!'

And she carried on crying and would not eat until her father and the elders spoke to her with soothing words and slaughtered a white goat to bring peace to her troubled heart. Then she ate some food, which pleased the intombis who said a bride must not be skinny, she must have strength to bear the white man's children.

Her own mother suspected that she had been bewitched by the other jealous wives of the Chief. She lamented and said with shame that her womb was not good enough to carry a daughter fitting the Chief's heart, for he had thrown her to the white zombies! Who ever heard of a man who carried no spears and wore no tribal gear? What a stupid isoka he would make for her beloved daughter, whom she had thought would marry a Chief's son of Sobuza's tribe in Swaziland. But it was too late – the Chief had spoken.

Preparations began. The maids of honour worked frantically; clay pots as huge as drums were made, with smaller ones for daily use; wooden spoons for daily cooking and eating; table mats to serve food on, and a whole lot of grass sleeping mats, as the bride wouldn't dream of sleeping on a bed.

The big day came with all the hysteria of drums and chanting. Feasting took a further whole week, and James Michael had to don a bheshu and full Zulu gear as he was given 'a princess from a royal kraal of the Great Chief Myeni' in marriage. What happened at night time in their own hut will of course never be known, but it is good to let your imagination run riot. There must certainly have been misunderstandings on both sides.

This bride from Ubombo then was my granny, my father's mother, and she was given the name Chithekile, meaning 'the one who was forced to leave', 'the banished one' or 'the one who was spilled out'. Sometimes she would even try running back to her own people, but her husband would 'rescue' her even before she crossed the Esikwebezi river, and ride back home with her. Then all would be well for a while. Eventually she tamed down, soothed by brown sugar and sweets and shining trinkets and beads, to become the gracious Mrs Rorke. She learned to sew and cook the white man's food, and wore starched lace petticoats, crocheted by her own hand. Home-made bread was the main pride of her life, and she made the best scones and brewed the strongest Zulu beer for her husband and his friends. She developed a great fondness for Joko tea, and so she was often known as 'Gogo Joko'. Rumour has it that she became so prejudiced against her own origins that she used to call the Zulus around her 'kaffirs': they had no brains, they were lazy, they did not want to change their way of life! Now that she was the white man's wife, she wanted to be an example to her fellows and teach them all how to sew clothes and make bread and scones.

Some grew to hate her, though she was still respected by many. They knew that she was not only the wife of the brave soldier Rorke, whose path they dared not cross, and before whom they all trembled in fear owing to his violent Irish temper, but she was also the Great Chief Myeni's daughter, and still sometimes called 'The Princess'.

My own mother came from a very similar background. Her father was George Nunn, and his father, an Englishman, had been noted for making the spears for Dinizulu's impis. Of high rank, he was the King's blacksmith and answered to Dinizulu for the number of spears he had manufactured – a hard task in those days when there were no proper tools to fashion these heavy metal spears and assegais. He had the same lustful eye for Zulu women as my other ancestor.

So my mother's father's nickname was 'Mgodini', meaning a large hole, because his father took out hot iron from a big hole somewhere in the mountains between Ulundi and Isandhlwana, where Zulu intertribal wars raged fiercely in the nineteenth century. His love for the bush led him to become a game warden at Mkuzi Game Reserve. I might add that I am as proud of my mother's ancestors as of my father's – they too played an important part in our country's history – and you will be hearing a lot more about this side of the family, particularly about my mother herself, whose name was Winnefred.

Like my Rorke grandfather (who had married a white woman, Louise Carter, before his black princess), George Nunn also had more than one wife. First came my mother's mother who was a Miss Dhlomo and who died of malaria after bearing him five children: Rosie, Winnefred (my mother), Gracie, Beatrice, Mary. Later he married by law a Coloured wife called Irene Wilson. Irene Wilson gave him two sons: Benedict and Henry.

Benedict in particular was such a beautiful plump child, with blond hair and blue eyes like violets, that my cousins and I used to fight over who was allowed to carry him. He is still alive and drops in on me now and then, bringing me a packet of brown sugar or some other grocery item.

All these people became closely knit. They looked after one another's material and physical needs with utter dedication and concern, and planned and organised their lives together. It is a pity there is not more in the history books and archives about the original bold and fearless men and their Zulu wives who started it all. 'The marginal man' – that's what the Coloured has been called. It is a pity that so little has been written about the interesting way some of us came into the world – with raw sex certainly not the only factor.

More than half of this book is my mother's story, and it's important for me to explain why. We were very different in temperament. My mother was a rather docile woman. She was shy, and never voiced her opinion. She always wanted to please everyone else except herself and in many ways this meant that she was left to her own devices, with no one to blame but herself. Jessie and Juliana, my sisters, were just like her. I, on the other hand, have a lot of my father's domineering, demanding qualities, and his determination – all this topped with an Irish temper.

My father, Benjamin Rorke, had taken my mother as his wife after his first wife, whom he had loved passionately, died suddenly of a heart attack. She was only thirty years old. He grieved at her death, but life had to go on so he started looking for a spouse. His older brother and uncles found him a girl who had had two children by a man who turned out to be just a drunk. She was almost an outcast – in those days it was a disgrace for a girl to be left in the cold – and worse still, with two brats. My father took her in and married her. She was twenty-eight years old and he was thirty-eight. I was their first child, born on Christmas Day 1937.

Of course it was barely a marriage. Or so it seemed to me. She was abused and scorned, and she was little better than a servant who conceived for her master. When I was nine years old I could barely stand the torture of hearing and seeing my mother being sworn at and occasionally sjambokked like an ox. She had no clothes except what rags she was handed down by my aunties who did not really care whether she lived or died, or if her children lived or starved to death. This was how I saw it at the time. Later when I came to know the full story I realised that it was all more complicated. I hadn't been able to understand why my father seemed to hate and distrust my mother so much – and us children too. When I heard my Aunt Irene's story – shortly after my mother's death – I realised I would have to think through all my memories again.

After her death I discovered I had the need to find out more about her life. But how? Even her brother-in-law, Wallace Rorke, who now lived in Eshowe, seemed very reluctant to fill me in on some of the past. He always evaded the issue when I asked him, and spoke endlessly about the war instead. He never forgot the terrible trauma it caused him. At the same time, as Sergeant Wallace Michael Rorke, never stopped relating what a brave soldier he had been. And then he would tell me to please leave him alone to rest his mind, and not bother him with stupid talk.

I had almost given up hope, when I remembered that Auntie Irene – actually my cousin, though much older – was now in an old-age home where I'd be able to speak to her about my problem. I coaxed her for weeks but she wouldn't buy my nonsense. 'Why do you concern yourself with the past, my child? The past is better buried and left alone. Sometimes the past brings back more pain and confusion and even hate. Leave it be! Don't dig up old bones!'

But something she said about the food at the home got me thinking. I was determined to know the truth. I marched up one day to the old-age home, which was not far from my house, armed with two chicken wings and four madumbis nicely boiled up, with shallots and green chillies to taste. After seeing her beady little grey sunken eyes give a twinkle I knew I'd won. 'Wallace, my brother, is a very proud man. But so am I, I've never wanted to accept that my granny was a black woman. I've always thought of myself as a white woman. For years I've lived in Durban and put my childhood days right behind my head. I hate to think about them too much, but my child I know I am dying and you are so determined. I feel it in my heart to tell you the truth about Uncle Benjy and his wives.'

She asked me to sit her up, and of course, being a distinguished Victorian lady, asked for her make-up, and her hand mirror which was so old but very dear to her. As she said in a whisper: 'Careful, don't break it!' my heart actually leapt for joy! I knew I had won.

With a little croak here, and there a little whisper, and a nudge, a shaking of her head, eyes popping out, occasionally a grimace and a startled look of fear, there came a sudden burst of words and a feverish demand for her lipstick and powder as though she were on stage. And after she had been talking for some time there was a heave, a sigh, a gesture with her feeble hands. 'Agnes my child, I am tired now. Come back tomorrow.'

I was bubbling, as I half ran home to write the first chapter lest I forget. I wrote it as though my mother were speaking it, telling her own story. The next day found my aunt in a better mood. She spoke as if she really wanted to get this load off her heart. They say when you are about to die you tell the truth, and you are then relieved, to die in peace. I thank Auntie Irene for relieving me, for setting my mind at ease, even though I cried almost every night when I thought of what my mother and my father went through. God forgive me a thousand times for hating my father, I had no idea!

And as I wrote every word came with such an overwhelming truth and my heart and my mind began to understand some of the things my mother used to do. Of course, living with my family, knowing them, hearing them speak in anger and hate, I knew exactly how to write my parents' story. I could not only hear the words as they spoke them – I could see how their mouths moved to make the sounds.

PART ONE

Winnefred

Benjamin Rorke

Chapter 1

Winnefred speaks about her mother and her father, about growing up in their home, and about her first lover.

W HEN MY FATHER GEORGE NUNN was a game ranger at Mkuzi, in the early years of the twentieth century, he always had meat around in his house and therefore visitors never ceased. He was also a renowned musician – he played the concertina very well, and so as young girls we had quite a few smashing parties. Everybody came. The wagons and horses, the sledges and horse-drawn carts were all a familiar sight at our home. Oh, my father was so handsome, a whole six feet something, not an ounce of fat, all muscle and big bones. His eyes were like the striking blue of the Pacific Ocean. His nose was like a medieval knight's and his moustache and mouth were curved like a Philistine's. Ladies would faint when he sang and played 'Red River Valley' on his concertina.

He built his home at Matshemhlope, which means White Stone Mountain, and that was where I grew up. It was built from white stones, set in-between two koppies in a garden of nature's choice. For nature chooses many different forms and shapes of living, and no one can interfere or tell her what to do. This house was unusual, breathtakingly rugged and beautiful, and when I was a child it almost seemed unreal.

I was one of five daughters, all considered outstanding beauties, though I say it myself. Rosie, my elder sister, was courted by a Mr Dunn from the famous Natal John Dunn house, and I was courted by a Mr

Jacobson, also a descendant of John Dunn. And this is how it came about.

I remember that first night he came to my home. My mother Roselina asked me to make the tea. I wondered who these people were, who had ridden for three weeks to Nongoma. There were three of them, but this one small little man spoke so fast and the others just kept nodding as he said: 'So you see Mr Nunn, we heard about the job at the sugar mill, and so you see Mr Nunn, we have no place to lay our tired carcasses, our hindquarters are swollen and so are our hoofs. And so you see Mr Nunn, even our eyes are crying as we walk, our ears are singing, and drums are beating inside our brains, and so please Mr Nunn, have pity on your poor sons, and give us a place to sleep, and so Mr Nunn, as soon as we become working men, we will kindly and willingly be paying you Mr Nunn your board which I think will have to be five shillings a month, as we are going to earn fifteen shillings a month. Uhuh-heh-heh.'

As I walked out with the tea like a little lady, I could see three very scruffy-looking men – of course all men looked scruffy in those days, as they were always riding and working very hard – but these had a muddy kind of scruffiness on them, as though they had been rolling in the dirt in their clothes. And as I thought those thoughts, half-giggling to myself, I put the tray down beside them. My father, who was puffing on his pipe, nodded for me to leave, but I could hear the man sighing. Then he carried on with a new tone in his voice.

'Oh Mr Nunn, we've had such bad luck – the tractor rolled right into the crocodile's jaws, and he ate up our pig's-meat and our Jo-sacks and all. The Dutch man couldn't drive the tractor properly, he was still learning. So you see Mr Nunn, we were right at death's dark door. And now the worms are grinding in our stomachs.'

Oh my word, is that why he sighed? There were no sandwiches or scones on the tray.

'Imagine almost being eaten by crocs,' I whispered to my sisters, who were busy cooking on the huge black Welcome Dover. 'You know those men came out of the croc's jaws.'

'You always talk rubbish, you don't even know what a croc is.' That was Rosie. 'Peel the potatoes, and stop dreaming of crocs.'

I heard a hint of agitated sarcasm as my father called me to collect the tray. 'And try to hurry up with the supper; fill up again and bring that mealie-bread.'

The little man's beady eyes followed me and disappeared with me into the kitchen. The other man seemed to be about thirty; he was a tall, thin fellow, with a sallow face with no colour. It was a face all in one tone. He had a large nose hooked on to his cheeks, and blue eyes, and a large skull, supported by a very weak, thin chin. He looked like he was missing his mother. The third man was totally harmless, just a square block of dead, dead flesh. They were all bootless, but the tall, thin one had a few pieces of leather bound about his feet, which could once have been a boot. He kept looking at me sideways whilst trying to push his feet further under the long wooden bench. The others did so as well – there was ample space under the bench, my father's tool-box lived there. A few cobras, and some hedgehogs and frogs sometimes lived there too.

We gave them a good heap of supper, and hot water to bath. They washed their soiled khaki clothes and asked my father for old blankets to wear so they could hang up their washing near the coal stove.

I couldn't sleep thinking about how the poor man was nearly eaten by crocs. I wished he could teach me to talk so fast. He must be very clever, I thought, I had trouble even speaking slowly. My sisters always said my breath smelled terrible because I didn't talk. I didn't know how to start conversing, let alone open my mouth.

I knew my breath smelled. Scrubbing my teeth with carbolic soap never helped, even with a rinse of gum-tree leaves. The smell wouldn't go away, it would just smell fresh for a little while; but if I carried on with gum-tree toothpaste, I'd have green gums and he'd notice I'd been using it. So what? Everybody used it. The nuns at Nkamana School had taught us how to patch very neatly, so I woud patch my pinafore and starch my petticoat with mealie starch. Tomorrow, I must start looking like a lady. I was twenty years old already.

Samson, the square man, had a voice which sounded like grain. The sound of grain being poured into an old enamel basin is something else in comparison with tossing a fish in a frying-pan with fat. Which is how Bingo, the skinny man, sounded. They spoke simultaneously, shuffling shyly, looking for the right words as though they were hiding under the table as chairs.

'With the ladies' permission, can we ask your parents to grace our company? Yes, only the ladies' permission. With the ladies' permission – can – can our company ...'

They looked at each other woefully and tried again.

Teddy, the man I had decided in my own mind to call the Parrot, sensed the stupidity of his friends so he chirped like the gramophone squeaking without a new needle.

'Excuse me, please, ladies, we would like to invite you to ride with us to Manzini on Saturday next week. There will be a smashing party. One of the Henwoods' daughters is turning twenty-one.'

Now everyone who knew the Henwoods understood that they were like Royal Family, very wealthy people. So Teddy, Bingo and Samson were trying to impress us by letting us know that they were acquainted with and socialized with very rich people.

'Mama, Mama, Mama. Please, please ask Father for permission for us to go to Manzini.'

'Hawu maSwati!'

'Mama, there is a twenty-first birthday party at the Henwoods'. Mama, please, beg Father for us, we want to go with Teddy and Bingo and Samson.'

'Mama Nkhosi! You girls are going with fools. Iziphukuphuku. They always seem to be in shock.'

My mother shook her head in disapproval of these iziphukuphuku until her hair combs fell off. She had so many of them, securing her hard, tight hair in a hairnet, that it sometimes looked like she had no hair, but wore a cap of steel clips and hair combs of all shapes and colours. She also wore big earrings shaped like roses or dahlias, and a string of water pearls given to her by her husband's grandmother, who was very wealthy and went back to England to die there. She was a stunning woman – very fancy – and fair-skinned with huge rolling eyes that were always ready to cry, or else twinkle when she was ready to laugh. No wonder my father really loved and respected her. Their five daughters are proof of this. Even though he was a Casanova he never made outside children.

So she huffed and puffed, flouncing up and down, taunting and criticizing in her own language. She would show these so-called 'blue-bloods' that her daughters could surpass anyone in beauty and comeliness.

My father would agree, as it turned out.

'Girls, remember George Nunn is your father. I will not be disgraced.'

He gave us two shillings and sixpence to buy yards of cloth to sew new frocks. As for Teddy, Bingo and Samson, their savings for Christmas never reached their homes. They went to the store at Pongola and came back with Five Roses packets full of their new clothes: three-piece pin-striped double-breasted suits, ties to match. Zobo pocket watches. Battersby top hats.

Our outfits were lovingly packed in Father's old battered leather portmanteau. We were actually off to the Henwoods, this was like a dream come true. The boys had asked for a lift on the cart that belonged to the mill. This mule-drawn cart always went to deliver post at Manzini, it travelled light and so could take a heavy load with ease, but we had to walk three miles from home to the mill. My mother was just as excited as we were, and even my father managed to beam.

My mother Roselina was shrieking: 'Winnie, don't forget to grind some gum-tree leaves and put some of the pulp into a small container to take with you. Rosie, please don't laugh too loud, try to laugh like a lady. Your eyes get too small when you laugh too much. Gracie, stop being too saucy and talking too much till your freckles look like ants on your face.'

We could hear the echo of her voice as we headed for the mill. 'And don't look at the boys, wait till they look at you first, and don't ...'

The Usutu River was swollen, but this was where the cart crossed every Saturday morning. The boys were over the moon. This was far better than Christmas. We sat giggling with excitement, hearts pounding, visualizing all sorts of romantic encounters, whispering in undertones: what colour must his eyes be, what colour must his hair be, how should his moustache be curved, how should his tobacco smell, how long must his hair be ...?

The boys whistled such joyful tunes but the Parrot did the best. He couldn't stop chirping and when he whistled the latest tune, the fastest jive beat, he kept throwing amorous glances backward.

'Give me five minutes more, only five minutes more, let me stay, let me lay, in your arms.'

Samson and Bingo were serenading the mule to trot a little faster. Gracie was hysterical and Rosie nudged her hard and told her to stop or she'd wee all over her broekies. She always wee'd on her broekies when she laughed too hard. What on earth would the boys say?

Plonk, plonk, plonk, went the mule. The river crept along like a silent snake, her dirty colourless eyes riveted on her prey; she had a hideous, ominous stare. Her body had a blueish, blackish glint in the afternoon sun – and then she pounced. Blnk, bu-bu-bu-blsh-sh-sh-sh.

We all gave one last haunted scream before departing from the earth and gasping for breath as the monster swallowed us. Teddy, Bingo, Samson, Rosie, Winnie, Gracie. Oh, and the mule.

We could hear one another's hiccups and gasps and half screams, and then no more. I knew we would all be dead in a matter of seconds. Oh God, please save us. I wanted to go to the Henwoods, not to a watery grave. Teddy's voice sounded like a dying pig.

'Gracie, hold on to Winnie. Rosie, hold on to Samson.' And he was submerged again. 'Gasp-gasp. Haaa-aaa. My suit. Catch my suit. Bingo, B I N G O – O!'

Gasping and vomiting, I clung on to my beloved sisters, who were gasping and vomiting too. We couldn't scream, we were all choking and gasping so painfully.

Gracie managed a piercing shriek. I knew she was dying.

I cried out loud: 'God bless her, my poor sister, she is dying now, all through me. Rosie, Rosie!'

We seemed to be sinking even deeper, as I heard Samson gurgling and gasping. But his tough arms were around Gracie, and Bingo, who was so tall, had the reins, standing on the tip of the cart, as he pulled with all his strength. Teddy helped him along and, gurgling and shouting for dear life, told Rosie to hold on to Samson.

'Heave her up. Heave her up.' All of a sudden we could all see one another's heads, we seemed to be floating. Finally the mule came up as if from the belly of the monster. She coughed and sneezed and water spewed out of her mouth, as though cursing under her breath. She boldly swayed, and pulled us out of danger.

Nobody screamed now. We were all sniffing and gurgling for breath, coughing out all the water that had almost filled our bellies. The mule shook her body so violently I thought she would topple back into the river, and Bingo jumped to shoo her further up. She let out an angry wail and carried on into the thicket, and Samson snorted like an angry bull: 'You damn bloody fool. We'll never catch that mule again. We could still have reached the Henwoods' place by tonight.'

Only then did the full impact of what had happened to us, or rather what could have happened to us, take shape in our dim and distorted minds. Oh my God, we nearly all drowned. What happened?

And with that, with one thing uppermost in our minds, we all started accusing one another of having been negligent and careless, we girls shrieking abuse at the boys:

'Damn bloody fools, idiots, what kind of men are you anyway? How can you boys let us drown? You all can't even drive a mule cart. You all are going to pay for our clothes and my father is going to shoot you all one by one, he trusted you, now look what you've done.'

Samson said: 'Bingo, you said you know how to drive a mule cart, now we're all in big peril.'

'Ja, because you said you smaak the stukkie.'

'Ja, you also said you smaak Rosie and you said you smaak Winnie.'

They seemed to forget that we were all ears. Forgetting our sorrow and wet clothes, and the suitcase that had flowed away, we all burst into gales of pure heartfelt laughter.

The sound of a roaring tractor brought us back to our woe; so as we boarded the tractor, we were very silent, very wet and very hungry.

My father gave the boys hell, and a sjambok hiding. We could hear them pleading for mercy and my mother went in to speak for them.

'Oh, my husband, please leave the boys now, they've suffered enough. I've always known that they were fools.'

A week after that episode, we were still mourning the loss of our clothes and talking about what could have been at the Henwoods' mansion. The boys were just as sad, they hardly exchanged glances with us, let alone words.

A week or two later, I was fetching the clothes in from the washing line. Deep in thought, I was wondering about growing up and falling in love, when I felt a hand touching me. As the washing all dropped down on the soft lawn, Teddy's grip was far tighter than the one I had for the washing.

'Winnie, I love you babe, be mine, until the stars no longer shine, until the moon drops down dead.'

I wanted to laugh, but I thought of my bad breath so I just kept very still in his strong arms.

'Do you love me too?'

'I'll tell you tomorrow.'

We courted for a few weeks. After one month I was in the family way. No one knew, apart from my sister Rosie. Then one day I said to her: 'I am giving birth any minute, please, warm some water for me, and tell Mama.'

My mother came in shrieking. 'What do I do, where do I hide my child, and my grandchild?'

She started to and fro, but everything was over in no time, and I gave birth to a bonny boy. She immediately wrapped the baby up and told me to pad myself up as she was taking me to her own home, to her mother. I was the second born, and not married to Teddy. This was a disgrace to her name as Mrs Nunn. My Swazi granny must hide me, till the baby was weaned.

I was crying, and didn't hear my father's voice as he peered into the bedroom, red and blue like lightning with rage. 'Where do you think you are taking my child to, you stupid, stupid savage?' he said to my mother. 'Do you think I want my child raised by some more savages?'

She darted outside to cry and wail in the garden. The second baby came one year after that, and still Teddy said nothing about marriage.

Chapter 2

Winnefred tells of their move to Esikwebezi, as well as the stories of Benjamin Rorke's marriage to his first wife and his grief over her death. Winnefred has her first encounter with Benjamin.

MY FATHER'S ELDER SISTER ROSIE met and married Walter Rorke from Ngome Forest Reserve. She trekked along with her people all the way to Esikwebezi where Walter had built himself a home. And my father George was to trek along there with his own daughters as well – but his Swazi wife would be left behind in a beautiful white-stoned grave just near her beautiful white house; for she, my mother, had by then died of malaria.

When we shifted to Esikwebezi, I missed my mother terribly. And also my home and the sweet sad lonely memories of Teddy, my first love.

My father soon found himself a very young woman who was from Nkamana or thereabout. She fell in love with this middle-aged man, who was the most awesome male she had ever seen. She had grown up without a father – in fact she had never seen him, as he had left her Zulu mother and went back to England while she was very little. And so she had no brothers and sisters, and had been brought up by the missionaries at Nkamana Mission School. Her name was Irene Wilson. She herself was not a beauty, but she had features that were unique and a beautiful spirit. She was hard-working, and anxious to please her husband with all her abilities.

My stepmother and I grew close in Esikwebezi. We were both new-comers in this new land. The master of the homestead was Walter Rorke. He had a brother, the youngest one, whose name was Benjamin, and who lived with his old father and mother at the homestead at Ngome Forest. I had heard all about Benjamin's wedding to Katrina, a beautiful girl from Utrecht, who spoke Afrikaans. Her wedding was very special as she came by chariot, all the way from her home, to mar-ry a prince, the most striking, handsome man anyone could dream of.

Messengers came from Ngome to say Benjamin and Katrina were going to Utrecht to see her dying father, who was very old and sickly. Benjamin asked his brother Walter for help in looking after their two small children, as they didn't know when they'd be back. Katrina's fa-ther passed away; but when they returned from the graveyard, just as they entered the house, Katrina had a heart attack and died.

Benjamin was beside himself with grief. His little daughter Ivy was only six years old, and his son Stephen was only two and a half. His old father was grieved too; and his mother who loved Benjy, him be-ing the last born, wouldn't eat for days, especially when she heard that he had wanted to throw himself in the grave as he couldn't believe that his young bride was dead.

Benjamin mourned his wife Katrina for a full three years. He be-came thin and gaunt, and silver threads began to glisten out of his black shining curls. His cheek bones became more hollow, his brow creased at every gaze – he often gazed into nothingness – and often tears would fill his dark brown eyes. One never saw the jawline break-ing into easy laughter anymore, showing off a row of glistening pearls set in such perfection. He was now heading for thirty-seven and was the most breathtaking heart-throb of a man there ever was.

His friends and his father's friends had tried in vain to entice him to go hunting, but he showed no interest. He would cuddle his little chil-dren and say, what if a leopard or a lion mauled him, they would be orphaned – he couldn't go hunting. They brought beautiful young ladies to the homestead to befriend him but he simply showed no in-terest.

One day I heard the sound of thunder and I shouted to my mother to bring the washing in for me.

'Now Winnie, why must the washing be brought in as it is not yet quite dry? Children's clothes must be properly dried out, and it is not yet sundown.'

'Oh my Mama, can you not hear the sound of thunder?'

'No, no, no, Winnie – it is the sound of the knight's horse's hoofs; there he is taking off the saddle from his horse whose name is Frank and not Thunder. Winnie, come and gaze at your knight, he truly is bewitching. Oh, this is what you call a man. Winnie come on, come quickly, and look at him before he disappears into the house …'

He visited his brother Walter many times. I had been scared to look at him properly; but on one particular day – it was very early in the morning as the sun slowly brushed away a fluffy cloud and opened her eyes to gaze upon mother earth – I took a long look at this knight. He seemed to have come out of the sun, even his horse looked unreal, shining from the first streaks of sunshine. They both looked like they had just arrived from another planet. I stood dumbstruck on our little verandah, and wondered if he could see me. I didn't want him to see me in a long hooded nightdress so I darted inside to wash and change into a floral pinafore dress, and went straight into my garden. I wanted him to see me in the garden. So he'd think I was an early bird, and loved gardening, and would think of me making a good wife.

Out of the corner of my eye I could see him striding into the cattle kraal which was just on the bank of the river, quite near our homestead. I took a bucket and headed for the river with some of my children's washing so he would think I was a good woman, and hardworking. I wished with all my heart I had never met Teddy. Now I was spoiled. No man would even talk to me. Benjamin knew all about me by now but he never even looked at me the way a man looks at a woman. I was quite pretty. Just not fancy, as I had no fancy clothes, so I was plain Jane. I felt so foolish, trying to get him to notice me – tears welled up from my broken heart. (Oh Teddy, I thought you loved me.)

I sensed someone behind me as I was on my knees washing the clothes and deep in thought; my pinafore was tucked in my drawers and instantly I pulled my dress down to hide my bare knees. I kept my eyes glued on the little pants I was washing. I never looked up. I was terrified of what I might see. I had never gazed at his face. Why would he come to the river? Should I get up and run away? I was always told even by my stepmother that I was stupid, I just agreed to everyone who asked me to do anything for them. Like my cousins would ask me to crochet something for their trousseau, and I would leave whatever I was doing and agree to do what they wanted first. Everybody took advantage of me. I was always smiling with my hand closing my mouth, nervous about my bad breath, even though there was the new Colgate toothpaste. I still held my hand across my mouth when I was speaking to someone. Oh my, I hope he doesn't speak to me – my heart was pounding as he washed his hands and asked me for soap and said he would like a cup of tea as he left home very early, at the first cockcrow. I got up stumbling, half toppling over the bucket – to look straight into the knight's face. I had never seen such a handsome man – he was frighteningly good-looking. I was dazed.

He sensed it and said: 'Don't be afraid, go and make the tea.'

I knew that he had heard all about me. I didn't want his pity, so I thought, I'll show him that I am not stupid. I was shaking, but I managed to say: 'Excuse me, sir, bush tea or Five Roses?'

'Young lady, I will gladly have Five Roses, so long as you personally make it.'

I practically ran up to the homestead, and my stepmother had the kettle boiling on the coal stove as the houseboy made fire very early in the morning. Did he want to test me to see if I was capable of making proper tea? When he strode on to the verandah in his riding breeches, the whole house shook. My heart almost stopped. I didn't realize he was so tall. My stepmother said under her breath: 'The giant is here.'

He sat himself on the wooden bench on the verandah and it actually creaked under his weight, a whole six foot something of lean muscle and bone. I took the tray to him only because my stepmother encouraged me to, she whispered and said: 'Be a lady and offer to milk and sugar his tea.' She took a new tea cosy and new tray cloth and new china, it was very important those days to serve tea the proper Victorian way.

He thanked me for the tea and thundered away. Even his walk was nerve-racking. I was dizzy with excitement and terrified that I had made the wrong impression as he said not a word, other than: 'I hope to see you soon. Goodbye young lady, goodbye Mrs Nunn.'

It was only later that I heard the full story of the mad bull Ndlovu, a name which means 'elephant'. This was the bull who had come from Utrecht with Katrina. Sibiya, the herdboy, had told Benjamin that he'd have to castrate the bull.

'Ntuli's young heifer got gored by Ndlovu, my heart bled when I saw how he fought and killed it; now you'll have to pay him back with one of Boesman's calves and the younger of the two will have to be castrated in order to plough next season. The other day Ndlovu uprooted the old lavatory down by the gum trees and he charged the women coming from weeding in their fields at Mahalahaleni. Carrying the thatched lavatory on his horns he was a terrifying sight, and they tell me old Nomandwali went off screaming, running for her life. Her isidwaba was ripped off her waist while climbing up a madoni tree to safety, and she had to wait up the tree to hide her shame, until Ndlovu decided to run madly into the donga, where to the great relief of all of them he was stuck, and he stayed there from sheer exhaustion.'

'Yebo, Sibiya. I understand. I will apologise to Mr Ntuli for the loss of his heifer and offer to compensate it with one of Boesman's calves, and I will castrate the younger one as soon as possible, and I will also compensate Nomandwali for her isidwaba with the very hide of Ndlovu as I am going to shoot him personally for my own wedding feast in July.'

'What nonsense are you talking about? Do you really think the fat nkhosazana from Wakkerstroom will return to marry you, after you treated her so shamefully?'

This was a young woman who had been so enthusiastic in the pursuit of Benjamin after his wife's death that she had given him a gold watch – but he had been still so smitten with grief, and possibly also repelled by her enormous appetite and her laziness, that he had neglected to respond by proposing.

'A man never chases a woman away,' Sibiya went on, 'he takes her and keeps her and makes her happy by breeding many children, and the more women he has got the more he becomes a renowned hero. I can't ever understand the mind of a white man. To chase away a woman is a criminal offence. I think that Nkhosana needs to strengthen his male organs by eating the very testicles of the bull and drinking a little warm blood from the bull's heart.'

'Oh Sibiya, you tire me with your endless chatter – and as for eating bull's testicles, I have enough sperm in me to make another twenty children. I am my father's son, he made twenty children. And he always tells his friends, every Tom, Dick and Harry of them, that he will never know how many children he made on his runs through the Natal territory. So please, Sibiya, stop worrying about my strength as a man. I am really going to get married in July as I've met the right woman from my brother's wife's family. I've not personally asked her to be my wife, my brother will talk to her first and then he will give me an answer – next week when I go to visit him. I've told my father who is very happy because he knows her father. Even though she has been let down, and left with two children, who are both boys. But she is very young and can breed more children for me.'

'Oh Nkhosana. I thought you were dreaming, hoping that the lady from Wakkerstroom would return to marry you. But I do wish you could have married her too, she was so beautiful and rounded, she had desirable buttocks, and thick legs. She would have been comfortable in the winter. It is a blessing for a man to have many wives – in case one dies, or gets very ill, there's always another one. If Nkhosana had two wives, you wouldn't be mourning so painfully for the dead wife, there would be the other one to console you.'

'Oh Sibiya, you are the worst savage I've come across. My father said you must teach me to fight with sticks, and to learn all your hunting tricks, and teach me to respect the elders – but not teach me your barbaric lust for many women. You have eaten too many bulls' testicles. Sibiya, you are my best friend, my brothers have all gone to be married, and I see them often but not often enough, so I would love to please you. Sibiya, help me to stop crying, and to accept that my wife will never come back again.'

'Don't worry my Nkhosana, you are my brother younger than me, I have to protect and look after you, the way your father picked me up orphaned by the wars and made me a big indoda.'

One day, as my father was busy on the huge carpenter's table outside under the pear trees, grinding some piece of machinery, Ndlovu the mad bull appeared with branches all over his head and headed straight for my father, who ran round and round the table until he managed to duck under it. But Ndlovu gored the very table and lifted it up on his horns, and ran straight down toward the river with both the table and the grinding machine bolted to it – as though, satisfied that he had got my father at last, he was going straight down the river to dump him among the rocks. Oh my God, Benjy's father and mother nearly fainted watching this frightening episode through their bedroom window. His father ordered Ndlovu to be shot there and then, but he disappeared into the forest.

The story of Ndlovu was heard far and wide. Everyone was terrified

of the bull who had come from Utrecht. Some said he became demented at Katrina's death and missed her scent and that is why he became
so angry. 'Where is my Katrina, I came with her here to this wild land.
I do not see her. What have you done with her, where is her grave? Am
I to believe she is dead, when I see no grave? Bring her back at once
or I'll kill everyone.'

This became very juicy news. Even the old gogos chattered and
whispered between handshakes and while releasing sniffs of snuff.
They should slaughter the poor bull and take the heart to Utrecht to
rest next to his wife's chest. Just dig a little and put the heart on top
of her; her spirit cries for her kids and her youth and her young husband, they both loved one another so much. It was Red Stone, an old
imbongi who was nearly one hundred years old, who told my father.
He told him all about this grief of the bull, but my father told him it
was a lot of bullshit.

Chapter 3

*Winnefred tells the story of how she agreed to marry Ben-
jamin Rorke.*

AFTER THAT VISIT MY AUNTIE ROSIE and her husband Walter sent
for me. They wanted to talk to me. I went up to the homestead as
soon as possible, because I thought I had been rude to their brother by
not offering him to stay for lunch. I was scared, but when I saw my
Auntie Rosie smiling I felt relieved.

Walter was a dominant and staid man, who resembled a stern German Brother. As I was brought up in a home with a very primitive
mother I hardly knew how to speak proper English. I prayed the Hail
Mary and asked her fervently for correct answers, and told her how
lonely I was. Please Mother Mary help me to say the right words.
Clasping my 'kerchief in my hand I sat down on the bench next to my
Auntie Rosie, while her husband Walter sat opposite on his favourite
oxhide-strapped rocking chair made by his own hands. He was massive. His face was surrounded by hair on all four sides, making him
resemble a lion. Even his moustache looked like a lion's. I had seen one
at Mkuzi Game Reserve when I was eighteen years. I trembled then,
just as I was trembling now.

'Winnefred, my brother Benjy came to visit you yesterday only because he wanted to have a good look at you. Of course, he is fully aware of your misfortune and has pity on one so young and yet so lonely. We have been trying long enough now to persuade him to stop punishing himself for the loss of the mother of his children, but he always has the same reply: "Walter, my brother, no one will take the place in my heart of the mother of my children. I love her more today than I loved her yesterday. She is not dead, but lives in my heart, how can I love another?" Then he sobs uncontrollably, his pain is my pain and my father's pain too. But we cannot all carry on grieving with him and for him. He has lost interest in himself, he's lost interest in the homestead and in farming; the cattle are dying of rinderpest, and he couldn't care. He just cries like a baby. We thank God that his mother and father are still alive and living with him in the homestead at Ngome, but they are old and will soon leave us. Winnefred, will you have pity on him and be his wife?'

We never answered or questioned our elders in those days, you obeyed and obliged, and never nodded or shook your head in response, so I was dazed and in my glory. I thanked Mother Mary silently for giving me a husband. From deep inside the rain forests of Ngome, I heard a deep murmuring penetrating through the misty jungle and as the sound got clearer in my mind, even my hot salty tears diluted with snot tasted divine, and I murmured: 'Yes, I will marry Benjamin William Rorke.'

Well, my agreeing to marry Benjamin when my uncle and aunt asked me on their own was all very well, but of course I hadn't related the matter to my stepmother yet. As for my father, who would only be coming back tomorrow from the game reserve at Umfolozi, he would be furious. He was just as much involved in everything that went on around him as she was, and just as touchy about being left out.

I can remember quite well how, waiting for Benjy, I burned my arm in the oven. The old Welcome Dover stoves had very deep ovens and I stretched my arm in without twisting the cloth around it. I was so cross with myself but at the same time thought: Now he'll see that I can bake. But what about being careless? Oh, he'll think: She is so foolish – couldn't she put a cloth around her arm to protect herself from burning?

I put on a long-sleeved blouse, and a long skirt with a figure belt showing off my small waist. So he'll think I've got a nice waist even though I have two children. The first thing I darted for was toothpaste and I scrubbed my teeth thoroughly. I am going to smile this time. I'll show him I've also got a nice set of teeth. He must not think I am dumb. I'll show him my teeth and I am going to ask him what are his children's names, just to show him I can talk.

I was shaking and my stepmother said I must act calm and make as if I was not hard up for him or else he'd have no respect for me. (Oh my gracious me! Does she really think I am listening to her?) But won't he see right through me? (I knew I was as transparent as glass.) Oh, my heart felt as though it was going to stop.

Irene put some lipstick and powder on for me, and a little 'Evening in Paris' behind my ears. I had a hairnet and a lot of hair clasps on my hair and kept patting my starched petticoat, and my pretty checked black-red-and-yellow swirl skirt – they were the fashion then.

It was three men in all who came strolling down toward our little homestead. Walter, his brother Benjamin, and my father. We hadn't known my father had arrived already – he must have come from the other side of the river and ridden unseen to his homestead. Anyway, there he was. You'd have had to have seen them with your own eyes as I did to believe that these were humans. There they were: giants, knights belonging to King Arthur. My father, George Nunn, shining like the angel Gabriel – Sir Lancelot. Walter Rorke, who resembled a noble emperor. Sir Galahad, Benjamin William Rorke, looking like the angel Michael. They strolled with ease and confidence as though the world was all theirs – no one dictated to them. Men, I mean real men. Amadoda. Hunks of muscle and bone.

Benjamin William Rorke: I'll never forget that vision until my dying day. He was bandy-legged so that his leather gaiters had a slight crease on the left leg. He must have worn a size ten shoe or boot. He had kruisbande that were genuine cow-hide leather, and a big thick belt with a big square heavy iron buckle. His holster and gun, slung carelessly on his hip, gave him an air of such striking breeding and machismo, I felt like running back indoors and not looking any further. Almost resembling a Norse Viking. Rather like a pirate he had tied a scarf around his head; black shining curls protruding at the nape of his neck; a well-trimmed moustache attached to his mouth, that parted occasionally to reveal his teeth. The sideburns met with the line of the twisted pirate scarf to show off a curly fluff of black hair and a very strong jawline. This was the Prince, the youngest son of James Michael

Rorke, the heart-throb of Ngome Forest. Almost like the Greek god Hercules in Greek mythology, his mysterious gaze had a disturbing sadness about it.

It was very fashionable to wear a pirate scarf and shirt in those early 1900s, so I presumed he wanted to show me that at least he wasn't just a 'bush baby'. Of course he had been to Jo'burg to work before he got married, so he had charisma. I thought in my heart this man was too good-looking for me, I didn't deserve him. Maybe he just wanted me to cook for him and his children. Ha, in that case I'd look after a thousand children and another thousand of him just as long as he marries me.

Their voices were coming from the dining room, I could hear them. So I peeped out from my room through the cracks in the wooden door. I had hidden of course. I would not come out until I was called. A child never sat in big people's company. I squeezed myself into a tiny corner for a better view.

He spoke with a deep voice full of unfulfilled love and an empty heart. I could see him more clearly now; his complexion was flushed. His deep childlike sorrowful gaze sent an arrow straight through my heart. I was crying. I felt so deeply sorry for him, there and then I knew I could die for him. If I could hold him in my arms, I'd surely collapse from sheer love. I was crying, very deeply and sorely, for myself and for this poor man's pain. What had we done to deserve such misery? I knew that I'd agree to serve him and love him forever.

I wiped two big fat teardrops from my cheeks and smeared all the powder away, but I stayed glued to the chink just to see him open his pouting lips and say: 'Mr Nunn, I humbly ask for your daughter, Winnefred Juliana, in marriage.' I did notice a shining mist in his eyes as his hand reached out to my father. He got up in full, and stood up to my father as though measuring himself to be worthy of his daughter's hand in marriage.

Oh my God, my dear God, so you do love me, I thought you had forsaken me. Oh, Mother Mary, how many years have I prayed to you – but you never answered me concerning Teddy. But now God has answered me. This man is going to marry me. Did I hear wrong? I am almost perfectly sure he said to my father: 'Mr Nunn, may I have your daughter Winnefred Juliana's hand in marriage?' He even mentioned my second name. Who told him? Which means I really heard the right words.

Forgetting my smudged tear-stained face I practically tore the door off its hinges, and ran straight out the dining-room on to the verandah and down to the river to sit in a little cove and cry so loud, I couldn't control myself. I kept saying, this can't be true, no man would ever marry me. Oh my God, thank you, I'll have my own home, my own husband too. All my sisters were married. I was left alone to become an old spinster. Now the Prince himself has offered to marry me. I'll be his wife. Oh my. I'll have his children. My head was drumming, many instruments were buzzing inside my mind.

I knew it was him beside me, I tried to cover my head and face in my pinafore, but he said: 'Winnefred, will you marry me? I've asked your father and he said I should ask you for your consent. I am waiting for an answer.'

There were a thousand bees humming in my head and another thousand butterflies in my heart as I managed to find my vocal cords and said a very solemn, very sacred, shaky 'Yes'.

'Thank you, lady, you've made me a very happy man. Can I please kiss your hand to show my gratitude?'

I meekly stretched out my well-worn hand for him to clasp with a vice grip in his massive hand and he gave it a squeeze. I almost thought he wanted to crush my fingers but at the same time a surge of warmth went through my whole body. It felt as though I was swimming in hot chocolate. I wanted to sip some, but I was afraid to burn my lips. Why can't he just squeeze me and kiss me on my lips? But this of course was not Teddy. This man was well bred, and had manners. You did not take advantage of a girl.

He did not sit down next to me. Instead he lifted me up, to size me up, and said I was very small, and he thought I needed to be fed properly. He joked about having plenty of milk at his home and plenty of fresh spring water and all the beautiful flowers. All the time he talked, I never once looked at him. He let go of my hand, and lifted me up and tilted my face and kissed my cheek like a child. I blushed so much, he could sense it and said jokingly: 'Your cheeks are red like tomatoes,' and put me down abruptly.

'Would you like to marry me in spring or next month in July as I have to plough in spring? Whatever you want, please tell my brother Walter. I'll be going home now to my children, who I am sure you know about as I know about yours, so we are very well suited for each other. Goodbye my dear. I'll see you soon.'

He was gone so fast that I wondered if he ever was there. Was I dreaming or imagining? Oh no, no, no, he had been here, right beside me ...

I stood on an ant-heap to watch him sauntering toward his brother's house; the ant-heap caved in just as he entered the verandah. The feel of fresh red damp sand from the ant-heap on my feet reminded me that, from now on, I would have to behave like a lady and learn to wear shoes every day. I ripped off my sandals, throwing them into mid-air. I was dancing and hopping, laughing and crying, full of red sand, and my heart full of joy.

I heard my stepmother call me so.

'I am coming, Mama.' It was my own mother, the Swazi woman, to whom I was responding. Oh Mama I am going to get married. Oh Mama I am so happy. I didn't know anyone could be so happy.

'Winnefred, come at once. Your father has to speak to you.'

I looked at the rugged mountains, where for months I used to gaze in tortured expectations for Teddy, and thought: No more gazing at the mountain pass, till my eyes are sore from crying. No more tears on my pillow, no more pain in my heart, no more running to hide myself when people come to visit. Dear, dear God. I love you.

Tears still streaming down my smudged face, my father caught me up in his arms and I buried my happy tear-stained face in his chest. I knew he was crying, as he said: 'Winnie my child, you've got a lot of work to do, what with a wedding coming in a month's time. I am going to build another room to accommodate the visitors. Freshen up now, and help your mother in the kitchen. She's crying for you. I wonder if I'll have any supper at all. I'll personally catch the red hen, and cook the dumplings myself, so you two girls will have time to talk about things.'

The Rorke girls came running from the homestead above, Irene in front shrieking. Sarah, Louisa, and little Maggie – her cheeks flushed as pretty as a doll's, big round black eyes shining with tears falling on to me. 'Can I be your bridesmaid? Uncle Benjy just told us you've agreed to be his wife.'

My father said he was going to slaughter a sheep for supper for the whole family to celebrate. Sarah and Louisa and Irene were just crying silently.

'Oh Winnefred, now we'll be one big happy family and Wallace and Alfred and Denis will all be your pageboys. We've got to start sewing the wedding dress, tomorrow we're going to Loeffler's to buy the voile and we're going to pass by Auntie Jessie's to start cutting and measuring and sewing straight away.'

'Do you like him, Winnie? He is so handsome but they say he is very cheeky, and stands no nonsense.'

'Ohooo!' I said: 'I've never seen such a handsome man. I'll marry him even if he sjamboks me every day, with two children I think he comes as a bargain. I'll have him lock, stock and barrel and promise to love him till death us do part.'

With all the chatter and laughter, I felt like a human being. I was befriended at last; my cousins, who previously had barely spoken to me, were astonished to see my teeth and hear my laughter. We all scurried up to the homestead to help cook the supper. My father forgot about the hen and dumplings and my stepmother dressed up to kill, with starched petticoats and hair-clasps and red lipstick, and just kept laughing like a young girl down at the river.

Walter took out a halfjack of Oude Meester left over from Christmas to toast at the long wooden supper-table; my father serenaded everyone with music from his concertina; the younger boys strummed home-made guitars, and the herdboys joined in with penny-whistles and mouth-organs while roasting the entrails of the sheep around the fire outside on the hearth. Oh, my heart was bursting with joy. We danced and swayed until eight o'clock.

Chapter 4

Winnefred gets to know her aunt Jessie, who is to become her sister-in-law, and other people at her homestead, including Nathi. Zimzim the Giant befriends her.

YOU COULD SEE THE MIST on top of the rain forest at Ngome early in the morning. I gazed as if noticing the forest and the mist for the first time. That was going to be my home in the bush. Everyone told me it was like paradise: everything stayed green right through the year. I said a little prayer and cried again for joy.

My father was already measuring out the new room as I greeted him with his morning tea. He shone with joy, and gave me a smile and a huge hug. 'Oh my child. I am so happy for you.'

Irene, Maggie and myself practically ran all the way to Loeffler's store. I chose pale blue voile – I couldn't possibly wear white as I already had children. Mrs Loeffler helped, choosing the right colour range, and lipstick. Oh, she was so jovial and rotund. She had been given the nickname 'Mamba' for her sharp inquisitive eyes and very sharp tongue. She had a raucous laugh, that caused her little piggy blue eyes to gleam, as she bent over toward us and whispered hoarsely in broken English: 'Herr Rorkeh, vairy goot looking male. I wish to marry myself, but now too old. Gott be good to you, Fräulein Nunn.' And she stretched out a pair of bloomers and a garter, and winked mischievously.

When we said goodbye to her, she bent down to whisper hoarsely: 'I give it you piggy, for wedding present. Come, you take home.'

I said: 'Thank you very much, Fräu Loeffler', and she thundered in guttural Zulu to the boy to bring the pig from the sty at the back of the store. We screamed with sheer shock to see the huge monster in the yard. The old pig wallowed and grunted with her long nose; not a single tooth showed except black stumps, and she was totally blind from old age.

What on earth were we going to do with her? She couldn't see her way down the dongas, even the Zulu herdboys whom we asked to help us drive her home looked scared, shook their heads, and shyly walked away.

Mr Loeffler came outside and blurted out something in guttural German to his wife, perhaps saying she had no shame to give someone a wedding present that was so ugly and fearsome. She grunted back at him in equal distaste: 'She eating all the other childrens.'

'Did you hear?' I whispered to Irene. 'The pig eats children, my God. How can I even dream of accepting such a pig as my wedding present? I've got two children of my own. How can anyone eat that pork?'

Irene said: 'Let's take it now, and drown it in the Bululwane River as we cross over to Auntie Jessie's, and save a lot of trouble.'

Maggie, who was far more educated than we were, said: 'Oh no, she doesn't mean it eats real children. She means it eats the baby piglets in the sty.'

We laughed so loudly that we were almost hysterical. Mamba stood at the door, and wailed: 'Hambani-ke. Iziphukuphuku. Get away from here, you idiots.'

Luckily for us, there was someone we knew from down the valley to drive this huge old sow, her long teats sweeping the ground, to the homestead.

I tied my parcel of material and make-up around my neck with a plaited grass rope so that it wouldn't fall into the river, and we took our clothes off to swim across, as it was quite swollen from the last autumn rains. Arriving at Auntie Jessie's, we were panting with excitement, running straight through the house calling for her, peering into every room to blurt out the news.

'Oh, my goodness gracious me. What's chasing you girls? What's wrong, have you lost your heads? How rude, where are your manners, girls? Running like savages!'

'Auntie Jessica, Benjy is going to marry Winnefred.'

I stood shyly, with my parcel still strapped round my neck. I felt sheepish and quite foolish. I really didn't know Auntie Jessie that well. I'd only seen her occasionally at her brother Walter's homestead, and thought of her as such a gracious, gentle lady. To present myself to her like this was embarrassing.

She said her father had sent the message already and she embraced me and said: 'Winnefred, I wish you all the luck you'll need and all the courage you can muster, as my brother is very spoilt, conceited and arrogant. Sometimes he really believes he is a king. Being the last born he has always had his own way, and my father spoiled him too much. However, he has mourned long enough. You'll have to be obedient, and be at his beck and call. If you truly love him maybe he will change; with all his emotional tantrums he has a large heart, and can be very kind.'

We stayed for two days, fitting and measuring my wedding dress, and talking and planning, bubbling with joy. She also had to sew Benjamin's wedding suit, which was to be a grey pinstriped three-piece and white shirt, with pirate collar, and white silk scarf. Oh I could just imagine what he'd look like.

And as though she could hear my thoughts, she said: 'He is a very handsome man, you are a lucky girl. Many women have lost their hearts to him in vain.'

She gave me a beautiful porcelain wash basin and water jug with potty to match, also many embroidered tea cloths and a pair of calico sheets with crochet lace, edged with embroidery; a bedspread, fully crocheted, with matching pillow covers. I was to come back in two weeks' time for final fittings, and so, happily and gleefully, I thanked her and we ran back to Esikwebezi.

On my next visit I told Auntie Jessie about the pig; how Uncle Walter and my father were disgusted at such an unpleasant wedding present, and how they had slaughtered her on the very next day after her arrival. She hardly had any bacon, but her meat was very tasty, and very very tough. Auntie Jessie shrieked with pure amusement as she told me that that pig was more than ten years old – she had bought one of her first piglets when she had moved to Ngome, and that was when she had met her husband, Mr Strijdom.

She told me to go into his study to greet him but first she looked me up and down and said I should tidy my hair and powder my nose, and not look like a golliwog in her husband's presence. I had to present myself as a lady.

I went in shyly, curtsied in front of him and almost gasped for breath, seeing this massive soldier. I was tongue-tied, eyes protruding. He looked up and said in Afrikaans: 'Alles van die beste, meisie. Hier is 'n troupresentjie vir jou.' He put a one pound note in my hand.

I was dumb and curtsied and ran out faster than I came in. Auntie Jessie smiled when I was back and said: 'Everyone is so afraid of him and yet he is the kindest man on earth', and her eyes shone with love. I kept that one pound note for a very long time.

Auntie Jessie nudged me gently to one side, and ushered me into her bedroom. She shyly pointed to a small solid steel bed, looked at me with much love and tenderness, and whispered: 'This is the soldier's bed where we made our only daughter, Georgina. I couldn't conceive another child as I was past thirty. He sleeps on it when he is home. We hardly use the double brass bed ...' – and she stuck her neck out to show me a king-size solid brass bed fit for a queen. It had the most beautiful embroidered white bedspread with pink crocheted roses, and lace edging all around; there were matching curtains with white starched embroidered lace edging, tiny little rose petals peeping shyly. The room even smelled like little roses, with a hint of lavender. Streaks of giggling sunshine were joyfully playing hide-and-seek on the white-washed walls, clinging on to the curtains – which responded with a nudge, and tenderly whispered: Embrace me, I'll keep you warm; come closer, and I'll whisper sweet soothing intimate melodies in your ear. I'll stroke your pretty face with my frills and flutters, your eyelashes with a gentle breeze, then gallop away into the moonlight like a gallant knight.

Oh dear God, I felt a lump deep in my heart, a chasm that had so long stayed empty seemed to fill up with emotional thoughts and dreams, feelings which I thought had died long ago. As though she could hear my thoughts she motioned me to sit down, and said: 'I've kept this room like a shrine.' She flushed girlishly. 'This little room was where we first made love. This was the soldiers' barracks, and he was their commander. When we married, we just extended around this room. I treasure the memories. I sometimes sit here alone when he is away on duty, and say all the fond words to him, never forgetting to tell him how much I love him. I am not well schooled, I cannot read or write much, so my love story is carved in the bits and pieces of cali- co, lace and embroidery. The bits of iron and steel on that little bed have kept me in chains, bound forever to my husband. Oh yes, he hardly uses the brass double bed when he is home, but I still fit snug- ly beside him on the little iron bed, just as comfortably as I did ten years ago.'

Fat tears rolled down my cheeks as she hugged me and said: 'My dear, dear Winnefred, I didn't mean to make you cry. I want you to forget past pains and be happy for the future. You must think of this little room as your own on your marriage night. Pretend you are here and it is the first time and, of course, the past is gone. It will be the first time for you and your knight in shining armour. He has captured your heart. You've told me how you feel about him. Oh Winnefred, sometimes love is as cruel as it can be kind, but it is better to have loved and lost than never to have loved at all.'

We were nudged by haunting painful strains of Mozart, sighing and lamenting, sneaking through the open passage door which led into the dining room, where a gracious tall stately gentleman – the soldier I had just been introduced to – stood in a trance, gazing through the open little window as though observing the scenery for the first time. I could see the rain forests, frighteningly aloof, mist hovering over the thick green blanket as though concealing some dangerous secret, like an ominous volcano.

Auntie Jessie's sewing room was just as beautiful as the bedroom. Everything was neatly folded and to my surprise, Benjamin's suit was all pinned up and ready for final stitching and pressing. She did the finishing touches on my gown, and told me to hold my tummy in as I was going to lose a little more weight from excitement, she'd need to make it tighter.

'Katrina had a tiny waist. My brother really hates women with pro-

truding stomachs, although of course it'll be different when you fall
pregnant. But you must tie it up properly, with a grass woven strap.
The old ladies at Ngome will teach you as you have no mother. Can
you make proper dumplings? My brother seems to love them, and I
hope you can make bread on the hearth outside on the fire. He designed an oven with stones for Katrina. She was good at baking bread
and roosterkoek. My dear girl, I have to warn you he loves his food
done well and on time. Every meal has to be served at table, and he
loves to eat vegetables boiled or rather underboiled, don't ever serve
him cabbage bredie. Just boil it: no pumpkin fritters, just boil the
pumpkin.'

'Yes, Jessica, I'll do everything you've told me.'

Oh, but she went on and on.

'When he is in the fields try to bring his grain coffee yourself, to
serve him properly with boiled milk and lots of cream and roosterkoek. He loves wild spinach and wild honey, you must always make
him amaviyo' – karob juice – 'in summer, and lemon juice. Always use
honey to sweeten his porridge or his tea and all the wild fruit juices
that he likes to drink. He mostly drinks bush tea; he loves eating meat
braaied, even wild rabbit must be braaied.'

Everybody ate braaied meat: even the cane rats and porcupines had
to be cut up for a braai. Did she really think I was so stupid? My father
was a game ranger, we saw many animals with their eyes popping out
ready to be eaten up and put on the braai. Oh, my word. I wish she
could finish with my fittings and let me go home now. I was bubbling
over with news to tell Irene and Maggie, and my stepmother.

Auntie Jessie gave me a maid who spoke Swazi to accompany me
home and carry all the presents she gave me. This time it was dresses,
shoes, necklaces, hair clasps, crockery and cutlery, like a real mother
giving her daughter a trousseau to start off with. I was so grateful and
wept as we said good bye. I was to pass by for my wedding dress on
the day we rode up to Nongoma Court House to be married. She
would dress me up. I couldn't take the dress home as it might be taken
by the river when we crossed. We never knew when the Bululwane
might swell up as its source was in the rain forests.

I was dying to speak to this Swazi girl my aunt had sent with me.
Her name was Nathi, meaning 'we too' or 'us too'. I was so relieved
to find someone I could really express my feelings and fears to, and
best of all Auntie Jessica had said I could keep her for as long as I

wished. She was an orphan. Mr Strijdom had picked her up and brought her home to his wife to be fed and taught to be useful around the house. And Jessica said as I was not very fluent in Zulu she would help me with the children.

Nathi told me her whole family had been killed by other Swazis because they said her granny was a witch. She ran to hide on top of a huge tree until they left but by that time everyone was dead. Over the next two days she walked for miles, eating berries and drinking water, never meeting anybody of her own tribe. If she saw anyone she would hide, because she didn't know if it was the same people who had killed her parents, until on the third day she saw many funny people riding horses. She tried to run, but the big soldier in front chased her and picked her up on to his horse. She screamed and screamed, trying to break away from him. He tied her up with riem and gave her something to eat, and water to drink. She says she fell asleep from sheer exhaustion. She was only ten years old.

Both her little fingers and toes had been cut off, leaving only stumps. She told me very proudly that it was their custom. Her granny had ordered the ritual to be done to appease her ancestors. Oh well, I wasn't perturbed either as there were many worse rituals that were done to appease the ancestors in those early days.

As she finished her story, the sun was sinking over the rain forests at Ngome. The mist lay thick like a shroud covering some massive graveyard. It was so foreboding, and yet so hauntingly mysteriously beautiful. I wanted with all my heart and soul to be there, to be a part of this mystery.

Nathi must have believed I was quite crazy, as I practically ran down the hill to cross the Esikwebezi. I wanted to reach home where my children were. She called out: 'Don't leave me, please don't leave me behind. They'll catch up with me and kill me. They'll know me by my missing small fingers and toes. Oh, please don't leave me. I've got nowhere to go.'

I stopped so fast I nearly fell, parcels on my head and all, and I said in clear Swazi: 'Nathi, I'll never leave you. I am only in a hurry to see my children. Come now, I'll wait here by the crossing of the river. Woza manje, shesha. Come now, hurry.'

Her sad eyes lit up but she never smiled or laughed. The deep pain of seeing and hearing her people being killed was not going to be erased from her memory for a very long time. That's why Jessica gave her to me, for me to mother her and for her to be part of my family, especially since she would have the children to look after. I felt very sorry for her, I'd protect her the best way I could, so I held her closely when she crossed the river and told her I was her new mother now.

Everyone was laughing themselves sick about something I had no knowledge of as my children came falling over me and asking where I'd been. I gave them a few Zulu Motto sweets from Auntie Jessie, then I heard the news. It was about the pig. Benjamin had heard about the old ugly pig from Mrs Loeffler, and he said he was going to shoot the woman. How could she do such a disgraceful thing? Irene and Maggie came running to say that their father Walter had to stop him from galloping up to the store to tell Mamba a thing or two. Just because he was marrying a second-hand woman didn't mean that she deserved such a wedding present.

But the height of the joke was old Zimzim the Giant's reaction. He was the overseer, who made sure that all the cattle were safely in the kraal and who looked after odds and ends around the homestead. He himself looked like the one-eyed giant: he had protruding eyes, both his cheeks were bitten off, so that even his nose was just a little sunken piece of flesh with two holes for nostrils, he was pitch black and his head seemed extra huge because of his protruding forehead. His teeth looked like a whole mealie cob, with rotten broken mealies attached to it. He laughed now, like hail stones falling on a zinc roof, because he said he had had the best of the ugly old swine's meat – so why was Nkhosana complaining? Oh, he was highly amused.

I'd never seen Zimzim before from such close quarters. He usually stayed near the kraal, sitting under the trees waiting for the cattle. I had heard that Walter found him on the banks of the Black Umfolozi River, wandering around with crushed leaves made into a thick paste covering half his face, tied with other bigger leaves, and with grass twine plaited by himself. He recalled wandering too far into the dense bush and coming near very big boulders, where a huge giant pulled him inside a cave. And as he started eating on his cheeks a huge black mamba gave the giant a terrific fright. This gave him the chance to crawl out of the cave, and run off bleeding. Remembering that lions and other wild animals would smell the trail of his blood, he quickly picked healing leaves, and feverishly stuffed them into the wound. Terrified of what might happen next, he climbed up a marula tree, from which he could clearly see a wagon across the river, and people chopping trees and collecting firewood. He knew the safest spot where the rocks were so high you could cross the river without the crocodiles being able to eat you. Walter and his crew took him on board their wagon and delivered him to their homestead, one shaky piece of left-over giant's supper.

Thus he was fondly and lovingly christened the Zimzim – the ogre. He became the chief herdboy, and never left the kraal. He sat in the gateway always waiting for the cattle to come home from grazing, and then would go along to the boss to report them all safe and sound. He had never seen his face and had no wish to observe it in a mirror. He knew full well that he was bewitched; by feeling his face when bathing down at the river and at night he knew that he could never hope to lobola any maiden, and so he gradually became inkabi, an ox. An ox is meant to plough, and is very strong; so was he. He could work very hard and is known to have pulled the plough in place of a sick ox.

The Rorke girls had become withdrawn and elusive. I had imagined a far more girlish response when I came back from fitting my gown, such as 'Ooh, aah – how does your gown fit? Is it a Queen Victoria neckline? Is it plunging, with lots of lace and frills?' and 'Ooh, I wish I was getting married,' or 'Oh my, when I get married, I'd love my gown to be silk or satin, not organdie.' I thought they might even talk to me about my wedding night. I know I was no virgin, but it would have been nice for me to share my joy with other girls as I had no sisters. They were all married. I was so alone, and thought they'd be overjoyed at my wedding to their widowed uncle. It made me feel sad, but I said to myself I'm still going to marry him, even though they don't like me.

A few days after that, I noticed the Giant cuddled up behind our homestead. He always had some old rags tied across his face to cover his scars. I went up to him to greet him and ask him if he had been sent for something. He shook his head and said in a voice sounding like a grunt from the old ugly swine: 'Please give me an old scarf to tie my face, before you go to be married to the cheeky Nkhosana at Ngome, so I'll remember you by it. I know you've been a lonely girl. I know how it feels to be lonely. I hope you try to make the best of your marriage, as already the girls are whispering down by the river that they would never like to be given away to a man who doesn't even love them.'

Oh my word. That's why they were becoming so distant. Even when we met at the river on wash days they would do their washing on the opposite rock from mine and hardly exchange a hearty laugh or giggle. At least I knew now, but it didn't bother me at all. I thanked Zimzim very much and gave him one of my late mother's head doekies. He thanked me with a handshake like a plough.

Chapter 5

Preparations for Winnefred's wedding. Beer-making – and the effect on the farm animals of the filtered-out mavovos or dregs.

BENJAMIN RORKE ARRIVED ON HORSEBACK the following week to announce that the wedding was to be held on Friday 28 July, 1934. We were to ride to Jessica's homestead where I would change into my wedding gown at five in the morning – that was when he would join us. We would then make the three-hour ride to Nongoma Court House to be married at nine o'clock. After the ceremony, with the ride back to Ngome, we could expect to reach the homestead at about six or seven o'clock in the evening. The wedding feast would take place in the morning and go on till Sunday afternoon, when the guests would start riding back to their homes.

Well, it seems everything was arranged for me and I had no say; but I was excited and did all the preparations with the help of my stepmother and my new maid. My father bought me a huge kist. I filled it up with all my presents, and with some of my own mother's tray-cloths and beautiful beaded milk-covers and crocheted tablecloths. Oh, I was in my seventh heaven. I thought of the days to go and counted them on my fingers and wrote on the wall above my bed: It will soon be the last time I sleep alone. Will he want to share a bed with me even when I am an old woman?

Actually, none of the men ever shared a bed with their wives, there were always two beds in the bedroom. Even my own father never shared a bed with my mother. Oh well, I thought, I want to share a bed with my husband and I am not going to be shy, although everybody must have told him I am stupid and shy. I am going to show him that I've got pretty nightdresses and 'Evening in Paris' and Colgate toothpaste in my kist. I've got pretty pink bloomers with elastic around the legs, not those long cotton ones with ribbons and lace around the legs which make them so hard to take off. I'll show him. I am younger than him. This is the twentieth century.

I stood behind the house, drying my thick hair in the sun, and gazing at the additional mud room that my father had now completed for the wedding. It looked like a porcupine trying to dig into a hole, with the thistly spiky grass still sticking out of the mud bricks being the quills – only this was a square porcupine. It was so small it had only the two beds and a little cupboard with the water jug and basin on it, but my kist also fitted into the corner, and a pile of grass mats that the women and girls had given me as presents.

And while I sat drying my hair there were a pair of fowls also sitting tied up right next to me who kept talking to one another, the red rooster saying in a deep husky voice: 'I am tired of being tied up. I want to make chickens. We'll get old without children. Try and turn around so I can reach you – what are you waiting for?'

I giggled as I thought of myself.

And the hen meanwhile seemed to be gazing up into his lustrous red and yellow eyes, trimmed with a golden halo. She looked at him longingly and said in her very best girlish tone: 'Oh, well, you know there are rules, Tom. You are the man, you are supposed to untie me, you have such a strong hooked beak. Such a beautiful red comb it looks like a big red rose. You've got to show it off to me all the time; just admiring your shining plumes, and your comb so puffed up and red, is enough to make me ready to wait for a lifetime.'

Tom retorted, and rebuked her angrily: 'I am sure they are taking us very far away, and maybe we'll never be together again. Why else do you think they've tied us up?'

'Well, then, stop complaining, Tom. We'll soon be together in a beautiful new place and never have to eat these mavovos again, and then we can make dozens and dozens of children when we eat fresh mealies. Oh Tom, we'll be so happy.'

'Oh my dear, dear Matilda, that is the best news I've heard, and the loveliest thought for the day. My, indeed, we shall have dozens and dozens of children. But, eh, oh, Matilda, do try to turn around.'

Tom and Matilda were both very drunk with the mavovos, the dregs, that they had been eating from yesterday when the Zulu beer was being squeezed and put into the clay pots and huge dried-out calabash containers. These amagobongo were ready to be transported to Ngome; tomorrow the wedding feast was to begin and no wedding is complete without meat and Zulu beer. Uncle Walter was leaving this afternoon to slaughter two oxen for the feast, and after the wedding vows at Nongoma Benjamin was going to shoot Katrina's bull.

Everyone was rushing around frantically doing whatever needed to be done. Even the pigs in their sties wanted to do something after eating so many mavovos. At least they enjoyed my wedding feast. They were screaming and shrieking, grunting and giggling, falling over one another, trying hopelessly to make extra porkies. Oh how hilarious, everyone was in love. I was not the only one.

The girls couldn't stop giggling and asking me about the wedding night.

'What if Katrina comes as a spook in the night while you are with her husband?' Irene said hoarsely.

Oh Nkhosi, where will I run to? Oh Irene, don't scare me so much.

My hair was generously greased with a mixture of pig's fat mixed with brilliantine which was very fashionable and new on the shelves. Mamba had ordered it for all the Rorke girls as it seemed we were her only civilised customers.

Before Walter left for Ngome, he shouted for Mehlo ('Eyes') to grease the wagon thoroughly with pig's fat – mixed with a little paraffin so as it wouldn't get too thick when they reached the cold rain forests. Mehlo, who was in charge of the wagon and inspanning, seemed to be buzzing around like a huge black fearsome dung beetle pushing a big lump of dung. He was stout-legged, bandy and muscular. He had got the name 'Eyes' after a spitting cobra spat in his left eye while he was herding Uncle Walter's cattle. On the spur of the moment he turned on the cobra, knocked it dead with his knobkierie, and took it home to his granny. She cut it up and gave him the hot liver and heart to eat so that he would never again be bitten or spat at by a poisonous cobra. He was rushed by Walter to Auntie Jessica's hospital where he was successfully operated on and sealed up, leaving a scar where there should have been an eye. He became the head blacksmith and burned off all metal irons needed for the wagon and ploughs and horse-shoes, bridles, saddles, riding breeches, riems, chains, straps, strops, lassos. He knew everything about the farm and so he was loved and respected by all the occupants of Walter's homestead, and he wore the dried-up cobra skin around his left wrist for the rest of his life.

All the girls and Auntie Rosie, together with my children and my maid, my kist, my grass mats and Tom and Matilda (still tied up) were to travel in a wagon pulled by six donkeys. The huge wagon, pulled by two oxen, was to take my double bed (made by Uncle Walter), my umtambuti wardrobe, and many cousins from across the river and some from Nunn's Halt, who were to be guests in the Porcupine Room together with my stepmother and her children.

My stepmother screamed like a dying pig: 'Girls, come inside at once.'

Irene and Maggie and Sarah ran up to their own homestead. My stepmother practically pushed me into my room and spoke as though a piece of sweet potato was stuck in her throat. She actually flushed red.

'What is it, Irene?'

'Oh, oh – your future husband has just arrived. He is not to set eyes on you yet, until you are married. Now stay indoors and help me pre-pare the fowls and scones and dumplings for your father – and you have to have your own padkos, but you must not eat before you wear your gown, in case your stomach swells up and your gown won't fit nicely.' She croaked like a young frog, and whispered in my ear as if I was deaf: 'Winnefred my girl, I hope he doesn't forget his wife's death certificate and the wedding ring. Where is your birth certificate? Oh, your father must have it in his Jo-sack. Your father never forgets any-thing. Oh, and don't forget to pack your white wedding shoes. Your fa-ther said they would fit you even though you didn't fit them on. He doesn't know what size you take and it's bad luck to put them on now. You'll change everything at Auntie Jessica's homestead, and don't talk to your future husband until you are married. Please see that you brush your teeth when you leave Auntie Jessie's place and please talk up. Try not to mumble, the magistrate will think you are dumb and he'll just get up and walk out the Court House if you don't talk up. He'll say you are wasting his time so please, if you want to get married to Ben-jamin Rorke, open your mouth and say: "Yes I do." And when the magistrate says "For better or for worse, till death us do part," you must say "Yes I do."'

I couldn't sleep even with cups and cups of hot milk, so I took my rosary and prayed and asked Mother Mary for guidance and protec-tion on my journey from spitting cobras and mambas. I also asked

God to let my own mother see me from above, getting married at last. (Oh Mama, I am so happy, yet so scared.) This was going to be the last night I slept on this little bed. I was soon going to face the biggest challenge of my life. A man obsessed by the sudden death of his young wife, who had left him with two young children; an old, ailing father-in-law, with an even worse old, ailing mother-in-law, who dies at every asthma attack. A homestead that's been left semi-derelict for three years without a woman's touch. New people, new customs, new surroundings – but most frightening was the fact that everyone was saying I was going to have to have the patience of Job to be able to live with the most handsome, arrogant, spoiled, censorious Prince in the whole wide world.

I'd had so much pain and change in my young life. Now I had to leave my father who was ageing and not so sure of the love of his young wife, and who was now dependant on his brother-in-law to keep an eye on his homestead while he went out to work, sometimes for months. And now I'd found myself a permanent home. I was going to miss my little home and my stepmother – who was almost as old as Rosie, my eldest sister, but we got on so well.

Oh, dear God, thank you for so many things. I sobbed with my rosary on my heart – but silently, so as not to awake the guests in the Porcupine Room.

Chapter 6

Winnefred's wedding day: waking up, dressing at Aunt Jessie's, the ride to the altar and the ceremony. And after, the ride back to the farmstead.

THE KNOCK ON MY BEDROOM DOOR was so urgent I jumped up like a scared cat. It was my beloved father with a cup of tea for me. His sharp steel-blue eyes looked like a troubled sky with sparks of stars dancing to and fro, searching my face. He softly said: 'My child, you are going to get married today,' and then turned around so abruptly I knew he was hiding tears.

I stood by the little verandah and wondered what was going on at this time of night. Everyone seemed to be getting ready for the gymkhana. There seemed to be a circus and a merry-go-round all in one yard. Being July, the moon and stars sang a melody which vanished, sound and all, into a huge blue sky. There were spooks darting from across the mountains of Ceza and Nongoma, bluish-reddish lights competing with the paraffin lanterns, which seemed to be dancing from one end of the homestead to another. Horses were being hurriedly saddled, wagons were creaking and moaning under heavy loads. Donkeys were yelling for dear life, cattle mooing, believing it was time to get out of the kraal, cocks crowing like broken violins, pigs screaming for more amavovo. There was a huge fire gleefully burning on the hearth, big drums of water were being refilled by giggling women happily singing Zulu wedding songs. 'Hama-ma-ma. O mayebabo, mayebabo.'

The whole homestead was buzzing with activity: children screaming with fright, young girls shrieking with sheer delight, men's voices booming with abusive language at the younger herdboys, telling them to vuka. Someone shouted for someone else not to forget the bride's brooms. (It was customary in the Zulu tradition for a bride to have her own brooms.)

The whole scene was frightening. I realised I was about to venture into the unknown. I had never imagined something like this would ever happen for me. My cousins all hurriedly kissed me one by one to say good luck. God be with you, Winnefred. Don't be scared, Winnefred. Ride carefully, my girl.

My father was already on his horse as I jumped on to mine with sheer confidence, and my young heart leaped for joy while the spirit of the wild pioneers and also their determination urged me to fly with the crisp morning breeze. I rode like a witch on her broom, out to put a terrible curse on some unfortunate person.

And as the stars slowly one by one allowed the greyish blanket of dawn to cover them and sing them a lullaby, promising them new threads of shimmering sunshine to kiss their eyelids until it was time for them to awake again, we galloped into Auntie Jessie's homestead. Benjamin Rorke was nowhere in sight.

I jumped off the horse as though it had a curse, and running to the gate I bumped straight into Mr Strijdom. I nearly collapsed.

'Benjamin must be waiting at the Court House already. He took his suit without fitting it on and rode off without even a cup of tea.'

'Thank you, sir,' I said; but my heart found it hard to settle back in its right place as I darted into the house, shouting for Auntie Jessie who was right in front of me holding my beautiful dress over her arm.

Pulling me in with her free arm she said: 'Oh, my goodness gracious me. You look like a golliwog. Come on, change quickly. Benjy is halfway to Nongoma by now.' The lanterns were dancing all over the ceilings, the verandah was lit up with its own huge lantern. The ladies and young girls were all singing wedding songs for me as I was dressing. The gramophone was blurting out some wedding march that sounded like 'Bring my terug na die ou Transvaal, daar waar my Sarie woon,' and as that number died another one came up: 'Please come back to the Red River Valley. Oh please come back to a heart that's so true. I'll be there in the Red River Valley, I'll be waiting my darling for you.'

Auntie Jessie was humming while she dressed me. 'Oh my goodness, you look heavenly – like an angel. Now turn around. Let's see the back when you ride. Don't sit on your dress. We'll put an old sheet underneath so that the horse's perspiration won't mark your dress. You will remember to powder your face? And put on your lipstick? There's a little mirror in your bag. Of course the dress is fully frilled and there's enough of it to spread on to the horse's back so it won't crease too much. Tie your bonnet up tightly in case the wind blows it off.'

I looked round for the bonnet and my eye caught the most beautifully made specimen – designed for a princess. It was so high it looked like a little koppie surrounded by all kinds of flowers and shrubs, dry ones and green ones, spiky ones with thorns and some that looked like spiders, others like butterflies. Oh my word, how was I to keep it from flying away with the wind?

The soldier was ready to gallop to Nongoma. He had promised Auntie Jessie to be at the magistrate's office before eight to fix up the papers for Benjamin to get married quickly 'so that he can be at Ngome Forest while it's still light for Winnefred to acquaint her eyes with her new surroundings'.

It was usually a half-hour ride up Mahashini Mountain to Nongoma. I knew I could never make it in half an hour as I had to look after my flowing wedding dress and keep my high bonnet from flying off my head; but I didn't want Benjamin Rorke to walk out of the Court House without me so I rode like a witch in her shroud, on her way to pay her penance to all the ones she bewitched in her life-time. (Oh God, help me not to be late.) I was strong and young and very healthy, so I pushed and pushed my horse up the mountain. She uttered loud bugle-like neighing cries, as she practically galloped up, flying like a bullet.

This was a wild mountain horse, a real climber who was quite used to climbing up and down the most dangerous precipices. My gown flowed behind me covering the horse's whole back.

I turned just a little to peep and my bonnet seemed to transport itself like a balloon right up to the sky. I couldn't stop to see where it landed. Oh my word. Auntie Jessie had told me to fasten it tightly with my scarf. I couldn't risk not being married in time. I panicked as I saw to my utter dismay that the huge bonnet was landing right on Benjamin's horse, and he was standing on the horse trying to retrieve it. He had been waiting for us on the mountain.

The soldier, Mr Strijdom, saw what was happening and rode back to fetch the hat as Benjy would probably have hurled it into the deepest donga. My spirits were in utter disarray. I thought: Now he knows deep in his heart and mind and soul that he is indeed marrying a total fool. My heart was bursting with self-pity. I was sobbing painfully and helplessly while the soldier was saying: 'Maak hom vas met die bandjies en hou hom dan vas met jou hande' – and so I pulled with one hand and got both ends of the bows and ribbons pushed into my mouth and held them tightly with my teeth. Still sobbing silently.

'Dis nie nou tyd om te huil nie, asseblief, meisie – don't cry.'

I kept my teeth securely fastened on the bonnet, wondering if I'd make it like that through to Nongoma. As long as Benjamin doesn't turn around to see me – how will I wipe my tears? What about the face powder, will there be a place to wash my face? I still have to put on my new wedding shoes. Where will I change? I found it quite difficult to breathe with the snot from sobbing running so freely. I couldn't reach for my handkerchief, the snot was leaking down my chest. I stopped sobbing very quickly, knowing that if I carried on my wedding dress would have a snotty patch on my bosom and I'd look like I was breast-feeding. At the same time I couldn't dream of getting married bareheaded. It was totally unthinkable, so I tightened my grip till I felt my jaws were getting numb.

Somehow my father rode up against me and pulled the reins and stopped the horse. He quickly gave me a chance to tie my bonnet securely with my huge white scarf. Oh my word, what a relief, thank God. You could see the red, white and blue flag, blowing happily above the Nongoma Court House. Benjamin was nowhere in sight. Oh my word. Did he turn back another way, straight to his home in Ngome after realising what an idiot he had nearly married? I felt my heart beat and patted the pearl necklace from my own mother, feeling very foolish indeed. Imagine riding all this way for nothing.

My heart leaped as I heard the man say: 'Winnefred Nunn. Winnefred Nunn. Your turn next. Are you here, Winnefred Nunn? Next please.'

My father pushed me on to the verandah and through the huge oak doors, with my riding boots still on my feet, my face messed up with dust and snot, lipstick all messed up, terrified eyes protruding, hand across my mouth – I found I couldn't walk properly. I was shaking as my father led me right up to where Benjamin stood, like the King of England. I was afraid to look at him lest he saw my smudged face and ran out of the Court House in sheer disgust. Oh Mama, where are you? Please help me, dear God. I can't go through with this marriage – first of all this man doesn't even love me, secondly I can't talk.

I knew I looked like Cinderella, with her white slippers full of fine Red River Valley dust, the same dust all sprayed over my wedding gown. My hair looked like the judge's ringlets, only powdered with red powder, peeping out on either side of my unforgivable bonnet. My eyelashes were powdered red to match my ringlets. I had distinct perspiration patches under my arms, as far as my chest, displaying a neat outline like the map of Natal in red dust. That's when I caught a glimpse of myself in a huge mirror hanging laughingly on the wall opposite me. I think it was put there for all brides and grooms to take a last glance at themselves before tying the knot.

I turned slowly around, not looking up, and lifted up my gown to reveal the most unusual wedding shoes, and then I darted, like an exposed witch, through the door; but a firm grip right round my waist ushered me back to my place. As the man shouted 'Order in court' I realised the man who had captured me was Benjamin Rorke, the kind bridegroom himself.

I knew I was going to faint as he said tenderly: 'Don't be afraid, come back and marry me. I do love you, don't worry about your dress, it's you I am marrying, not the dress or the shoes. Come on now, it's getting late, we have to ride back to Ngome to your new home.' I heard every word he said.

'Benjamin William Rorke, will you take to wife Winnefred Juliana Nunn as your lawful wedded wife, till death you do part?'

'Certainly, sir.' His voice sounded like an aeroplane, as though he wanted to get all this fuss over with (because he had done it before) and fly home to his ploughing.

I don't think I'll ever forget my wedding, not till my dying day. I never looked up to see the magistrate or anyone else in that court room, until we walked out and I ran to my father to hide my face in his chest. With my father's heart beating for mine, my mind slowly crept out to remind me that someone had put a ring on my finger. Slowly I allowed my eyes to look at my finger and, well, lo and behold! The ring was on my finger.

Oh my God, I'm really married. Mama, I'm Mrs Winnie Rorke. Oh Mama.

And then, slowly, my eyes bloodshot with dust, I started wondering who the man was who put this ring on my finger. Oh maSwati. Oh all you Swazis as a nation, come and gaze at this man. Is he real? Am I dreaming? What is he? Where does he come from?

I rubbed my eyes, feeling the sand grating like rough salt, as hot tears mixed with red dust ran down my cheeks. I couldn't control myself. I ran away.

My father ran after me and caught me just as I was turning the corner of the Court House. To my surprise, round the corner I saw this little square river made of stone, full of greenish mucky water. A few horses were drinking greedily from it. I tucked up my wedding dress, which looked like I had taken it out of an ant-heap, and after trying to get on my haunches I succeeded in cupping my hands and scooping up some of the slimy water to wash my hot flushed face. It was as though I had on a red clay mud-pack, as the water turned a reddish-brown colour going back into the greenish thick slime. I even washed my feet, and Daddy brought my wedding shoes, tucked under his coat so Benjy wouldn't see them. I moistened them with spit until they slipped on. And Daddy said: 'Oh my girl, I wish Roselina was here.'

Daddy looked so forlorn and uncertain, he kept twitching his moustache and twisting it around and around – at the same time puffing violently at his pipe. Teeth clamped on the pipe, steel blue eyes gazing toward Swaziland. I knew he was pining for home just as I was.

Then Benjy, my husband, tucked his arm under mine, and mustering all of his English gentlemanliness and poise he said: 'Can we please have something to eat? I'm starving.' He smiled down at me and for a delirious moment I thought he would at least kiss my cheek. Kissing in front of elders those days was unheard of. I even thought: How foolish can I be? How can he kiss me after washing my face in the trough? But he didn't seem to disapprove, as he also washed his face and hands. Oh well, perhaps just to put me at my ease. He did notice my shoes but never uttered a sound, maybe he was too hungry – or perhaps he thought Katrina's shoes were ten times better than mine, perhaps she wore golden or glass slippers.

My husband ate a whole chicken, my father ate one too. As we had brought two I had a little bit off the bone. I wasn't hungry in any case. I was happy when he said: 'It's time to ride home.'

I took my wedding shoes off, slipped my riding boots on, and leapt on to the horse without a care about how my dress looked, or who was watching and what they might say.

However, there were a few ossewas with nooientjies and ounoois and oubaases who gazed at us. I think most were disgusted at my dress – but they admired my handsome husband.

One ounooi who seemed to have ten petticoats on and a bonnet higher than mine said: 'Ag siestog, sy het seker geval van haar perd af.'

'Magtig Hannah ou vrou, kan jy dan nie sien nie die vroumens is nou baie dronk?'

'O ja, Hendrik, ek dink ook so. Foeitog.'

From on top of my horse I looked at my husband as he strode toward his own. He lunged forward like a rhino; he seemed to take two steps forward each time instead of one. His sideburns were trimmed in line with his moustache, which curved right down to his panting mouth; thick eyebrows covered the creases on his forehead, and his eyes glared piercingly straight at me as though saying: Look at me properly, woman. I am not the type to be taken lightly. Be careful. I am a full-blooded, half-caste English Irish stud.

And then something lurched up out of my mind. I was gazing at the building beside me that resembled a huge brown mountain with a big mouth, and eyes, and ears. Suddenly I realised what had gone on inside that building. I looked at it with a shudder. I could hear myself repeating after the magistrate: 'Yes, sir, I will marry him.'

My eyes seemed to take everything in all at once. I noticed the huge stones that the Court House was built of and remembered my own father and Benjamin's father were its builders. I was proud of them both. My eyes caught some inscription on the huge door. Of course I couldn't read, but the sign shone in the mid-morning sun. My head turned and I gazed at the mountains all surrounded by dense bush. Hazy clouds like purple smoke arose from as far away as my eyes could see. I could hear my mother's voice, coming from the mountains of

Swaziland, whispering softly: 'My child, I am here with you. Don't be frightened.'

I felt another tear running down my cheek as I looked to the left so that Benjy wouldn't see me crying. I noticed a group of Zulus dressed in their bheshus; some had tribal feathers and some were with round black rings on their bald heads. Some looked quite fearsome, talking and nodding their heads – but some took snuff gently and gazed wistfully at the mountains as though they knew and felt the pain of missing something just like I did. Then I listened to the unusual sound of the wa-was or nkankanas with their long huge beaks, flying over the court as though saying to me: 'Come and fly away with us.'

As we galloped towards the steep hills of Mahashini Benjamin Rorke stopped, and turning around on his fearsome stallion beckoned me to stop too. Then his voice boomed over at me: 'My dear little lady, you'll have to ride with me. I cannot lose you now.'

My father agreed and jumped off his stallion to grab my reins and lead my horse, a mare, at a trot behind him. Of course I leapt up without his help. I wanted to show my husband I was no weakling. He sped off as though he had just stolen me from my father's kraal. I heard him call, caressingly: 'Thunder, my brother, my friend, please go, boy, go. Get up and go.' Thunder snorted, and perked so violently that I held tighter around my husband's waist. The very ground shook, and we disappeared in a cloud of dust.

Hayibo, what a horse. I felt as though I was being transported upward into heaven, my heart surged and leapt together with my prince and his stallion. We would have reached heaven a very happy trio. Thunder lurched and snorted, his nostrils sending fumes of fire and smoke like a dragon, heaving breathlessly toward the looming mysterious rain forests of Ngome.

I suddenly felt a cold shudder creeping up my whole body. I didn't really know this man I was marrying; he was neither the boy next door nor had he been courting me for three years. But what I knew and could sense was that he was no commoner. He presented himself like a real prince. He came of high breeding, even on his mother's side. His pride was not the stupid pride of haughty times, nor was he proud and arrogant because he chose to be. He was brought up that way. I thought of Uncle Walter and Auntie Jessie. They were fine, well-bred people – most of the early pioneers preferred to take Swazi women for wives. Zulus were very feared. To dare think of a Zulu wife meant you were tampering with Chaka's belongings. Swazis were known to be more peaceful and tolerant, and not a war-like tribe; therefore most English and Irish and Germans and Scottish pioneers took Swazi wives or concubines, too scared to tamper with Chaka's Zulus.

In no time we were crossing the Bululwane River, entering the northern side of the wide open prairie that spilled down from the rain forest on the other side of the hill. And there, I knew, was the homestead tucked away under the Ntendeka cliff. As Benjamin was speaking loudly enough for me to hear, I tried to lean around to listen to him; but he wanted to point out the homestead to me and his massive shoulders blocked the scene so I just shouted: 'Oh yes I can see it now,' and held him even tighter. I didn't really know what else to say. I'd never seen such plush pockets of grazing land. I could see this was indeed the land of milk and honey. We had lived in much rougher terrain and at Esikwebezi there were no forests.

He squeezed my hand and shouted: 'We'll soon be home, don't worry, my dear.'

Then I really started to panic. All kinds of different thoughts ran through my mind. What will I do when we get there? How was I supposed to present myself to his father and mother? How do you do, Mr and Mrs Rorke. I am Winnefred Nunn. Oh no, not like that, I am forgetting that I am now also Mrs Rorke. Auntie Jessie told me not to worry as they know who I am. Oh my God, please help me to answer properly and to speak up and smile. I wondered if my teeth had pieces of fowl meat lodged in between them. What about my soiled dress? I was so embarrassed and very very confused and frightened. What would they think of me? A real golliwog with no proper upbringing? Oh well, at least my stepmother will be there and Irene and Maggie and my Swazi maid.

I kept running my tongue across my teeth, my hands were clenched tight. I couldn't release my grip or else I'd fall headlong on to the rough stones. But at least we were not taking the road through the dense forest, as I had been told it was actually dark even in the daytime there. My thoughts were spinning round and round in my head. My heart was pounding. I was sure he could hear it through his shoulders and into his own heart. No, no, no. Don't panic, Winnefred. Stay calm, you are now married. You've got to be brave and face the future.

As the faint smell of Benjy's perspiration swirled around my nostrils, I held him tighter and thought: Well, he is here with me, what more do I want? I loved him more now than ever before and I laid my cheeks on his massive strong shoulders, and felt quite safe. And soon the hillside became dotted with round grass huts and cattle grazing all around, with little Zulu boys in their bheshus, and then we rode out on to an open meadow where a much larger herd of cattle were grazing, unconcerned about who was marrying who. We galloped through them and as we went on up to the homestead I could hear singing and shouting, merrymaking, joyous laughter – and we saw people running toward us to meet the bride.

Chapter 7

The reception at the Rorkes' homestead. Teddy Jacobson makes a reappearance. Winnefred's wedding night.

THE SMELL OF BRAAIED MEAT caused my taste-buds to water and I felt very hungry. Smoke seemed to flow from everywhere in the yard. A little cottage emerged, so quaint and unusual. It appeared right in front of my eyes, part of a larger homestead. The main house was built of stone, of shale, under a shimmering zinc roof. A heavily-thatched little mud brick house stood on its own just around the corner. There were also other huts on the yard: several rondavels, two huge nqolobanes – granaries on stilts where the mealies and other grain was stored. My eyes were caught by a verandah running round the main house, with flowers growing right up the heavy wooden poles. I wanted to go and touch them.

Fowls and chickens mingled with the many people – all busy, moving up and down, in and out. The Zulu women sang as my stepmother and my children ran up to me, and my husband lifted me off the stallion and carried me to the verandah. My heart was so full of joy, I just cried. Irene and Maggie and the other aunties that I'd never seen before came and kissed me and welcomed me home with huge bunches of wild flowers. My children were all over me. 'Mama, are you married now? Where are the sweets?'

I was ushered into a bedroom which was standing ready with my huge wooden bed and cupboard and my porcelain wash basin and jug all in place. A beautiful floral outfit had been laid out for me on the high mattress. Everyone fussed around me, urging me to have a wash, and change to go and meet my new in-laws. It was about four in the afternoon and I would still be able to see everything in the house before dark. The door from my bedroom led out into a little passage that led to the dining room, where the table was decked with all kinds of food. I was really hungry. Hurriedly I dressed. My perfume and lipstick were put on for me by my cousin Irene. She couldn't stop giggling and smiling, asking me: 'How did it go at the Court House? Did you talk loudly, did the magistrate hear you, did you say yes I do? Oh Winnefred, I am happy you are married.'

My handsome husband ordered me out of the bedroom on to the verandah. He had also changed – into a white frilled silk shirt and black trousers. Oh, I nearly collapsed.

'Come on Winnie, you must meet the old people.'

I knew I looked good, as he gazed at me from head to toe. He had crooked his arm and held it out for me to put my arm in his as we slowly stepped out on to the open yard – across the yard where everyone was waiting to see me walk hand in hand with my husband – then to the old people's room to meet them. The aunties whom I'd never met followed behind in their flowing gowns and huge hats, ribbons and bows and buttons and brooches all shimmering gaily; aunties smiling and chirping like squirrels. Gentlemen in tweed suits and tight waistcoats, with Zobo watches dangling on silver chains across their chests, moustaches all neatly in place, hats in hands, all proudly followed behind us.

James Michael Rorke sat on an armchair; next to him, his wife. They looked like the King and Queen of England. Aah! He really and truly was an aristocrat. His wife, whose name was Joko, looked like a real queen. She sat up stiffly, wearing a starched lacy collar, a white silk blouse adorned with pearls, a fully gathered blue georgette skirt. Her head was raised proudly, her hair in a net. She was quite yellow in complexion, unlike my mother, who was more mahogany. Still, her skin was quite smooth for her age. Meanwhile her husband, the white man, stood up from his chair with the aid of a walking stick. He was wearing a grey suit, with a silk white scarf around his neck. His eyes shone, his white hair was immaculately groomed.

Smiling, to show teeth that were still creamy white, he said in a very strict, icy tone: 'Congratulations, Mrs Rorke.'

And he sat down again as I curtsied and said in a dying voice like I was receiving the last sacrament: 'Thank you, sir.'

Mrs Rorke stood up as well, huffing painfully; her chest heaving up and down. She said: 'O, maSwati. At last my son has got someone to look after him.'

And her husband chorused saying: 'Now, my son, I can die in peace.'

He was very old but still strong whereas his wife looked very thin and frail, but still very shrewd and aware of the situation. My husband ushered me nearer to them to bend over so they could each hold me and kiss me on both cheeks. It was dusk by now and so the lanterns were lit as they led the way to the dining room. Benjamin practically carried his father and Walter carried his mother, and so they got them both seated at the long wooden table set with all kinds of food.

Benjamin's father said to me: 'My girl, please pour us a cup of tea.'

I knew this was the test and I found the challenge very amusing. I knew perfectly well how to pour out tea from the tea-pot. My mother had taught us and she had been taught by her husband. By now I was past the stage of being frightened and confused. I just wanted to be happy. The child in me gleefully joined in the fun and merrymaking and of course I knew table manners, such as how to use my knife and fork properly. I also knew that if I was asked a question I should not forget to say 'Yes please,' or 'No thank you,' or 'I beg your pardon.'

Of course I was starving, so I tucked into almost everything on my plate. I was too shy to look up to see how everyone else was eating or who was there and who was not there and what they all wore, but my childish inquisitive mind kept urging me to peep just a little. (No one will notice, everyone is eating.) My eyes wandered a little and glanced toward the far corner of the verandah, near all the vines and ferns – and there, almost hiding, shyly pressing himself into the bamboo fencing around the entrance to the dining room, was Teddy.

I felt nauseous and all the food seemed to be stuck in my throat as I tried to snap out loud and clear: 'What do you want here?'

I lurched up, so as not to vomit on the table. Of course no vomit came out but only a vile word I never knew I could use. My father, who was sitting next to me on my left, my husband, who was on my right, and my in-laws, who were next to them all, looked up startled. Before my husband could stop me I hurled a bowl of rhubarb thinking it would reach Teddy. But it landed on the bald-headed man who stood not so far from him, and who turned out to be none other than Bingo. The huge bowl cracked on his bald head and the rhubarb flowed freely down his face on to his immaculate white silk shirt.

Bingo shouted to someone: 'Run, Teddy boy, run away.'

I was actually screaming at the top of my voice: 'Daddy, shoot him. What is he doing here after what he done to me? Does he think he'll get his children? Never, never, not over my dead body. My husband will look after me and my children. He married me knowing that I've got two children. I'll kill him, tell him to go.'

Benjamin Rorke, my husband, took me in his arms and held me close to him as he whispered and said: 'I knew that he would be here at your wedding. He spoke to me and my father and your father. He begged to see you getting married and apologised for all his mistakes. Everyone belonging to your people knows that he is here, and my people too. Now please behave yourself and stop crying. Don't spoil your day.'

No wonder everyone kept so calm. Why hadn't I been told?

I screamed at my husband for not telling me. 'I wouldn't have thrown the rhubarb at him. Now what are people saying about me?'

'Ah Winnefred, I am so proud of you. I think my parents are just as proud. You've got guts and a defensive spirit. Now I know you do love me. You've shown everyone present at your wedding that you've got no more love for Teddy. I, your husband, ordered them not to tell you. That's why he was hiding away from you. He has told me a very sad story. He was told by the doctors at Nongoma Mission that he had got TB. That's why he couldn't marry you, and he wants permission to take his children to see his mother and sisters. He lost his father last year. Winnie, my dear wife, don't be upset or angry any more. He heard that I have two children and thought it best to take his two to reduce the burden of being my wife and having to look after my children and yours as well, and also my dying parents. Both my father and I and also Walter my brother think he has done the right thing. Your father agrees as well. He forgives Teddy and so do we all. After all, he is a very sick man.'

And now I was trembling. How could I swear at the poor man like that, calling him a bastard, and meanwhile my in-laws are so proud of me and my husband?

There was total silence. Everyone carried on eating as though nothing had happened. These Rorkes had power over everyone, they commanded respect, their word was law. I admired them but I also felt a bit terrified of the future with them in control. Everything concerning my welfare was done without my knowledge or my opinion. I really didn't matter as I could not speak for myself. They knew I was stupid and it surprised them to hear me defending my rights and my feelings so openly. At least now they'd know I was no fool.

The merrymaking carried on. I never caught sight of Teddy again, but I asked my husband to let my children stay with me for at least another week, to which he agreed.

The high-pitched laughs of the ladies in their stiff collars, with rouge thickly laden on their cheeks and lipstick smeared across their mouths after eating, were all about Durban. It was the only topic of conversation. And one lady, a very pretty woman, had actually seen Durban. She didn't live there but she had gone to work as a housemaid for Goodrich, the land surveyors. Her name was Nettie and she was my husband's sister. Oh my word, she was a glamour girl!

Then there was a square man with a mouth so wide the food kept spilling out on both sides of his moustache. He chewed away greedily, and kept wiping the food away with his handkerchief instead of with the table napkins. I wondered where he came from and shyly asked my husband, who told me that that was his brother-in-law, Jacob Dunn. His sister Louisa, Jacob Dunn's wife, was the tall square lady with a huge navy hat all adorned with feathers. She looked quite queer, with a broad mouth almost like her husband's, and huge teeth flashing with every mouthful.

Further down the adjoining table were the Rorke boys, all very strait-laced, sitting with their chests out and their stomachs in, eating like blue-blooded English princes. My husband tried to tell me what their names were, but I couldn't see their faces. A pile of meat was heaped almost to the ceiling where they sat.

There was a man who had a face like a lion. His head was so large, his whiskers so untidy – and his eyes kept roving to and fro in the general direction of the wooden meat-platter. Even though he had half a ribcage in his grip he was trying very hard to devour the whole thing, bones and all, like a hungry lion. He practically snarled and grunted like a pig with every morsel. Fat spattered on to the frilled lacy blouse of the lady next to him and she protested in a high-pitched voice: 'Aha, man, Bransby, just try to chew properly, you're like a big greedy pig.'

'Ag, Mildred, you are always treating me like a child in front of everybody.' Munch, munch. 'It's better that I marry the beautiful lass in Durban; you are just too silly. You've never even seen the sea.' Munch, munch. 'You know the sea?'

Now everyone was looking at him: eyes alert, mouths gaping. They knew the sea was a huge large dam that had no end, and anyone who spoke about the sea was very clever indeed.

'You see, Matilda, if you look for the sea, your eyes go blind, because the sea is red-hot fire.'

'Hawoo. This man is drunk from too much meat,' Nettie screeched. 'You've never seen the sea in all your life. The sea is blue like the sky, not red.'

'Ah, get away, Nettie. What do you know? You're a child.'

His name, my husband said, was Bransby Jack Dunn.

I was in a much better frame of mind by now. I had pushed all the other confusing thoughts to the back of my mind, and was listening to all the gay laughter, and the smell of braaied meat brought me back to where I rightfully belonged. This was to be my home, for better or for worse. (Yes, sir, I will marry him.)

Trying her best to speak proper English, Auntie Angela was cooing about her new sewing machine from England. 'Oh my, it's a bomb I tell you, I've made Bob a new suit. He would have come for the wedding, but the cow went missing with her young calf and so he is going to search for her in the dongas near the spruitjie behind the mountain. Oh, no one here has got a machine like that. Bob said they made only one for me in England. I think otherwise only the Queen has got one.'

My father-in-law and my father seemed to be twitching their whiskers in deep thought and talking very softly. My husband was flying in and out the house. He seemed to be all over at once. Uncle Walter kept reprimanding his children about table manners. Everyone was so happy eating away. Soon the next instalment of braaied meat was brought into the dining-room on huge wooden platters. Ooh, it smelled delicious.

My eyes saw that the part that only men were supposed to eat had been given a prominent place. The wooden platter was placed in front of my father and my husband, and Walter cut the testicles into pieces. My husband took the largest piece, Walter second, my father third.

My father-in-law was most amused. He smiled and said he had eaten enough testicles; now he was ready for the ants to eat up his own.

To which his wife retorted, half in Swazi and half in English: 'Oh my husband, and there has never been a greater stud, but you are rude at table.'

You had to ask for an excuse to use your fingers at table, so we all did. The old man, my father-in-law, nodded in anticipation and asked politely if he could retire, as it was past his bedtime and he could not eat braai at this untimely hour. Every one of his daughters, those who were present, fussed over him. Louisa was the eldest and – still in the wedding hat of many feathers which graced her huge body like an umbrella – she fussed and faffed until Walter and Benjy got her parents up safely to their own quarters.

Benjy came back with a mischievous grimace. He looked so young and reckless as he led me to the bedroom to see his children fast asleep. The little boy Stephen was so pink and delicate, with long eyelashes that almost filled his entire cheeks, and he lay there so peacefully. Little Ivy, the girl, had lips as red as if she had lipstick on. Even her cheeks were rosy and round. Oh my God. To think they had no mother. My own were sleeping at the bottom of the double bed that came from Esikwebezi. I kissed them, first his two, then mine. My heart was overflowing with love and pity for this young prince, who had lost his young wife, leaving young children for him to care for on his own.

Benjamin sat down abruptly on the edge of the bed and bent over to kiss his children. 'These little ones are my life. I can't say I don't miss their mother, because I do. But most of all, I am angry and very confused. Why did God take her away from me? I always think maybe I said something wrong to Katrina or I did something wrong as she gasped her last breath. I didn't even realise she was dying, maybe I could have saved her.'

His brother called him to give a speech, and he refused quite angrily, saying he had no time for stupid speeches. Walter must give the speech. Instead he opened 'His Master's Voice' and it blurted out 'Please come back to the Red River Valley.' He sat a while near to the gramophone and became very quiet.

Nettie was shrieking for 'Give me five minutes more'. The jive, she said, was in fashion in Durban. Everyone who found space jived until they were huffing and puffing and perspiration ran down their faces, mixed with dust from the dung-smeared floors. The Zulu beer came in huge black clay pots, the men and the boys were all dancing on the verandah, some of the aunties were swaying to the concertina and guitars – played by the uncles and even the herdboys and some visitors who had helped to braai the meat. The concertina was pressed by my father and Bransby Jack Dunn was strumming the guitar. He was so full of meat he had his shirt buttons all loosened, showing his drum of a stomach. The Zulu beer was working wonders, everyone was swaying their own versions of whatever came to mind. Some were crying on each other's shoulders and the young girls who watched laughed and laughed, until they cried tears.

Bransby Jack was now at his best, he tickled the guitar strings with a coin and everyone thought it was thundering as he boomed: 'Oh, it's crying time again, she's gonna leave you.' My husband was not a dancer but he asked me to dance this number. He just held me and swayed around and around. We were so distant there seemed to be an island between us. We couldn't reach one another's hearts. Some more braaied meat came in heaps, followed by more Zulu beer. The bare-chested Zulu boys with their bheshus on were very far from sleepy.

My stepmother, who was over-tired, crept up to me and kissed me on the cheek, and whispered to her husband. But he was preoccupied with concertina-pressing, squeezing the notes gently, his eyes closing slightly, chewing on his pipe. He dreamily answered my stepmother with a nod as she disappeared in the crowd. He said I should go and sleep, the time was almost the first cockcrow.

Then my husband's arm was around me and he whispered in my ear: 'You must go to sleep in the girls' room, with Louisa and Nettie. They will look after you, you are tired. Tomorrow I've got to be up early as Walter must go back home. I have to shoot the mad bull before he leaves. Good night – sweet dreams.'

My troubled heart sank. I thought you were supposed to share a room with your husband on the first night of your marriage. Ah well, there were so many people to put up, where would we sleep anyway? But where was he going?

Auntie Louisa – his eldest sister, Jacob's wife – nudged me to come with her to our rondavel. Weaving through the crowd was rather embarrassing without my husband to speak for me. Somebody asked me where I was born and who my father was, and Louisa answered politely for me. In no time we were stealthily heading for the outside toilets and trying to negotiate the lanterns and the huge bonfire. The merrymakers were still singing Zulu wedding songs welcoming me to the new homestead.

I missed Auntie Jessica. I didn't know Louisa at all. In fact she made me nervous. But my nervousness disappeared as she burst out laughing and hiccuped, bending over toward me. 'Oh my girl. Have you ever heard of a man who wanted to sleep in his father and mother's bedroom on his wedding night? He is so selfish, like a spoilt, arrogant child. We've all pampered him far too much. I bet you he is now in Father's arms, crying for Katrina. And Father will give him honey or some wild fruit which he makes sure the herdboys collect for him.'

I nodded shyly and said: 'I understand his loss was great. He has told me about the love he had – and still has – for Katrina. But I promised to be faithful and true, and I'll love him even in pain or sickness, till death us do part.'

'I am happy that he's told you about Katrina, but he could have spent this night with his new wife.'

'Well, he finds it a bit hard, he is not ready. But I really don't mind, my life belongs to him now and forever.'

'You know,' she said, 'he said he was nervous about being intimate in case he called out Katrina's name instead of yours. He spoke about this to Walter, and of course being his eldest sister they didn't mind me hearing so that I could have some sort of explanation for you. But I know better! He is dead scared of women.'

I listened carefully.

Louisa continued: 'We also discussed his children. He has asked Jacob and me to take them and care for them. We are grateful because as you know we have none of our own. Walter is going to take your children when they return with Teddy from seeing their grandmother. My brother Benjy disapproves altogether of the idea that your children should live with Teddy and his family, as he knows that Teddy is a dying man.'

'Yes, Louisa, that goes to show that he is a very caring man where children are concerned, but I did ask him to let my children stay with me just for one week before they go.'

'Oh Winnefred, I am afraid the old people have discussed this already. Jacob and I are taking your children with us together with Teddy in our wagon, right to Mangete. From there it's nearer for Teddy's mother to ride up to our homestead to see her grandchildren. Then at Christmas time Walter and your father will come to fetch them. Ploughing will then be over.'

'Oh well, everything seems to be arranged for me. So there's nothing much I can say.'

I thought what a close family this was. Everyone looked after the other's interest and welfare. My father-in-law ruled his household with a very stern but concerned and loving hand, especially where children were concerned – and look, they accepted Teddy because he was sick. They all felt sorry for him and treated him with love and respect.

As though she could read my thoughts she said: 'The old man sent word last month for Teddy to come to Jessica's homestead for treatment for his TB. He really has confidence in her healing powers using herbs, although he was dead against this at first and said he'd have none of his children becoming involved in savage and barbaric cults. Oh my, he used to rant and rage and blame "the savage" – who of course was my poor mother. She taught Jessie how to boil herbs for stomach-ache and colds and flu. This went on until one day a poisonous spider bit my father on the hand. He became swollen and blue. Jessica boiled some leaves and made him drink the juice and made a thick paste from the parboiled leaves. She wrapped them tightly around his arm, which was purple and red – it looked terrible on a white man's skin. He kept it on overnight and the next morning the pain and swelling had gone. There was a little blue dot where she squeezed out the pus. He'll never forget that. From then on he started to believe in herbs. Teddy has to stay for a while at Jessica's hospital. Who knows? Maybe he'll heal up.'

Half-falling asleep, but still inquisitive, I asked her: 'How did Father know about Teddy?' But the answer came from skins that seemed to be drawn over very rough terrain. I never knew a woman could snore so loudly.

Chapter 8

The next morning. Discussion of the fate of Benjamin's children, and then also of Winnefred's children. The wedding feast. The Chief comes to inspect Winnefred and to give her presents. The following days with the end of the festivities. Benjy rides off to Utrecht. More departures. Nettie the city girl.

AND IN NO TIME AT ALL, we were ordered to rise and shine. The wedding feast would wait for no man. At first I didn't know where I was. There were about ten of us in one rondavel. Some were on grass mats on the floor and some were piled up like sardines on a huge brass bed.

Louisa was still pulling skins. When they heard her, everyone started laughing so loudly that she sprang up with a snarl, looking a bit like a tired, hungry dog. She shrieked: 'Jacob, where's Jacob? Oh my gosh. Of course, it's the wedding. I thought we were at home. Oh gosh Winnefred, we must dress you up. Have you had a wash and a cup of tea or coffee? Hurry up girls, come on. Wake up.'

By the time the sun peeped out of her blankets, we were fully dressed and greeting her face to face outside.

The air was thick with the smell of braai so early in the morning, but fresh and crisp sweet-smelling air crept in occasionally from the misty rain forest. I lifted my head to take a look and inhale the sweet air. Dear God, I whispered, thank you for all this beauty.

Oh my, the activity. Everyone was up and about. The wagons and carts reached as far as the cattle kraal, where herdboys were busy driving out fat, healthy cattle. The cattle kraal was circled with nsinsi trees and they were all in bloom, each carrying a mass of red bunches. A huge black bull was tied to one of the trees. The mad bull. I hadn't been told that it would be shot at my wedding feast.

My husband, looking like a cowboy with a headscarf and one earring, came up to me smiling, making my heart miss a beat.

'Good morning, Mrs Rorke. Did you sleep at all?' And he planted a kiss on my cheek as he said: 'Now I am going to shoot the bull. I hope you are not going to be scared.'

'Oh no, my father shoots so many buck, I am not scared of a gun.'

His parents stood near their rondavel and he asked me to go and greet them. Auntie Nettie was standing with them, gaily chatting away. In rather a thin voice I said: 'Good morning, Mr and Mrs Rorke.'

My father-in-law, looking fresh and sprightly on his walking-stick, said: 'Nonsense my child, you must call us Dad and Mama. You are our child now.'

My mother-in-law smacked me on the cheek with her flabby lips. 'O maSwati, did you sleep well my child? He he.' She knew I didn't sleep well because she had hidden my husband in her room.

Everyone was standing outside. I caught a glimpse of Teddy and Bingo, with my father standing near their wagon. Jacob and Bransby, the Rorke boys and Walter their father, and many others, were there too. The Zulu women and girls closed their ears as the gun rang out twice loud and clear. The echo along the Ntendeka cliff was heard right through the rain forests of Ngome.

That was the end of the mad bull. Everyone started to sing and shout. The men were singing praises to my husband. Wena wegebu likaJimu. Oh you from the brave warrior – a branch, a piece of rock from Rorke's Drift. They went on and on, the women ululated, and my husband came back to me and held my hand while everyone who was there came to us to shake hands and wish us well. Some Zulu girls brought gifts of beads and woven grass mats and bangles. Some brought pumpkins and cow-pears in woven baskets as food gifts. Oh, it was so touching, my heart was filled with joy.

My children were holding little Ivy's and Stephen's hands and they made a ring around me and just danced as they didn't know how to sing. Oh, little Ivy was so pretty in her pink floral dress and bonnet. Stephen was in a little suit of blue linen with a hat to match. He was so painfully pathetic, so frail and small. I went to pick him up and his little sister wanted to be picked up too. So I held them one on either arm, squeezing them to my heart. I couldn't let Louisa and Jacob take them just yet, until I'd got two of my own. Then they could have them.

I felt as if my heart was tearing apart. And I broke down and cried bitterly as my husband took the children from me and led me to his parents in their rondavel. Then I burst out, unable to help myself: 'I can't let Louisa take these children. Please, please – I'll look after them myself. At least let me get my own first – then Louisa and Jacob can take them.'

The old man became very quiet and my husband's eyes were watering. My mother-in-law was softly weeping too. My husband held the three of us together and whispered: 'Thank God. Oh thank you Winnie. I was hoping you'd say that. I am not ready to part with my children yet. If you agree to look after them, then they can stay with us. Louisa can take them when you start your own family.'

My father-in-law said: 'If it's what you want, my girl, your wish shall be granted. I can see you have the heart of an angel. This beautiful country here at Ngome is so rich that the soil yields enough food, and we won't go hungry. This is a land of plenty and your husband loves ploughing; he is my son of the earth and soil. I know now I'll die a happy man.'

Everybody seemed to be crying. All the family members were holding one another, and my father-in-law held me even without the support of his walking stick. Tears were streaming down his flushed cheeks, and he whispered: 'God bless you my child.'

And so the mad bull was slaughtered for my wedding feast. It seemed so fatal, such bad luck. Was I going to see black all my life? Was darkness my destiny? Oh, you know how the Zulus are. Everything has a meaning – and always to do with ancestors and death, good luck and bad luck. It was as if my married life had been doomed – was to be marked out by ill fate. Hayibo! This thought made me feel deeply troubled and quite frightened. Maybe because I was Catholic.

The sun was laughing and singing. So were the guests, everywhere you looked something was taking place. Colourful people, some white, some brown, some mahogany, some pitch black. Oh my, what a beautiful day. No one would guess what pain and loneliness some of the people were going through. Katrina's children were really miserable, I think. How on earth do you tell a child so young that their mother has gone to heaven when they don't even understand the word? If I had to tell my own children by Teddy that their father was going to die, what would I say? They hardly knew him, and were frightened to go near him when Louisa tried to introduce them to him. She said they ran away to tuck their little hands in their grandfather's.

In those days everybody was called by their nicknames, even grownups sometimes. So my elder child was called Bighead, and the smaller one was called Winkie.

I asked: 'Bighead, do you want to go with your father to see your granny – far, far away? You'll ride on the big wagon.'

I told them now that their father was very sick, they should go and look for him by the wagon or somewhere in the yard and say to him: 'We love you, Daddy' But they ran away in the direction of the cattle kraal to be with the other little boys where they could play with mud, making their own herd of cattle and wagons and carts. Oh, they were never short of things to do.

Before we went to lunch, Louisa spoke to me in our rondavel as we changed our outfits for the day. She told me that Teddy was going to stay at Jessica's hospital to be treated.

Louisa said to me: 'Winnefred, my father was quite smitten by the way you were so sympathetic towards his son's children. Now he says that you must have the say where your own children are concerned. He thinks you are an angel sent from God to take care of his son. You're lucky. He's a very proud and domineering man, and one has to be careful not to arouse his Irish temper. You'll be leaving his homestead, with children and all, early in the morning.'

I was thrilled at the thought of staying with my children in this beautiful country. Bighead was just telling me he had seen a big fat frog. 'Mama, Winkie mashed up my pretty worm. Mama, I saved a pretty butterfly and a big grasshopper, but the other boys said we must roast him on the fire and so we ate him up. Mama, they said they're going to trap birds and roast them. Mama, I like staying here. Please Mama, can we stay here for all, all, always.'

Lunch was just as yesterday, the table laid with heaps of food. My father-in-law was very attentive to me, and kept saying: 'Have some more, my child. Have you tasted ... ?'

My own father seemed far happier today too. Everyone seemed so happy and more relaxed. Oh the braai was smelling so nice, I asked my husband to get me some. He was so jovial and so very very handsome, his eyes shone as he darted out to tell the boys to bring in the wooden platter.

It was some hours later that the Chief arrived, having been invited to see the new makoti. He was very critical and scrutinised me from head to toe before grimacing to show his beautiful teeth.

'Wena Hamu, o hayi! Makhosi akwaMiyeni kwaze kwakhanya emuzini kaMbiji, siyabonga Makhosi!'

He then threw his sticks on the ground and leapt up to stomp so hard on the ground that it shook, and then all together his fierce-looking entourage joined in harmonising, some beautiful Zulu wedding theme.

I was shivering with awe and admiration. I stood shyly at my husband's side and bowed my head out of respect for the Chief and his entourage. The house of Zulu was indeed a force to be reckoned with, and highly respected in this part of the country. Fortunately, good relations had long been established between the Chief and the family. It was Aunt Jessica who told me the story. Against his will, and much to his sorrow, the old man James Michael Rorke had shot a leopard. He loved everything about the forest and its animals, and the leopard was a creature for which he had feelings akin to adoration – but he had no choice. He came face to face with the animal while clearing a road, and when it lunged at him he had by reflex action rolled to one side and shot it almost in one movement. Jessica mentioned that he had fouled himself in the process, and had to hurriedly find a spring to wash himself before his three Zulu companions could notice and incorporate the story in his praises! They, however, were deeply impressed with his deed and accompanied him home shouting praises about this man who had killed a leopard. When the Chief had arrived on the scene, my father-in-law had presented him with the skin.

Prior to this event, according to Aunt Jessica, the home at Ngome had been plagued with strange happenings. It had been built close to where a group of warriors had been buried in a donga after a battle; as a result the family were haunted by strange shifting lights of various colours, which went on to some extent even after the Chief had arranged for proper reburial. But Jessica says that when the Chief leapt forward to accept his gift of the leopard's skin, she could see the flames of the ghosts disappearing into the ground under his feet. All seemed well after that. Only my mother-in-law was angry about the gift and never quite forgave her husband for giving away wealth that she considered his and his children's.

Now the Chief had come to inspect his friend's son's new bride. I was presented with a cow so I could feed my children with amasi, and a huge gula calabash to make the amasi in. This was a considerable honour rendered to the house of James Michael Rorke of Rorke's Drift. Was this not his son's bride, the prince's wife? The ancestors have blessed the house of Rorke with another wife because the first found favour in the home of her own ancestors, her weak heart having taken her into their dwelling place where she will live with them forever. The Chief's stunning wives ululated as they came forward, each with a gift: some with clay pots, some with woven mats, some with chickens and foodstuff. Oh ohh. I'd never seen anything like it, let alone seen a Chief with ten wives. My husband whispered to me, saying there were two more to come when they were of age.

The rest of the day was spent greeting new people and laughing gaily as my husband was in a happy mood. We all retired early as everyone was tired. Louisa and the girls with Nettie were all cuddled up in the rondavel already, waiting for me and my husband to pop in to say goodnight. He said goodnight to all of us and said he had so many chores to attend to he'd probably only sleep after midnight.

We all slept till eight o'clock the next morning, which was very late. I sent Bighead, my son, to look for Nathi in the crowd. She came along all smiling and grinning, saying what a wonderful time she was having. She was happy that she was not going back to Esikwebezi or Bululwane, as the place was very dry and it was far to fetch water and wood. I gave her some of my personal washing to do and my boys begged me to let them go to the river with her.

Today was the last feasting day. I wished it wouldn't end, but all good things must. Most of the wagons and carts and sledges were gone by now. Even the crowds of Zulus were gone. There were just a few people hovering around cleaning up the mess.

My father-in-law sat under the window of his rondavel with my mother-in-law, facing the warm winter sunshine. He beckoned for me to come to him. 'Good morning, my child.'

Mother said in a trembling voice: 'Good morning, my child', with a heaving chest and heavy breathing. She said: 'Tell her, my husband.'

'Your husband has galloped off to Utrecht to see Katrina's grave and to tell her people that he is married. He spoke to me about it yesterday, but said not to tell you as you might be offended. He'll be back presently. Not to worry, young lass: he is a very good horseman.'

Oh I was shocked all right, but I managed to say I'd have understood if he had told me; and quickly offered to make them tea. I hurried out of their sight toward the kitchen, and asked one of the maids to fix a tray for me to serve the old people.

What if he didn't return? What if a lion mauled him or a wild pig or a mamba bit him and he died in the wilderness with no one in sight to help him? Oh God please look after him for me and bring him safely back. I wasn't angry or upset. I knew the dedication my husband had, the loyalty and respect he had for human beings – and how the deep Christian upbringing he had received demanded that he should do what was right for everyone concerned. What he had done filled me with love and respect for him. Now he would be able to come back and live a full life of his own with me without a guilty conscience. Going to Utrecht was not much worse than going to the store. It took the whole day just to buy sugar and tea. He'd probably be back on Tuesday morning.

I took the tea-tray to the old people and, like a lady, poured it out for them and said nothing more about the matter.

My father-in-law spoke very softly, almost in my ear, as I bent over the tea-tray. 'You'll have all the years, lassie, don't let your heart be troubled.'

My own father knew that Benjy had gone to Utrecht and said not to worry, it was the correct procedure, and then said goodbye to me, hugging me tightly and whispering: 'God bless you my child. I'll see you at Christmas. Your mother will ride in the wagon together with the other ladies. And please look after your children.'

'Yes, Daddy, I will. I am going to miss home and you and mother. Tell my sisters about my beautiful wedding and the handsome young prince I've married. I'm sorry they couldn't be here to see it with their own eyes.'

He galloped away smiling to himself. At last his child was married.

After supper we retired to our rondavel with Nettie – alone as all the girls had gone back to their respective homes. I kind of missed Louisa. When we said goodbye she cried and her mouth looked so ugly I wanted to laugh, while she was genuinely sad to leave her parents and brother. She said she knew her father was going to die before her mother because he was much older than she was and she was very strong. 'Oh Winnie, please, look after them with all your love and patience. God bless you.'

Jacob had been snoring in the wagon when I said goodbye to Louisa. Teddy shyly came to kiss my hand and say goodbye. 'Winnefred, I can't thank God enough for giving you a good man. I'll die in peace knowing that someone is looking after you and my children.'

By now I was beginning to think of Louisa, wondering if she was upset about her brother's children. She had been so happy to think that she would be fostering them. And perhaps she felt hurt even though she didn't show it. Oh well, she would have them when they started school.

I turned around to look at Nettie, who looked tired. Without her make-up she looked quite different; even her manner of chirping like a parrot had stopped. Her voice was hoarse as she said: 'Oh my, I am so tired. I'd never like to marry a farmer. Ooh, all this work. Oh no no. I'll marry a city lad.' And then, as though remembering something, she added: 'Did my brother tell you that he was going to Utrecht?'

'No, but he told the old man to tell me. He thought I'd be offended.'

'Hawu, what a fool – leaving his wife for two nights. It'll be four nights by the time he returns. I wonder if he thinks Katrina is going to get up from her grave? How can he speak to the spooks? Katrina is a spook now. She died three years ago. Eh he he! These farmers are so stupid and old-fashioned; me, I don't tell my friends in Durban where I come from and I'll never tell them that my mother is a black woman. I tell them my father is a white man, and that's that. Imagine living in the bush all your life! I'll never come back here again. Durban is a beautiful city. There are lamps in the streets. Boy oh boy. The beautiful fashionable clothes. Oh, I'm telling you, Winnefred, you should have come to look for work in Durban instead of marrying this stupid fool brother of mine. He can't even read or write but he thinks he's the King of England. I don't know how you are going to live with him. I feel very sorry for you.'

'Nettie, I love your brother with all my heart.'

'Ha ha – "love". You make me laugh. Hawoo.'

'Nettie, don't talk like that, he is your brother and the farm is your home. I couldn't go to Durban to look for work – who would look after my kids?'

I heard her pulling skins, and I laughed till I cried tears, thinking of all the things she had said. Hey, this was a city girl indeed. Then I think I was soon pulling my own skins too.

Chapter 9

Conversation with Nettie down by the river. Benjamin consummates the marriage.

NETTIE WAS UP EARLY to wake me up with a scream. 'Heyi wena, you're married. Makotis don't sleep till late. Come on, let's go to the river and I'll teach you how to have an ice cold bath in the Ngome springs. The water stays ice cold all round the year.'

We were at the river when Nettie continued: 'My boyfriend is a city boy and we will live in Durban; not here, that's for sure. I'll never even bring him here. The leopards might eat him up. Have they told you that there's leopards in the forest? My father shot one some years back, but you can still hear them growling and groaning and wailing in the night when they come down the cliff in search of our cattle. Oh my God, Winnie, you must never walk through the rain forest by yourself. I'm telling you your kids will never smell you again.'

I did start getting worried, so I said: 'Your brother will look after us, he's got a gun.'

'What, do you think leopards are scared of guns? How do you know he's not eaten up already?'

'Oh no, no. Nettie, please stop now. You are making me scared.'

'One can come out right here, coming from the big forest, coming to wait till it's dark. Can't you see, we are surrounded by forest.'

We were now both naked as she looked around us and screamed: 'There it is! Winnie, run for your life!'

I froze and just collapsed in a heap, quite naked, as she laughed herself sick. 'Oh Winnie, you are such a coward. I am only playing. Haa, you really are a coward. How on earth are you going to live here? Every corner you take you meet a mamba or a cobra.'

I was blue with the icy water and with fright. She took my clothes quickly and helped to dress me. Luckily we had finished bathing and she said in a very severe tone: 'Heyi wena, please for God's sake don't tell my brother that I gave you a fright like this. You can tell him when I'm back in Durban, then he'll never get me. Weee Nkhosi yami, he'll kill me.'

I was scared and cold, half shivering. I said meekly: 'I swear I won't tell him, please let's go home now, I am hungry.'

She had such a beautiful rounded body, her breasts stood out like pawpaws. She was unmarried and claimed she was still a virgin at forty years old. And I believed her. These girls grew up under such strict laws and they had both mother and father to keep an eye on them. All of them were ripe old virgins when they finally found suitors.

That night we had such fun laughing and talking about life in Durban and on the farm. She kept telling me what a fool I was. Did I know how to plough and milk cows? And she kept warning me not to tell her brother – especially about the rude talk, and her way of talking about her mother as a savage marrying a dirty old white man. Nettie was a scream, my sides were aching from laughing, but I think she was keeping me from thinking about my husband.

I bathed little Ivy and Stephen myself and fed them supper myself and went with them to kiss grandma and grandpa goodnight. And I had a lovely time with my own children trying to teach them to say the names correctly. 'Say Ivy and Stephen' – 'Alfi' and 'Fifin'. Oh, we were laughing with my maid, saying words in Swazi which made my children laugh, and teasing her.

Tuesday morning. The mist shrouded the bushes right down to where we had to fetch spring water. It was frightening. Nettie kept up the chatter about her brother as we walked through the long dewy grass. There were paths curling like rabbits' pathways, leading to their holes at the spring. We started chasing some colourful butterflies. Then Nettie noticed some wild guinea-fowl chicks busy eating the fat red ants on an ant-heap. There were so many of them, little balls of burnt orange and earth, rolling around the ant-heap so fast. Ooh. I'd never seen anything so exciting. Nettie was so carried away she forgot about being a Durban lady and screamed with delight. 'Catch them, Bighead, run and catch them.'

But he had no idea about what to catch and how to catch them. He tried running after them but Nettie was leaping like a springbok into the thickets, lunging at them like a real hunting dog. I was amused as I jumped at some coming my way and managed to get two in my hands. Nettie had caught quite a few already, all stuffed down her bosom, and said: 'Put them down your bosom, and try to chase them out into the pathway so we can see them. This is an old ant-heap. When we were young we always caught them right here on the same ant-heap. Oh Winnie, I wish I was young again to do all this.'

She had caught six and I two. My son was crying because he caught none. 'Mama, I want one too; please, Mama, give me one to carry.'

But before I could let him carry one, Nettie was perched on top of the damp ant-heap sobbing her heart out. I thought she never cried. I went up to her and asked what was wrong. My first instinct was maybe she'd been bitten by a snake.

'Oh Winnefred, no one knows how I long for home. I cry so much alone in the city, which is just a jungle of concrete and clay. I hate it, I hate it. God knows I'd give anything to come back home, but there's nothing for a young girl here. I'll grow old waiting for a suitor. No one ever comes to this part of the world. Everyone gets scared when they hear there are leopards in the forest, so they'd never venture to ride all these dangerous roads to find a wife. Oh Winnie, you are so lucky that you're going to live here. This is Paradise. There's no place on earth like home, sweet home. I tried telling my suitor to live here on the farm when we marry, but he says he had enough of hard life on the farm in Ixopo.'

I was amazed at her sorrow. I really thought she loved Durban – and then she just held me and we laughed and laughed. My son joined in. He thought we were crying for the runaway chicks and laughing for joy over the few we had. We didn't hear the hoofs of Frank, my husband's horse, because he was trotting slowly, wondering what the laughter was all about.

'Ah girls, I see you are in a good mood.'

We were half in a daze, not knowing if we had heard right. There in front of us he appeared in all his glory like the angel Gabriel bringing good tidings. I don't really know what he thought. But I was quite sure at the time that he was thinking: This is an imbecile. I've gone and married a common fool that laughs like an idiot. Ladies don't laugh so loud and raucously – Katrina would most likely never have laughed like a fool. She was always such a dainty lady.

He jumped off Frankie's back and told him to go on home. Sibiya would take off his saddle and fresh him down. The horse listened and galloped off on his own up to the homestead. Practically throwing his heavy weight almost on top of me, Benjamin sighed and stretched himself, turned around and did some push-ups on the muddy grass. Then he said to Nettie: 'Pretty lassie, go and fetch your baby brother some sweet water from the spring. Then run home and prepare a quick picnic basket with plenty of meat. There must be cold meat left over from my wedding feast. And make me strong Five Roses. Get Sibiya to bring it down here for me. By then he will have finished cooling Frank down. Hurry up, Nettie. I'm starving.'

I tried to muster my moral and modest behavior by shyly putting my hand across my mouth, but Nettie helped me out. 'Hey Mister Big Stuff, before you order me around, just tell me where have you been. Why didn't you tell Winnie, eh?'

Seeing her wiping her tears with the back of her muddy hand and trying not to squash the chicks in her breast, he burst out laughing. It was the loveliest sound I've ever heard, the whole forest echoed as though everything laughed with him. He looked so tired, his eyes had dark rings around them, but this made him look all the more lustrous and passionately impenetrable.

'Nettie. I am a married man. I think only my wife has the right to ask me such questions. Run now. I am telling you, Nettie, I am really and truly hungry.'

'Oh, you always get your own way,' she mumbled and disappeared into the bush where the spring was, my son trotting behind to see the big frogs.

In almost no time she reappeared. Benjamin was taking off his thick heavy riding-coat so that he could be free to do proper push-ups, saying his back was aching from riding.

'Thank you, Nettie lassie.' He gulped almost half the billy-can of water and stopped to pant like a hunting hound.

'Bring your coat, I'll carry it home as it might be too heavy for the prince to carry.'

'Oh no, Nettie, leave my coat and get me food.'

He did three more push-ups and sat up beside me. Folding my hand in his he said: 'I didn't realise your hands are so small, Mrs Rorke. May I please see your ring? Oh, my, my, so you are married. I was going to propose to this young girl that sat on the ant-heap with my sister, laughing gaily at the ants. Oh by the way, what is your name, girl? My name is Benjamin William Rorke, kindly tell me yours.' Then he said: 'I'll give you a little time. You can practise first by saying mine: Benjy, Benjamin William Rorke.'

I found my voice, which was lost in the mist, as he said softly: 'Do you love Benjamin William Rorke?'

I looked sideways and I heard someone say: 'Yes, I do.'

He pulled me towards him and said: 'I love you too.' He held me tight and kissed me on both my cheeks like a child, and said: 'I have to tell you why I went to Utrecht, and now I hope you'll understand ...'

Just at that moment we heard Nettie shriek: 'I've brought the prince his banquet.' She laid out the meat in front of him, all ready cut up in slices, and said: 'I had to cut the meat in slices so Winnefred can eat. I know you don't like sliced meat. Of course I've not forgotten that you are a savage prince, and love to eat a whole ox piece by piece uncut. Shall I pour out his lordship's tea? Oh, and I found some dates for you in your father's cupboard and some honey. He's so happy you are in one piece.'

'Nettie, I've not invited you to join us. I can pour my own tea, with the help of my wife. Oh, I am so sick of this parrot, I don't know when she's going to fly back to the jungle of concrete and clay where they keep them in cages.'

'Ha ha. You'll miss me, you fool. I'll not bring you dates from Durban anymore.'

I poured his tea in a big cream mug. Sipping noisily he showed me a picture of Katrina which he had just brought back from Utrecht.

'Oh, what a beautiful lady. She looks like Stephen. Oh, look at her eyelashes, and so tiny, so frail. Oh, she looks so sad.'

'Well, she had a heart problem, she couldn't live a normal life, but now she is in heaven.'

He showed me her wedding ring which he said would be Ivy's when she grew up and then he spoke about ploughing. He had to break in a new field and said he had never had a chance to go back to work in Jo'burg in the mines. There was just too much work on the farm. 'I hope you are well prepared for that, Mrs Rorke.'

I said of course I was not afraid of working in the garden. The nuns at school taught us well. He got up abruptly. I thought I had said something wrong, when he said: 'Come, let's shift away deeper into the bush, this spot is too open.' He gathered everything together and threw his coat at me, saying hastily: 'Follow me, come on.' He took four steps forward and we were in a cosy little spot right under a tree, full of fallen leaves. There we lay on the brownish reddish autumn carpet, specially woven for us.

'Winnie. I am tired of talking about everything except us. I think it's time to talk to my wife.'

He was on his haunches, as he untied his leather gaiters – and tossed them over his head. He was very silent as he stripped his Zobo from its chain. He started loosening his buckle. I started to shiver. I felt cold as he grabbed me and kissed me on my mouth. I had no thought of smelly breath – or rather, I didn't have any thoughts at all. I was void of all fantasies, of any awareness of sound or surroundings, any thoughts of past or future. All I had was feelings. I was sound-proof, and shock-proof. I only felt like I was dying and going very far away.

An unfamiliar voice called me back from the dead. 'Winnefred, let's go home, it's late.'

We walked up to the homestead in silence. I couldn't look at him. I was still in shock. I didn't expect him to be so passionately obsessed. He was like a wild raging animal. He had been caged up for far too long. He walked me out of the thicket on to the pathway leading to the homestead. He had bundled all the picnic things under his armpit and said: 'I'm very tired, I've not slept for two nights. Make sure to tell Sibiya to de-worm the sheep early in the morning if I'm not up by four o'clock, and please prepare me some freshly ground mabela maas for supper. Wake me up if I am sleeping' – and he lunged forward like a bull ready to invade another kraal, and disappeared into the yard. I staggered up and remembered that I was a married woman. I must regain my poise and cook supper for my children and my husband.

Oh my word, how was I going to face Nettie?

She met me coming up from the river with no water. 'Oh Winnefred, don't blush. This is what I'll never be able to do, make love in the wilderness – my suitor won't hear of coming here when we marry. Oh, you are going to have many healthy strong children. My brother hates

sleeping on a bed with his wife. He used to take Katrina for many picnics. He uses his bedroom only when it suits him. You'll have to get
used to that kind of life. He is a real stud. No time for sheets and pyjamas, he's never owned any. He wears long johns only when he's riding. My savage mother says her white savage was like that – so Benjy
takes after his own father. I am quite sure my brother was conceived
in the bush.'

Supper was ready. I went to wake Benjy up in his own rondavel,
which had been re-done for his particular purposes. All his clothes
hung in an open cupboard made of tree-trunks. Everything was rough-
hewn, and smelt of raw leather and fresh hay, which was what his
mattress was made of, pushed and stuffed into a sailcloth. The springs
of the bed were made of woven rawhide; the legs and the headboard
were of hewn raw tree-trunks with bark and all. In one corner were
his hunting knives, neatly arranged by size, hats hung up of many
sizes and shapes, broad buckled belts made of plaited leather thongs,
leather bags and pouches all carefully stowed in their places. Braces
hung carelessly stuck in their pants.

My eyes took all this in. On the narrow bed a bunch of curls was
half-covered by coarse army blankets. There was a sheet almost sweeping the dung-polished floor, scrunched up in a heap and looking like
a striped black and white mamba, and lastly a heap of men's clothes.
All these were like decorations on the long grass mats – the amacan-
si. My first impulse was to just put my hand on the curls, but then I
thought: My word, what a mess, so I started picking up the clothes
one by one, putting them in a neat bundle to be washed.

'Come here. First lock the latch behind you and come here.'

'I came to tell you supper is ready.'

'Yes, thank you, I know. First come here.'

I feebly shuffled towards him and he grabbed me by my apron. I
looked at him as he lay on the black and white pillow, all flushed. His
eyes, almost bloodshot, glistened like a leopard about to devour his
kill. Even his moustache and sideburns were curly, his cheeks were rosy
and pink. I remembered Sarah saying he was shy of women. That's
why he slept in his parents' bedroom. I wonder what she would say
now.

I tried to protest and said: 'I've got to see to supper first.'

But he hoarsely groaned and said: 'Nettie will see to it. The maids
will see to our children, as well as the old people. There are so many

helpers in this homestead. Everyone has something to do. Please relax and don't be shy. You are my wife.'

Chapter 10

Nettie and her parents. Ivy's questions about her mother. Conversation at lunch.

MY FATHER-IN-LAW AND MOTHER-IN-LAW called me after morning tea. They were so excited. I felt nervous and undignified, after spending the whole night with my husband instead of with my children and his. I hadn't even said goodnight to them, they really must have thought me very ill-mannered indeed.

Nettie was flat on the mat on the floor plaiting little Ivy's hair and little Stephen played with two oxen pulling a plough. My little Winkie winked up at me so excitedly holding a newly plaited whip in his hand, and shouted: 'Mama, Mama, look at my whip Biya made for me,' and Bighead had a six pairs of mud oxen inspanned and pulling a very lopsided wagon made of blue mud.

Nettie shrieked: 'When do you propose to prepare a decent meal for your husband? Eh, eh. My brother is going to die of hunger. Awoo.'

'Nettie, your brother is happy now, he has mourned enough.' This was my father-in-law speaking. 'Nettie, my lassie, you are such a bright spark. I love you so much, my child, but it near breaks my spirit to see you grow old without a spouse. When will you bring a man home, so that we may discuss marriage?'

'Oh Father, it's all your fault. You prefer to live in isolation in this God-forsaken jungle, full of all kinds of deadly beasts and crawling with poisonous insects and snakes. Does Father expect other people's children to journey for months to die here in the wilderness? I don't know what kind of a white man you are. All the English people are living in Durban. You are the only one living in the forest. I honestly don't understand your concern about your children. First of all we had no schooling, secondly we have no suitors for miles around. We are surrounded by our own relatives.' Then Nettie caught her breath. 'Oh Father, what am I supposed to do? I am getting grey and blind. Sibiya will have to carve me a walking stick. Oh Daddy, I am the only one left without a husband,' and she sobbed bitterly like a child. She laid her head on both knees and wiped her tears on her mother's pinafore. Her father patted her lovingly as she snuggled closer to them.

My heart broke for her; it was not so long ago that I went through the same pain and despair. I knelt down beside them and hugged Nettie, and tried to console her by saying everything would be all right. 'Look at me, God has given me a husband, even with two of someone else's children. Oh Nettie, please don't give up.'

Her father was crying, and he said in a croaking broken voice: 'My child, there are things that only the soul of a man knoweth. I swore an oath in God's name that I would never leave this soil, this is where God took a handful of soil to make my ribs and I became a man. I've sworn that my bones will be buried under those pine trees in this homestead and that's how it will be. I am so, so sorry my child. I hope you can forgive me one day.'

My husband's voice at the door sounded so sad as he said: 'Nettie, come here, my sister.' He opened his arms and she dropped into them still sobbing. 'Nettie, when my first wife passed on I nearly lost my mind, but I didn't. God sent me another wife. Be strong and have faith. Where is your faith? I am starving. Father, can I please slaughter the spotted sheep? She seems to be limping. I found a huge thorn in her hoof this morning as Sibiya de-wormed them with me.'

My husband took the boys toward the kraal to witness the slaughter of the sheep. Nothing is more interesting for little farm boys than to witness a slaughter. But little Ivy stayed with me and I befriended her by offering to sew a rag doll for her. She rolled her round eyes, looked at me pathetically, and said: 'Gaan Auntie vir my 'n poppie maak soos die ene wat Mama vir my gemaak het?'

I could hardly speak a word of Afrikaans, but I knew what she was saying, so I said: 'Ja, ja, my kind. Ek is Mama. Mama sal môre terug kom.'

Her eyes shone with confidence. She fluttered her eyelashes over those beautiful blueish, greyish eyes and said: 'Mama sal lekkers vir ons bring.' And she nodded her head as though she sensed I wasn't believing her. She wanted me to say: 'Yes, Mama is coming back tomorrow.'

Oh my God, please dear God, what am I supposed to say to her? This was the first time she had spoken to me. She honestly believed with her little heart that I could support her hope. But how could I tell her that her Mama had gone to heaven? And even if I did my husband would be angry; every family member said that he would tell her when she was older.

I held her but she pulled away in defiance. She felt I wasn't answering her and she ran outside. I ran after her and found her on her little haunches, crying behind her grandparents' rondavel. I tried to hold her; but she pulled away, crying so pitifully, and in a squeaky little voice said: 'Jy is nie my Mama nie. Ek wil my eie Mama hê, ek wil Mama hê. Waar is Mama? My Mama – you are not my own Mama.'

I ran away to hide myself as I was crying bitterly. With all the pain I'd experienced I'd never felt so utterly and completely broken-hearted. Dear dear God, please dear God, oh, what must I do? The pain in my heart surpassed all other pains I'd been through. I sat flat on the grass behind the main house and hid my face in my apron, sniffing and choking with hot tears. I felt so unworthy, so useless and selfish.

My husband found me still sobbing and said: 'Winnefred, I've brought the liver and heart from the sheep. Will you please fry it for me for lunch? I love to have it fresh. My father likes it too. Stop crying now, come along with me.'

But I blurted out in despair: 'When and how are you going to tell Ivy about her mother's death? She believes her mother is coming back tomorrow. Oh Benjamin, what are you going to do?'

He sat down beside me and told me that Katrina's auntie had come to look after them after their mother's death. 'So she really doesn't remember her own mother, but Miemie, the old lady. Miemie stayed here with her and little Stephen till she had to go back to Wakkerstroom to her people because the rain forest with its mist and rainy days was no good for her asthma. Winnefred, I'll have to wait until Ivy is older. You've got to help me by trying very hard to mother her. That's why I was so happy when you said Sarah and Jacob should not take the children just yet. Together we will do our best to look after them.'

I went to find Ivy, but she was with her little brother in her grandparents' room. They were playing with her tattered rag doll. I noticed two long wooden boxes there, covered with a white sheet. My eyes, still swollen from crying, almost popped out with fright. I thought they resembled coffins.

'Oh my word, don't tell me those are coffins covered up there?' I practically screamed the words out. 'What are coffins doing in the house?'

My father-in-law looked towards them, pointed with his walking stick and banged them twice, and said: 'Can you hear the hollow sound? They are quite empty, my child. I made them when I was stronger for my wife and myself. They are our last resting-places, so I made them very comfortable for us. I've even lined them with satin from the Arabs who used to trade with us some years back. So you see my children will have no problem looking for coffins in these desolate parts.'

I prepared the lunch myself. And I didn't forget what Jessica had told me, so I boiled pumpkin, sweet potatoes, and cabbage from the garden. Cabbage and peas, being winter vegetables, were green and would make the table look very pretty. And then there was the fried liver and heart, and the fried spek pieces to go with it, and brown rice (which was grown on a small scale on the farm just for the old man who couldn't eat very much mealie-meal). I was particularly impressed by the huge black coal stove and the shelves that were lined with canned fruit, even canned vegetables. There were green beans and beetroot and a lot of rhubarb jam, orange and lemon marmalade. I wondered who had bottled these.

'Ha!' I grinned to myself as I inspected one.

Then my mother-in-law nudged me from behind and said: 'Ha! You fight for the heart of the man by food.'

I didn't even know she was in the pantry. 'Oh Mama, I didn't know you were here.'

'Yes, my child, I must teach you to cook for the heart of my son. Katrina, she taught me very very many ways how the boere cook and my son he likes very very much the boerekos.' So she opened the pots and sniffed in sheer joy. 'Aah, you make the spek. Oh he likes that very much. Hawu, my child, you make very nice dinner. Your father-in-law is too proud to eat rubbish.'

My mother-in-law said I must go with Nathi and show her how to lay the table. Nathi knew a few things from Auntie Jessie's, but Jessica's table was only set for three. Here it was sometimes laid for ten or even more. I looked at the cupboards and shelves made of hewn wood. There were stumps of wood carved into a hollow with another one like a thick stick to beat whatever was put in it into a pulp. I had never seen anything like that. It was to stamp mealies to cook with beans and thick pork spek.

My mother-in-law was saying: 'Awee, he likes to eat that food like that. Makoti, you must cook it next week before we make the soap.

He is riding to Loeffler's store to buy caustic soda to make the soap, and you must learn how. Usually he makes it because he is afraid the poison might get on the woman's hand, and then how will she suckle the baby? – and if she cooks maybe the poison will get into the food.'

Oh my word, Mrs Rorke was indeed the wife of James Michael Rorke – the lady of the manor, the Missus, the Nona, the Nkhosikazi, the maitre d'hôtel. The Ndlovukazi – all the Zulus around held her in high esteem. She had worked very hard and had passed the grade, she had weathered well. Her husband looked up to her with respect. She had a will of her own, a determination to conquer, to cross the raging river. To make ends meet when there are no ends. She was no fictitious flippant flabbergasted savage, she was totally immersed in this illustrious life of being Mrs Rorke.

She found it compelling and fulfilling to such an extent that the Chief had asked her nkhosi, her husband, if she could teach some of his many wives to make bread and scones and teach them to make cakes out of mealies ground freshly into a paste. She would fry them in summer in lard with shallots or even isijingi (pumpkin porridge), which made a lovely tasty meal when she seasoned it up with lard and shallots, and teach them how to save meat by boiling and salting it before hanging it up under the trees.

Oh, so many little things that the white man taught her she passed on to her family. But the issue of the isidwaba, the skin skirt, was taboo. They had better not mention it.

Nettie had apparently been fast asleep; but she wasn't really, just subdued and deep in thought. Her father asked her at table if she would have some more spek with sweet potatoes, which was her favourite.

She said rather rudely: 'Father, I'd still like to keep my waist the way it is now, thank you.'

'Nettie, have you left your table manners in Durban? Please run and fetch them at once. Hawu maSwazi wena Sobuza, there's a child getting out of hand.'

My father-in-law thanked me for a tasty lunch. He went on to say that Benjamin had to resume his work as border guard on the rain forest territories as the ploughing would soon start and the rains with it, and the building of new huts would also begin. He himself had to be on guard lest the locals chop young saplings for their huts. And also to ensure they gathered the correct amount of beans, lest they over-harvest. That was his life here in the rain forest. He nursed it the same way he did his children and his wife.

My father-in-law went on to say Benjy's life would be more settled now as soon as ploughing was over. He had to ride to Ngoshe to obtain his badge from the court, stating that he was Sheriff of the Border Guard of the rain forests. This job meant that he was to report immediately to the Forester if he found defaulters, and they in turn were to be fined or charged or even dismissed from the rain forests according to the crime committed. He had to have a meeting with the Chief to discuss ways and means of curbing grazing land and working on soil erosion. He would speak to his son, telling him to learn how to take wild twine from the forest in such a way as not to disturb the undergrowth while cutting it, and then to weave it as if it were tying the rocks and stones together, making a wall to prevent soil erosion. Moreover, the Chief and the headman would have to be informed on how to build the structure, and they would all have to go out into the areas that were hardest hit by soil erosion to demonstrate to the locals, showing them that this was the only way they would save the land from tearing apart. Otherwise the dongas would cause more damage to the grazing pastures. He went on to say that the only way to get them to do some work was to do it with them. Then their interest would be captured and they would become excited and willing workers.

Benjamin answered by telling his father how he feared talking to the Chief as he would say he was a child.

'That's why we have to call a meeting, my son, don't you understand? The ways of the Zulu demand total respect and complete loyalty to the elders. You have to be very, very cautious. I sometimes fear for your free tongue. You have to learn that the Zulus have a decorous manner of speech, and are very suspicious. Everything you say and do concerning their welfare must be clearly understood, or else they think you are a wizard and want to cast some sort of spell on them.'

Nettie burst out. 'Oh Father, you tire us with all your Zulu customs. Tell us more about the European way of life. I am so tired of all the dedication and love you have for the welfare of the Zulus and not for your children.'

'Awoo, Nettie my child, the city is making you a hooligan, a tsotsi. You are not going back to Durban, you are going to stay at home and learn to plough and weed, and look after your old parents.'

'Haa, and marry the Chief to become wife number ten.'

'Nettie, behave yourself and go to your room.'

Nettie knew full well that her father was partially deaf in the left ear, and as she sat on the far right of the long table he never really heard what she said. She mumbled under her breath pretending to be busy collecting the empty plates, but making sure the clatter was louder than her voice. Oh Nettie, she was really fed up with life.

Chapter 11

Nettie's departure. Winnefred settles in. Talk of possible offspring. The Chief's visit. James Michael Rorke's father's death. His burial. The children are bundled off in various directions.

NETTIE WAS LEAVING FOR DURBAN. She had to travel to Jessica's homestead and from there walk to Nongoma to catch a railroad bus to Durban. Oh my word, I was going to be left alone in the bush. Nettie had been such good company. We clung together and cried bitterly. We both knew that even though our reasons for crying were different, they were very good reasons.

'Please write to me, Nettie.'

'I'll try, but you know I can't write.'

'Oh well, ask someone else who can, and I'll reply in no time at all – but you'll receive yours in two months' time as you know how long the post takes here.'

'Oh, it's better now we've got the railroad bus from Nongoma, so you can write to me often enough.'

We all stood under the trees watching her little plump backside wriggling away, turning ever so often to wave her handkerchief until she disappeared. Her father went back to his rondavel and sat on his huge chair and cried bitterly, saying he knew he'd never see her again. She had spent her last night at home in their rondavel in between them on their huge brass bed, like a little child. She had cried herself to sleep, and even then it was only after her father gave her some honey and warm milk and her mother sang her an old Swazi lullaby. Oh Nettie. I missed her already.

After Nettie left for Durban I really had to work very hard. I had no helper except the servants whom I hardly knew, except for my own maid that Jessica had given me. Surprisingly enough my husband dedicated a lot of time to helping me, getting his children to help too. His parents were also very concerned about my welfare.

Big Father seemed to be getting weaker by the day though. Little Ivy, who was eight years old, used to sit by his bedside and talk to him. She had gotten over her mother and started calling me Mama. We had become good friends and I loved her and her brother terribly; I seemed to care more for them than for my own. My husband worked so hard, ploughing and breaking in new fields and coming home tired, but still he helped where he could.

Early in September most of the ploughing was finished so he went up to Louwsburg to fetch his badge as Sheriff of the Border so he could start his duties in October, before the rainy season. I was excited. I loved to see him in his uniform. He was so handsome. I loved him painfully, even when he raged and shouted and strutted back and forth doing everything at once. Everyone had to move out of his way when he came galloping like a mad horse all over the yard. It never occurred to me that he was being over-demanding or aggressive in any way. I was proud of him because he was a hardworking man.

Benjy's father would sometimes call him to reprimand him when he overworked the herdboys or when he had been rude to Sibiya. His father loved Sibiya and so on many occasions the argument would be intense.

'Daddy, you love this savage of yours more than you love me. I am your last-born son, but if I ask you to buy me a shirt or even some long johns, you'll always say, "Oh all right son, I'll think about it." But let Sibiya ask for a shirt and he gets one.'

On a beautiful spring day in October, before Benjamin went to work, he took us for a picnic. We walked right to the waterfall under the Ntendeka cliff. The raging waterfall, tucked into the corner of the cliff beside the thick green forest, looked like a frothing white cloud flowing down from heaven, rushing to wash the souls of mankind. Oh it was frighteningly beautiful. Awesome. The cliff on one side looked like a huge pile of human bones. Some resembled huge legs, some massive heads, and the cracks looked like jaws and teeth, even hands – but all those were stuck together as if when God created man he had to take all the bones from there.

There were all colours and shapes of insects and birds and butterflies. There were ferns so beautiful I thought angels must have done the fine crochet work, spiders so pretty I wanted to touch them. African violets hung on every branch or rock near the waterfall, all getting sprayed by the vapour. There seemed to be a constant rainbow across the green forest, making a pattern like shimmering threads of golden hues dancing to-and-fro, and fairies playing the harp of golden hues endlessly. The humming bees danced to and fro to the sound of the thunderous cascading water.

My children were shrieking with joy. Benjy had little Stephen on his shoulders, changing every now and then with one of my sons; and then his hand held mine as we picked our way, while the maid carried a heavy basket on her head, full of food.

Stephen was getting stronger. He was so happy, trying to chase a butterfly and falling and screaming: 'Mama, catch it. Papa, catch it. We want to play.' Oh he was so handsome. His cheeks were rosy, his small little pink mouth pouted as he rolled his blueish greyish eyes and said: 'Mama, I is hungry.' Oh he was so sweet and so loving, I cuddled him up on my lap together with my Bighead and fed all of them together. My husband was too deeply engrossed in tearing the dead fowls' legs and munching gleefully and contentedly away.

Benjy pointed up the long greyish hill to show me the row of pine trees that used to be their old home. As we neared the homestead he pointed out the fields that were ploughed and the ones that had to be ploughed after Christmas. He pointed to the red mealie field and the black mealie field, and further down in the plain beside the waterfall river, the mabela field and the grazing land for the sheep and cattle.

My husband said to me: 'When I've gone to work, you must be aware of your fields. Don't let the neighbouring cattle get in to graze. Always keep an eye on things. Sometimes the bush blocks the view and before you see it a whole field will be wiped out. Then you and your children will starve. There'll be no reaping. The sweet potato patch is down near Mahalahaleni. It's lowveld down there, and dryer than up here, so they'll do well there. We get the best beans on that patch overlooking the kraal, and the round potatoes are there as well so they get enough manure from the cattle dung.' He drew a breath. 'Oh Winnie, there is nothing that doesn't grow in this land. Sometimes we get three mealie cobs on one stalk, and the pumpkins are as big as ant-heaps. Our cows get so much milk we are never without butter and amasi. We have watermelons and white melons to make jam. Oh, I love this land more than my own life. My life is not important without this land. Look at the oranges and lemons, the pawpaws and avocado pears and mangoes. Even the guavas and granadillas grow wild, and there are thousands of different kinds of wild fruit inside the forest and outside. We will grow old together still never having tasted half the fruit that the rain forest has to give.'

Suddenly he turned to me and said: 'I've noticed you are getting thinner. What is worrying your heart? I wonder if you're not starting to germinate my seed?'

'No, no, no. It's not that. I was hoping to start germinating, but I think I've been too scared and confused. This is such a new life for me. I had given up on getting married, but I'll settle down, given time to get used to living in Paradise with the most handsome man on earth.'

Oh my word. I should never have said that. He quickly ordered the maid to go on with the children and held my hand, whispering excitedly urging me to come with him to our first picnic spot. As I walked in front of him for the first time, he paid me a generous compliment. 'I love your slightly bandy hairy legs. I love your hips and flat English backside. Your tiny hands and feet, and the way your breasts heave up and down when you try to talk. I love the shyness, the way your little eyes droop, and you shyly put your little hand across your small mouth, your figure is still like a young girl's, and most of all, I love the way you totally submit yourself to me. I know I'll never get over Katrina, but it seems the wound is healing slowly.'

After making supper, I set the table and went to the rondavel to see if the old people would sit at table with us or have their supper brought in on a tray. My husband was having a hearty laugh with his father.

The old man said: 'Winnefred my child, you've broken the ice in my broken-hearted son's life. I haven't shared such a hearty laugh with him in a long time.'

'Thank you, Father, he has made me happy too.'

He was smiling. The old woman, Joko, was mumbling away and said: 'She'll come with me to fetch her husband's supper.'

And in the kitchen she looked me up and down, and grinned showing her beautiful set of teeth. 'Ah maSwati, you've made my son so happy, does that mean you are expecting?' And she bent to touch and felt my stomach, and said: 'Ha, there's nothing yet, but that's because of all the confusion. The body takes long to spill out the poisonous gases and then start receiving the cleansing. Only then will your mind be free to receive the gift of germinating. I think you are overworked. I must ask Nomandwali to come more often to help you. This homestead is too big for one little makoti to handle.'

Then Joko said: 'Your father-in-law is very sick. I've got to give him all the love and attention he needs, so I have no more time to see to many things around the house – especially my garden, which you must take over. Nomandwali will help you.' She planted a wet kiss on my forehead and took her husband's tray.

She brought the supper tray back personally so she could whisper to me: 'My child, when your husband comes back from ploughing tomorrow you must take his towel and soap and clean underwear down to the river. Sibiya will not be here, he has to leave for his new bride's kraal to offer to pay lobola for her. The white man has agreed to give him the cattle to lobola the young virgin and Sibiya can hardly talk with excitement.'

I knew that this was a plot to have me meet my husband down the river. Little did she know that we already had our mating spot. Oh my word, this cunning old lady. She knew from experience that the best mating whereby one will conceive is down at the river in the open air, not in a bed. She really felt I wasn't having enough time alone with my husband because of the overload of work and the children. Maybe she was worried that perhaps I could not conceive at all. Which would be disastrous in her culture. Oh well, I just hoped I could conceive, otherwise I'd have to visit Auntie Jessica's hospital.

The Chief came down riding his horse, dressed in full soldier's khaki uniform to see the white man, as he knew the old man was very sick. He sat with him in his rondavel and they spoke about the new fields down at Mahalahaleni, which the Chief had given the new makoti as a gift from himself. It was a very fertile piece of ground right on the river banks of the Empopoma, which took its water from the waterfall, and rounded Mahalahaleni to run into the Esikwebezi. He said I could plant red mabela which did well in that field.

I was called in to say thank you to him, and he chuckled with approval at the way I knelt down before him with the tray. It was set with hot scones and mulberry jam, which he enjoyed so much that he finished the whole bottle. It was rude to leave food unfinished that was set in front of you to eat, so he showed me the greatest respect by devouring everything on the tray.

'Oh haa, umnandi ujam, Nkhosikazi. Thank you very much, can you teach my wives to make such jam?'

I agreed very politely and he told my father how lucky my husband was. He always had women who made nice things to eat. The Chief said his goodbye to the old people and offered my father-in-law a young goat so that broth could be made for him. The method involved boiling the insides of the goat together with the rest, so as to get bitter broth from all the kinds of bitter tree that the goat ate from. My mother-in-law knew how to prepare the entrails the way her husband liked them. He would send the goat in the morning by herdboy.

The old man was getting weaker by the day. He enjoyed the bitter broth and ate a little of the meat, sitting up on his chair. Then he called his son and told him that he could not remember many things. His memory was fading very fast, even his speech was fading, and his eyesight was failing too. He begged his son not to leave him alone and go to work at the forest border – to wait, rather, until early in January.

The old man was withering away very fast but he still had hopes of seeing all his children over Christmas. It was customary for all the family to be together at Christmas and he spoke about the two oxen he wanted to slaughter at Christmas for his children. He told his son not to worry about feeding his children because he still had four gold coins hidden in one of the coffins. Joko had hidden them in true traditional style in a little calabash shuffed with corn grain. Oh how he loved and admired her skills!

The old man wanted Benjy to have the papers taken to the Court House at Ngoshe to bind his will and leave him the gold pieces and the livestock. Walter and James had their own livestock which he had given them as wedding gifts, and he had nothing more to give them now. He hoped they would understand. For of course Benjy, being the baby, should have the bulk of whatever livestock there was. The land belonged to the government. They could lease it from the government for as long as the government saw fit.

My husband rode to Ngoshe the following day with the signed document to have it legally stamped by the court, the witnesses being my husband and Sibiya and the Chief Mpontshane. This was why my father-in-law had given Sibiya his herd of cattle to lobola. He knew he was a dying man. He had no ailments on his body, he was dying from old age. He was one hundred years old. Ivy would sit on his bed and try to talk to him. Sometimes he would answer well, and she would be thrilled and come running to tell me. 'Mama, Grandpa can talk. Mama, Grandpa is calling you.'

I would sit and hold his hand and kiss his old wrinkled fingers that were lifeless, but his smile would get weary and he'd say: 'Please promise me, lassie, you'll look after my son. I am going to England and then to Ireland to see my granddad. I'll bring you back a pretty Irish frock. Oh lassie, you've got a beautiful heart. I am going to give you a gold coin for my first grandchild from you. Don't tell my Benjamin. You must ask Joko to hide it safely for you. Oh blimey, she knows how to hide well, she does.' And he would laugh in a very faint voice and then close his eyes and sleep.

Sometimes he would call Nettie, sometimes Louisa. When he called Jessica he would almost want to get up and beckon to her: 'There come the Zulus! To the pit at once. Oh God, don't let them take my children.'

And he would sob so bitterly and some days he would call Sibiya and ask for his horse, but Sibiya would say the horse is grazing far down in the valley. One day he insisted so painfully on seeing his horse, that Sibiya and my husband brought the horse inside the rondavel by breaking some of the wall away and taking the hinges off the door. It was the most touching scene. My father-in-law seemed to glow as he almost jumped out of his sick-bed. He ordered Sibiya to saddle up at once.

'I've got to gallop to Iswandlwana to Mbijane, to warn my father at once before the wagons cross the drift. Quickly, waste no time, they are coming, I can hear the stampede. Oh Thunder, my beloved brother, why are you so slow, are you feeling ill, didn't you eat? What could the matter be? Oh Thunder, my friend, my best friend, why do you leave me?'

The horse seemed to hear every word the old man spoke. He knelt down beside his bed and the old man hugged him with both his frail arms. Imagining he was riding him he cried: 'Thunder, Thunder, fly away – boy-o-boy – there's my friend, go boy go.' He gasped his last breath and happiness shone on his face as his eyelids closed with a contented smile.

Joko leapt forward to catch his body as he collapsed on the bed. His son threw himself on top of him screaming: 'Daddy, Daddy, don't ride away. Please Daddy, go after Christmas. You said you want to see all your children on Christmas day. Daddy, don't go. Please, Daddy.'

Joko gently and gracefully laid her cheek on her husband's and called on her ancestors to help her to accept her grief.

Sibiya led Thunder out. He prepared his things to ride to the Chief's kraal over the mountain to report the death of the brave white warrior; then he would ride to the forest office to report the death there. But under the pear trees he found Thunder lying with his legs up in the air, frothing and gasping for breath. The horse was dying and Sibiya watched him in horror, shouting for his ancestors, hands on his head.

I was left wondering where to start. The children were screaming, the old lady was quietly washing her husband's face and crying silently. My husband held his father's body full against his bosom, while his mother washed his face.

The three of us washed the old man's body and changed him into his shroud. My husband took the coffin out and laid him gently inside. Joko remembered the gold coins in the small little calabash and took them out. At the foot of the coffin she anointed the shroud with lavender which she had kept for this occasion, and brushed her husband's white silken hair till it shone, and kissed him on the forehead, and told him to keep her place ready as she would be coming soon.

The Chief came at once to send out his indunas far and wide to report the death of James Michael Rorke. It was 16 December, 1934.

The grave-diggers were there early next morning. By midday my father-in-law had been laid to rest under the willow trees, beside the pear trees at his beautiful Ngome Forest homestead.

His children arrived one by one from Durban and all over Zululand to pay their last respects to their beloved father. There were many friends, including a magistrate from Peddie in the Eastern Cape, who was his uncle's son; some came from Utrecht, from his wife's family. There were many oxen slaughtered for the mourners. The natives around Ngome mourned by howling the Ntendeka down; the echoes carried on for days. Jessica stayed for Christmas together with Nettie who still wasn't married. Sarah came with her husband Leonard Dunn and Louisa came with her Jacob, who looked as large as a house. There were prayers offered at the grave every day for a whole week. The priest came down on donkey-back from Nongoma. It was Father Jacob. Even though James Michael was an Anglican, he was blessed by a Catholic priest as there were not many churches except the Catholic mission at Nongoma.

Walter bundled up his beloved mother to go and live with his family at Esikwebezi; Louisa bundled off Ivy and Stephen to her homestead at Mangete and left together with Leonard and Sarah. My own father bundled off my children to Esikwebezi, to live there with his young wife.

Then I had no more tears to cry. I was childless, all by myself in the bush. My husband was so lost that he kept saying: 'Oh Winnie, why did they take our children?' and we would cling to one another and cry like two bush babies.

Many years later something happened which made me remember this time.

My eldest daughter Agnes was married and had her own five children. And she came home to Ngome with her boys, her face all swollen with a blue eye – and very, very depressed. She was quite traumatised.

I remember asking her: 'Where are your two girls Rhonda and Beryl?'

'Mama, they've taken them to the home for abused children in Durban. The welfare people took them, and Lemmy is blaming me for going behind his back, and giving his children away to the white people without his permission. He has given me such a hiding, I nearly died. I've come home for good. I am never going back to that murderer! I'd rather have my own father sjambok me till I am black and blue.'

And she cried sorely, clinging on to me: 'Mama, my children, oh God, my children, my two little girls, I won't see them till the July holidays.'

And as the two little boys clung to us crying, because their mother was crying, the memories came flooding back.

It seemed like yesterday that I had cried bitterly for my two boys and my husband's children. Then the thought hit me like a hammer. The Zulus had a saying that the first daughter takes the mother's womb – meaning her fate and the pain of it. Hawoo! Nkhosi yami! Wathatha isinye sikanina. She has taken her mother's womb. Oh Mother Mary, I hope it stops there, I pray she doesn't go through it all!

How observant the Zulus are, and how much knowledge is stored up in their sayings. It was just as well my child did not know what I was going through at the time.

Chapter 12

Winnefred meets Mtembu the inyanga. She visits her parents at Esikwebezi. There she finds her children alienated – and she hears about the new arrangements. Nyawo's teachings about the isifociya.

JANUARY CAME SO QUICKLY. My husband had to resume his duties at the forester's office. He came back wearing his uniform. I couldn't even feel the excitement of seeing him with his uniform. He seemed to have gone grey overnight. He had lost his zest for living. He was gaunt and lanky. The uniform hung on him like a scarecrow. I felt so hurt for him but I missed the children so much I would hear their voices everywhere in the yard and in the rooms. Ivy and Stephen's little voices, soft and forlorn.

Life had been getting too good to be true here in Ngome. I had been too happy for it to last. So what now? What happens next? After six months I wanted to see my children. I walked alone with Nathi, my maid, to Esikwebezi. I didn't want my husband to come with me. It would only break his heart as his children were far away in Mangete.

As we walked, across the river, we passed a vast kraal with many huts. This was Mtembu's domain. We saw an old, shrivelled man, wearing skins with hair still on them, digging on the river bank. He stood up to greet us, and seemed to know who I was for he sympathised for the death of my father-in-law, saying what a fine warrior he had been.

The old man, whose name was Mtembu, went on to say that he was a great healer – the greatest. If ever I needed to be treated for anything, even conception or childbirth, he would be able to help me. Oh my. I thanked him very politely and told him I'd come to him if I had any ailments but I knew many herbs which my own mother had taught me. He said to tell my husband he would be coming up to the homestead with the herbal mixture for the cattle, to de-worm them before ploughing season.

In no time we were crossing the Esikwebezi and walking uphill. We had a full view of the homestead. I could see my boys playing in the huge yard, chasing one another with little sticks. I was right behind little Winkie when he turned around. I grabbed him in my arms and sat right down on the ground in the middle of the yard.

'Oh my child, my own child.' He had grown a little taller. 'My child, my baby.'

I kissed his pink cheeks and held him tight, but he wriggled free and looked me straight in my eyes and said: 'Leave me alone, you're not my Mama, you left me alone. I cried and cried every day, but you wouldn't come to fetch me. Go away, leave us alone.' Both he and his brother were now chorusing: 'Leave us alone.'

I found myself running back down the road to Ngome. I thought of all the happiness I had had with them at Ngome. Perhaps I'd find my children all waiting there. Ivy and Stephen with grandpa and grandma and all the birds and butterflies and the big, big frog. Mama. Oh my Jesus. Oh Mama. Mother Mary have pity on me. It's enough. I'll rather die. At least I had a bit of love and happiness. Now it's best to die. If my own children refuse to talk to me, then what's the use of living.

Footsteps, swift and heavy, came up behind me, but even a firm grip on my shoulder couldn't make me stop. I ran even faster, sobbing bitterly, but my father overtook me at last and pleaded with me to stop at once. He picked me up and held me in his arms.

'Winnefred my child, come up with me and we'll explain what has happened. It's not what you think.'

He wiped my tears with his big hairy hands that always felt like rough stone. He almost bruised my cheek as he stroked me, to make me be quiet and stop crying. He cooed softly as we walked back toward the homestead. My father had a very soft tender voice. He never spoke loudly. His steel blue eyes always did the talking when he was cross. His eyes would emit fiery sparks like falling stars out of a fierce blue sky.

My Auntie Rosie and her husband Walter hugged me and both apologised for the children's behaviour. They asked me to sit down while the maid brought in steaming tea with freshly baked scones, and as I calmed down Walter said in a deep sad tone: 'Winnie, my child, we have spoken about you keeping your children in the new marriage. But we have all come to the conclusion that when your own children start coming, you'll have a hard time. It would cause many painful years and would not be fair to my brother as he has also had to give up his children. My brother is a very temperamental man. In the course of time he will definitely have a change of mood and cause you to suffer under the stress. So we as your family – your Auntie Rose and my brother-in-law, your father – decided that the kids should call Auntie

Rosie their mother, not your father's young wife as she will also feel burdened. We would like you to understand that there are many painful things in life that have to be dealt with in their early stages rather than waiting till they grow bigger and bigger. Often that way they cause more pain and misery in later years than if the problem had been solved earlier.'

I had to accept that. That was the truth, as I was not accustomed to asking questions or arguing. I just cried softly and nodded my head in response. Auntie Rosie, who never spoke, much like her brother, said softly: 'My girl, as time goes on you'll understand that a man does not like to bring up another man's children. You might end up with no marriage at all.'

Well, everything was done for me, I had no say. They called my children and told them that I was still their real mommy, but I had to part with them as they were going far away to a boarding school and would not be able to see me for a long time. Their father, who was much better after Auntie Jessica's medicinal herbal remedies, was ready to take them to start school next year and they would be together with Ivy and Stephen in the same boarding school. I didn't know what else to say. As I said goodbye to my children, I felt unworthy and sinful as though I was being punished for my shame.

I was very quiet as we walked home to Ngome, hurrying to get there before sundown. There was no excitement in my heart. I felt dead inside. I wasn't making too much sense, even to myself. Why couldn't I conceive another child? Was that also part of my punishment?

I couldn't cry any more. My heart seemed to have left me. Nathi, who was half-running behind me, said: 'Nkhosikazi, stop crying, and don't fly like a mad woman. Just walk nicely. Look, Nyawo is here with us now. Your husband sent her to meet us and to look after you. You are so thin, as if you are going to die. Even if a Zimzim came across you, he'd never eat you up. You would cause him to run away instead. He would surely think you are a spook.'

Nyawo ordered me to sit down on the river bank near a patch of incema rush. She said in a very stern, matter-of-fact tone: 'Do you see this incema rush? We Zulus make many useful items with it. Dishes to eat out of and mats to sit on – but only to be used by kings and chiefs. We women are not even allowed to sit on such an expensive mat. Yet after giving birth a woman is allowed to have a woven belt of incema. And this is tied tightly around her belly, to keep her guts in place and to remind her to respect her belly out of which a child has come, and to make her aware that the child is gone from her belly and will never return again.

'You tie the belt very tightly. Even when you are eating it stays on. Even when you are sleeping it stays on. You are not allowed to shift it at any time. The old people tie it on for you as soon as you give birth.'

I listened, still sniffing a little, to what Nyawo was telling me.

She continued: 'This is a Zulu custom, but we also use it as a proverb to convey many of the teachings in our culture. When we are in pain or when we are grieving for a lost one, even for a lost child, a Zulu woman has to tie her isifociya, her belt for life. When you are hungry from the fields – you've been weeding the whole morning, you are so hungry – and yet you know that when you get home, you have to first go down the spring to fetch water or to even collect a little bundle of firewood, then you tighten your life belt. You have to grind corn on the grinding stone to make the amasi or to cook phuthu? – you must make your belt tighter.

'The hunger subsides somehow, you'll get the strength to carry on until your meal is cooked and ready to eat, first by your husband and then by all your household. The incema has a way to curb all pain in your body; all you have to do is tighten your belt and you'll endure anything.

'Remember your babies are gone out of your belly. Never, never can they go back inside. You've got to let them go. Tighten your belt and stop thinking of too many hurtful things or else you'll allow weakness to take over your whole body and you will be sick.

'When you conceive your first child in wedlock, I will be there to tie your belt and I'll see to it that you never take it off. You see mine, it has been on me since my firstborn son. I've had six children. Two were taken by their ancestors but I just tied my belt more tightly.

'Come now, my child, your husband is waiting patiently at home for you. I'll go now as I cannot walk like a tortoise to grind the corn for amasi, and I'll tell him to meet you on the road to Mahalahaleni as I know how frightened you are of the bush.'

As we watched Nyawo walk briskly towards the homestead, Nathi asked me humbly: 'Did you hear everything she said?'

I said: 'Yes, I did.'

'And do you understand what she means? I do. I know about the life belt. My mother taught us when we were learning how to fetch water and carry our calabashes straight without wobbling and spilling the water.'

My husband appeared on the road in front of me, with his gun loosely slung across his shoulder. He was so withdrawn and gaunt, his eyes were all sunken in, his beard overgrown, his trousers tied with a broad leather belt to keep them from falling.

I ran up to him from sheer pity and he lifted me up like a child. I stayed like that, holding on to my life. He was my very breath that I breathed. I took a deep gulp of him. His perspiration. He had a faint smell of cream, mixed with all the fresh soil with dry fruit and crushed autumn leaves. Also just a hint of wild flowers, which give out a very strong scent from autumn till late winter. Whenever he held me like that I became devoid of words and thoughts and reasoning. I was just like a lame, sick calf.

Benjy said brokenly: 'You poor little girl, you are so thin. I am so sorry for all the pain I've caused you. I should have never married you.'

'Oh no, don't say that. Please not that. We both knew what to expect from this marriage. We'll work it out. Things will get better with time.' I thought of the life belt and summoned up more courage to say: 'I'll conceive as soon as I am over the pain of my children. Parting with our children is confusing and stressful. Your mother said that it will take some time before my body is ready to germinate with the seed of life.'

'Oh my Winnefred, I am not in any rush to have children. I know that you are not a barren woman and I am the strongest bull there ever was. So please don't let that be your worry. Try and get a little more rest and eat a little more amasi.'

We walked through the sparse forest which was almost bare of foliage as it was winter. What caught my interest was the way the scenery coincided with the way we felt. We seemed stripped of all happiness. The red patches of bare soil and cracked dongas were sparsely dressed in ugly dying bunches of thorn. The huge boulders and clusters of stones were whispering desperately and despairingly: 'What's going to happen to them?' The protruding thorns – long, sharp and white, and glaring at us, laughing hysterically – seemed to be saying: 'Katrina cries for her children. Where have you taken them? Why have you driven them out of their birthplace?'

I felt cold and scared. Benjy sensed my mood and tightened his grip on my hand. Suddenly there was a rushing noise right in front of us, made by a family of wild boar. He blocked my mouth from screaming and held me tight, whispering very very softly: 'Be quiet or else they'll think you are the enemy and charge, but if you're quiet they'll pass us by, hopefully without any interference.'

I froze and I knew I was wetting myself. I couldn't control it. My father used to tell us many tales of wild boar, and how they even fight with lions, so you can imagine how scared I was. My husband was as calm as the eyes of a calf as he loaded his gun and held it ready in case he had to shoot.

I said a prayer. 'Please dear God, help us if we have to get eaten: let us both be eaten together. Thank you God, amen.' I closed my eyes, ready to feel the first snapping off of my legs and wondering how I would endure the pain whilst the last drops of urine ran down my legs.

From deep in my mind, I heard my husband's faint voice. Trembling, he whispered: 'Thank God, they are gone past now. We can walk through safely. They still wander around from time to time, especially in the winter, looking for food. It gets too cold up in the rain forest and there is nothing to dig up except huge trees, so they prefer to come down to the lower and warmer pockets of bush and shrubs, and to the dongas. That is why I sent Nyawo to meet you. She knows exactly where the stinkwood trees are situated along the pathway and where you can climb up quickly in case of emergencies. Wild boars won't come anywhere near a stinkwood tree. Oh Winnie, please don't be scared. Let's go home and have some strong bush tea to ease our sore nerves and cool our thoughts.'

Chapter 13

Dejection in the marriage partners. Visit from the Chief. Benjy rides off to speak to Katrina's people. The sheep sacrifice.

IT WAS SOON PLOUGHING SEASON. The Chief came down to talk to my husband about some heifers he wanted to buy to lobola his sixth wife, who was twenty years younger than he was. Oh, he was so excited. He spoke about having a hundred children and that his tribe would surely be the most powerful tribe in all of Ngome. And why had I not fallen pregnant yet? Were the ancestors not pleased with me?

Perhaps Katrina's spirit was unhappy. Maybe she was highly annoyed. Every time she came to visit her home she found no children and yet she knew full well that she had borne two children for the house of Rorke.

'Did you offer her a sacrifice asking for her permission to remove them from their birthplace? O Makhosi akwaHamu! Oh, you white zombies really have no respect for the dead. You are both going to end up very sick if you do not give her some meat in repentance for sending her offspring to far-off lands without her blessings. Now my son, listen to me and prevent any more disasters by apologising to the mother of your children, lest your new wife gets seriously sick.'

My husband retorted in an angry tone. 'I am still mourning for my father. How can I slaughter now for my dead wife while I am broken-hearted concerning my father and his horse Thunder? Katrina is at peace. Leave her alone to rest. Her spirit has not come back to haunt this homestead. But if it be that she cries for her children – yes, Chief, I will ride to Utrecht to confer with her brothers and uncles to hear the truth concerning this matter.'

'Well spoken, my son of my white brother, the brave warrior who killed a leopard with his bare hands. I've not forgotten his total regard for humanity and respect for my people, and the love he had for the soil of the land. Nevertheless, I must warn you about the flame that flickers in your brain. You must learn to cool it off with spring water from the igobongo before talking to your elders.'

I made my husband's padkos. Two fowls and dumplings, some biltong and wild dried fruit and honey. Sibiya made sure to keep the white bucket full of honey. He knew my husband loved it. All through his mourning Sibiya would sit close to him and comfort him with honeycombs and wild fruit, and wipe his tears with soft flannel leaves, telling him to stop crying.

Sibiya would tell my husband: 'A man does not cry, especially one who's just got married. My brother, don't show a woman that you are crying. She will think of you as a weakling. Of course, I share your pain. Our father has left us.'

And they would both crawl away into their secret corner of the cattle kraal. I would see them sometimes and walk away to cry in my own secret corner.

Benjy rode off early at the first cockcrow. I watched him disappear into the bush and said a prayer, kneeling down right in the pathway.

I nestled into the sweet-smelling grass and cried to God to please bring him safely back to me and his home.

Work kept me from going crazy. I planned my vegetable garden. I had Nyawo teach me how to make grass mats and how to plait a nqolobane, a mealie granary, or an isilulu, one of its containers; how to stitch the grass on, as it was thatching time, in readiness for the summer rains. We spoke about many things.

My husband was to be gone for a whole week. He had to pass Vry-heid to see to some important reports on the rain forest, and also to ask for a new dipping inspector as the old one had moved to Ngoshe district. At night, alone in my room, when the paraffin lamp started making frightening skeletal shadows on the wall and the bare wooden ceiling, I would cry – missing my children, wondering if I'd ever be a mother to them again. I knew my Auntie Rosie would look after them well but I could smell them and hear their little chattering. I wanted to feel them, to cuddle them close to me. I also thought of little Ivy and darling little Stephen. Oh dear God, I could see all their faces in the dancing, laughing shadows on the walls. Eventually my head would feel numb and very light. My eyes would burn like fire and I'd blow the lamp out and sleep soundly.

My maid would wake me with a cup of hot ground coffee with thick cream, and say to me: 'Hawu, Nkhosikazi, a woman doesn't sleep until the sun shines. There is Nyawo waiting for you outside, ready with all the planting-grass.'

Sometimes I felt I was going to die, I was so weak and tired. Until Nyawo brought me some fresh blue mud which many pregnant women loved to eat. It is supposed to give you strength, so she told me to eat some every day and make sure I ate plenty of amasi, thickly laden with cream and honey.

Nyawo was like a mother to me. I grew so fond of her. In many ways she reminded me of my own mother. And there was Dinah, who was always comforting me with such loving words, giving me confidence. Hoswayo, the eldest of them all, was the matriarch and the head girl of the izinkhehli at her time; she reigned supreme even now. She comforted me with many jokes of her bravery and her strength. She could inspan oxen, she knew how to castrate a bull, she knew how to lasso a sick cow. She could treat its wounds or those of an ox that had been gored by a raging mating bull.

My husband came back looking like a ghost. I got very scared when

I saw him. I really thought he was going to die. We all did everything we could to help him out of his stress but he complained of a headache and said he was feeling giddy. He looked in bad shape as he lay on his bed, twisting and groaning in pain. I prayed hard and sent Sibiya for Auntie Jessica, who arrived by sundown with all her herbs. She soon treated him and said he had got nothing wrong with him. He was just too tired and worn out, he needed some rest.

I clung to her and begged her not to leave us so quickly, but she said that he'd be all right in a day or two. She kissed her brother and me and left us both crying as she drove off on her donkey cart. Oh dear me, this was a hard life, but I was determined to make it work. She left me with a bottle of strengthening herbs, and told me to carry on eating blue mud and lots of amasi.

A week went by before Benjy was ready to tell me what Katrina's people had to say. He said: 'These people up-country are just as crazy as this crazy Chief with all his crazy beliefs about ancestors. They all insist that Katrina's ghost has been appearing on several occasions, crying (so her eldest brother says) – he believes she is unhappy. We should slaughter a sheep at once to apologise for the way we just sent her kids off without her consent.'

'How on earth does she talk from the dead?'

'I have no damn idea. Anyway, she has not said anything to me. I dream of her often, but they are always happy dreams. I am going crazy with so many things on my mind. But Sibiya must go and tell that damn savage I will slaughter a sheep to appease his huge appetite for meat and beer. If it makes him happy I'll even slaughter an ox. I also feel I am tired of mourning and being unhappy. Perhaps a little fresh blood and gallons of Zulu beer will lift my spirits. The difference is that my spirits are very much alive! We'll see if Katrina comes along from her grave at Utrecht to join us.'

The next week was hectic. Preparations for brewing beer were not easy. All the ladies were excited. This was almost like preparing for a wedding, which made me think lovingly about my own wedding and how I had had to sleep alone for days because of this same dead Katrina who always seemed to pose a threat to my happiness. Oh well, perhaps now she'd finally be laid to rest.

I was quite excited and joined in the uproarious laughter and the hard work, learning at last how to brew utshwala, Zulu beer. Even my husband joined in occasionally, full of jokes about dead people coming to eat, and teasing Hoswayo by telling her and Dinah not to forget to invite their dead fathers, who were loved by his father – because his father wouldn't be happy drinking and eating without his friends.

To which Hoswayo retorted: 'Oh Son of the White Chief, your own mother was a Zulu. Why then do you mock the customs of your womb? We have listened to your father and done some of the customs of the white man like throwing away our isidwabas and eating sugar and salt, even bread and scones and tea. Why then do you so hate our customs? You should not treat this matter lightly for it is true that the spirits don't die. Even your white father told us that if we were bad witches our spirits would burn in a big, big fire somewhere in the stomach of the earth.'

Katrina's uncle was too old to ride such a long distance, but her two brothers came along. Oh my word, what a feast. The Chief was exuberant and jovial as he launched himself into a thunderous self-applauding gyration full of gusto, shrieking at the top of his voice, praising himself and singing praises to his own ancestors. Oh Mama, I wish you could have seen this. He looked like an eagle in his skin skirt swaying to and fro, everyone joined in the dancing. The woman all danced in the traditional amabhayi and isidwabas. Their topknots were well treated with impepho, a kind of henna. Oh my word. I gaped in sheer bewilderment, as my very husband who was dead against all this barbaric feasting and dancing had donned himself a bheshu and full attire, beads and feathers and all. And after doing some inexplicable jumping and hopping together with his Sibiya he flew like an eagle right up to me and grabbed me by my apron strings. We both laughed ourselves sick, dancing together in the merry crowd.

Ohh, ohh, they noticed us, and the screaming was so much it brought the Chief to a halt. He looked around, checking that the dancers were keeping up with the line of duty, observing the brave Chief's wild ritualistic ceremonial dancing. He gave one leap, almost disappearing into the sky, and screamed with joy. Darting like a springbok toward my husband and myself he lifted my husband's bheshu just to see if he had a mcwedo – a penis box – on, and to his joy Sibiya had made sure to fit him out with one of his. The Chief laughed and cried at the same time, saying: 'Your own father wore a mcwedo on the wedding of my fourth wife to show me that he respects our customs. Now I know you do respect our customs even though your boiling brains refuse to acknowledge it, but your big heart does.'

Everyone was happy, and as they drank more and more gallons of beer they became even more high-spirited. My own husband was already quite drunk when he said: 'Winnefred my wife, I've not been a man for so long, we will not be missed if we take a little cooling-off at our favourite spot down the river. But I cannot walk in this outfit. My legs and backside will be torn with thorns.'

'Benjamin Rorke, you are very rude. What will the Chief think of you if he finds out what you are up too?'

'What do you mean, woman? He'll be proud of me as he knows that that is what is expected of a proper man. And I must admit I've not been a man these few months. Now, thanks to the Chief, I've had enough beer and meat to make me think like a man – and now, my dear wife, I am definitely thinking of acting like a man.'

When we came back from cooling-off, the Chief was tired of dancing and sat on an isicepu mat made of incema. He called my husband to thank him for the feasting and offered him a gift of a huge carved khuzwa-wood wooden platter that could hold half an ox in it plus the gravy, because now he had proved himself to be a man who adhered to the Zulu customs. And he shook his hand and offered him a sniff of snuff from his snuff-box, taken on a porcupine quill.

And he jokingly said: 'My son, when you spill your sperm on the soil it grows up to be a healthy tree with many branches, and many birds sit on it and eat its fruit, and it gives shade to the many who pass by, and you can build your kraal with its branches and finally make your centre beam with its trunk. Well done, my boy, you even look radiant on your tired weary face.'

Chapter 14

Time passes. The tree. Winnefred falls pregnant. In successive years three daughters are born to her. A disagreement between the Chief and Benjy about compensation for damage to a field.

SUMMER CAME AND WENT. We worked very hard. I had learned everything there was to learn, even about making soap. I knew how to milk a cow and to hold the plough. My husband worked at the forest and came back every evening. His horse Frank sometimes disappeared to mate far away, with the result that my husband had to walk to work and sometimes had to sleep over at work when he was tired. But I learned to be brave. I knew how to cope with practically everything. I even knew how to kill a snake, and I killed plenty.

One day a buck came running out of the bush and I took the gun and shot it. I was so scared my husband would be angry. We were not allowed to shoot at buck; they were protected, as the Zulus were hunting them to extinction. But Benjy was quite happy when he found venison at home, though he did warn me never to do it again or else he'd have to put me in jail.

We had plenty to eat. The crops were always plentiful and we had enough milk to give to the neighbours if their cows were out of calf. Auntie Jessica visited less often; Nettie came one Christmas in 1936; and still I had not got pregnant. Nettie shared my pain as she couldn't fall pregnant either. On some school holidays I used to visit my children at Walter's homestead, but they really had forgotten about Ngome. My husband went to visit his children, all the way to Mangete by railroad bus, and came back to tell me how well they'd grown and how they loved schooling at Little Flower School together with my ones.

And so life went on and I became more and more confident in my surroundings and myself. My maid Nathi went back to Swaziland to look for some of her people. I never heard from her again but I had another maid who was given to me by the Chief to help me around the house. My husband had to rebuild the old people's rondavel and he added another room to the main house. Of course he got Sibiya to find builders as he had no time.

Sibiya had two wives; the young one had not yet conceived and he used to complain to my husband that perhaps he made a wrong choice. What could he do with a barren woman? He would say my husband and he were cursed with barren women, and cry for the cattle that my father-in-law paid as lobola for him, for the lovely girl whom he loved so much. Then he'd say he thought it was due to the older wife's curses.

'Oh Nkhosana, it's because I don't go to her hut any longer. I think she is using witchcraft. Why cannot my young girl fall pregnant?'

My husband would scold him very severely. 'Sibiya, you always told me to eat bulls' testicles and now it seems you are not strong enough to keep two cows happy in your own kraal. Shame on you. You are a coward.'

'Oh ah, Nkhosana. How can you say that? You fail to satisfy even one cow in your kraal. Hawoo. What kind of a man are you anyway?'

My husband would get very angry. 'The fault is not with me, Sibiya. My wife seems to be very weak, but I know she will bear me many children so just shut up and go about your duties and leave me to mine. Since my father's death you have become very troubled. Let your spirit not be angry with your first wife. Go into her hut and she will bear you some more daughters, so you can have many cattle for lobola. Remember our father's teachings. We must look after one another.'

And then they would talk about happier times, and then Sibiya would laugh about him wearing a bheshu and say he needed to make him his own with the hide of the black mad bull because he was just as mad as the bull – and laugh and tease him until he left for his own little kraal, which was about a mile away in the corner of the fields near the bush. His own huts were growing in number. He even had his own fields and cattle kraal, which my father-in-law had given him.

As soon as Sibiya went my husband would brood in Olympian silence and gaze into the crackling fire in the stove, looking so handsome and forlorn. I knew he was longing for his mother and father. He had taken his father's death very hard. Then I would try to appease him with some dates or honey as his father had, watching his hollowed cheekbones and his pearly teeth as he chewed very slowly – as though even the honey tasted bitter in his mouth. He would get up abruptly from his chair and say he'd like to retire to his own rondavel. I would know better than to say more and nod my head and say goodnight.

Another year went by. I became used to the routine and I felt stronger and more self-confident. I was also more confident of falling pregnant and, in the April of 1937, after three years of a hectic, unsettled, sometimes frightening life, my husband came back from visiting his mother at Walter's home. He was full of joy. Oh, he had grown so handsome at age thirty-eight, his sideburns had flecks of grey and his moustache had started greying as well. He told me how his mother said he had grown old and yet his Winnefred had still not given her a grandchild. He said he knew that I would conceive when he was ready. I must remember, he said, that he is the man and when he was ready he would make a child.

I was excited when he said to me early one Sunday morning that I should pack a picnic basket and we would spend the day at the waterfall. I made all his favourite food and packed the basket. He reminded me not to forget his heavy army blanket which his father had used as a riding blanket. We walked talking and laughing like children. He told me about many different birds and their nesting habits, and showed me different colourful butterflies, and told me the names of trees.

He told me too about a certain huge wild oak tree that was over two hundred years old. Legend had it that it could talk tree language. That's where we were going to sit, and we would listen to what the tree has to say to us. I kept saying: 'Where is it?' And then there it was, right in front of us.

It was dark under this tree with just a few golden streaks of sunshine fighting their way through to the soft thick brown carpet underneath it. You could hear the rushing waterfall almost on top of its branches.

Benjy said: 'I love this place, Winnefred. I used to come here often with my parents and my sisters. We boys used to have bets on who could climb the highest, and my father would give a pocket-knife to the winner. My father used to talk to the tree and he made us believe it talks back to you when it senses you really love its presence. Sometimes we would bring a whole sheep to roast here on the stones at the side of the tree, because he would say we must not pollute the tree. Then my mother would say that this white man is truly insane, and that she'd rather leave this white man alone with his mad children, and that she would start walking back home by herself. Oh, my father used to tell us many tales about all his experiences and wanderings, and many more about England and the sea.

'The last time I was here was with Katrina, but she highly disapproved of picnics for fear of snakes. The best years of my childhood were spent here; as a young man I've had nothing but pain and misery. I've grown old before my time, grieving and confused. Now I want to forget all my pain and remember the carefree days I spent under this tree.'

For the first time he spoke his heart to me. As we ate he complimented me on the way I'd become a little plump and drew me close to him on the old blanket, where we became lost in paradise. Everything that could make a sound sang at the top of its voice. The African violets and the many wild autumn blooms seemed to give off their best perfume. The waterfall sang the loudest as I gave my whole heart and soul to the man I loved so much. I had loved him from the first day I saw him. But this was the first time I truly opened my heart and my life to him.

Two months after that day I knew I was expecting. I became moody and cried a lot. But in the third month he started noticing the change and was beside himself with joy. He rode down to tell his mother, and he told me she cried and cried and said now she could die in peace. Sibiya used to tease him, saying he wondered which good strong bull's testicles he had eaten.

We were so happy together. For the first time he pampered me. He even trapped rabbit for me, which I really loved, and brought me sweets from the forester. Everyone knew by now. The Chief was pleased, saying it was because Benjy had slaughtered and appeased the ancestors – so they'd presented him with a child. And on Christmas day a girl was born. All the old women came singing their lullabies for her and brought gifts of beads for our little red-headed girl whom my husband named Agnes Margaret.

At her birth I believed I was the happiest woman on earth. Nothing would ever come between me and my husband again, I thought, as I held the little pink bundle in my arms, trying to push my nipple into her already gaping mouth. What a greedy little girl, she'll probably have her father's appetite. God couldn't have blessed me more than by giving me such an angelic Christmas present. My heart surged with such love for her that I ached inside my womb. It was as though I'd given birth for the first time.

But as my husband's breath and male essence caught my nostrils as he bent over to kiss the angelic child, I had a deep sinister foreboding feeling, mixed with joy and perplexity. As though my husband could sense my tenseness he softly said: 'You've been a good strong girl, I knew you'd give me many children,' and gave me a peck on my forehead. Then he ordered someone to hurry up and make me broth from a fresh chicken so I could get my strength back.

As the women sang to me they sounded like so many angels in Bethlehem, and I thought of my school days in Inkomana, just how beautifully we sang the Christmas hymns in Zulu. So I hummed and my husband joined me as we both sang 'Ubusuku obuhle' – 'Silent night'. I sang with such force my husband whispered in my ear: 'You'll hurt your womb, you're not yet strong,' but I was thanking God and at the same time offering my thanks to Mother Mary for my happiness and untold joy. I told her in my song how I didn't deserve such joy. I knew I had sinned by not joining the nunnery after my two sons were born out of wedlock, in fornication.

Soon my broth was ready, and my husband had ordered Dinah to see that I finished it. Pushing all menacing thoughts to the back of my mind, I just caressed my little girl, bubbling over with pride. I was truly Mrs Rorke, wife of Benjamin, the Prince of Ngome.

The very following year I had another little girl, Jessica. The whole family was so excited. My father came to see my children, bringing my two boys to meet their sisters. They had grown and didn't show much interest. Anyway, I was thrilled to see them. They stayed for a week, and I went back to see my mother-in-law to show her the second child. She was very happy and gave the children her blessings. She gave the child a Zulu name, Sindisiwe, meaning 'I was saved from being called barren' – and her name stayed as Sindi.

I went back home feeling very happy. And life went on. Every day was a new day with new ideas on trying to better living conditions on the farm, like making new beds out of hewn logs, with springs made of ox-hide plaited and zigzagged into the wooden frame, and digging a dam down at the river which would hold enough water to wash the napkins. My husband ordered the boys to pull a large square rock to be put at the side of the house where we could wash the napkins on cold days instead of going down to the river. We put up more washing lines made of barbed wire, thorny enough to pin the napkins on. Of course Auntie Jessica made all the children's clothes, buying the flannel she needed at the Loefflers' store and the towelling for sewing up the napkins. She even bought the baby powder and Vaseline and napkin pins there. Jessica was thrilled that the child carried her name. She gave me her first Singer sewing machine and told me her father had bought it for her from the Arab traders, Achmat and Abdullah. She asked me to treasure it and look after it and only oil it with paraffin mixed with pig's lard.

The next year I fell pregnant again and conceived another girl, Juliana, at almost the same time as Sibiya's third child was born, who was a boy from his young wife. Unfortunately for him he'd wanted a girl, so he and his brother, my husband, who were both intensely proud of themselves, were still in competition as to who should be regarded as the stronger stud.

Some time later the Chief came to say my husband's cattle had gone into his fields and eaten up half the mealies. Oh, he was most angry and said my husband should slaughter more cows in thanks for all the girls that he'd got. How come he had four girls and he, the Chief, with so many wives had none? What did he do to conceive so many girls? He must be consulting white spirits according to his own white customs and using witchcraft.

My husband heard this and walked up to the Chief's kraal to ask about the damage done to his fields.

The Chief believed that Benjy had come to mock him because of his girls. And maybe, said the Chief, Benjy was not even sorry about the field that would have been enough to feed his children through the whole of the summer. In the end he said Benjy must pay him back with six oxen or heifers.

My husband was shocked and dismayed at the Chief's sudden change of attitude. 'What have I done to you, Chief? Why do you treat me so badly? You know full well as a Chief that six oxen are far too many to pay for a field. I can pay three but not six.'

'Aah, we shall see about that. I'll teach you a lesson. I'll cool that hot head of yours with the strongest cold water straight from the spring in the middle of the rain forest.'

'Oh Chief, you need not be angry; I'll pay three heifers, but not six. You have a kraal overflowing with cattle. I on the other hand cannot keep more than fifty head of cattle here in the rain forest reserve. The law does not allow us to overgraze the land. But you, Chief, live outside the reserved land. Therefore you are allowed any amount of cattle – as I do not have to remind you, because the Chief knows all the rules and laws of the rain forest. If you think because you are the Chief you can do as you wish, then I'll go further to the white man's court at Ngoshe, but I'll not give you six head of cattle.' My husband said the Chief merely nodded his head and took snuff silently.

My husband told Sibiya to drive the three heifers to the Chief and tell him to go and report him at the court for the other three as he was not prepared to pay him.

Sibiya came back, not looking very happy. In fact he looked terrified as he whispered hoarsely to my husband: 'Please my brother, I am begging you to pay the Chief the other three. Please do not treat this thing lightly. He is so angry, he says you have dishonoured his might and position as Chief, and with your boiling brains you are going to cause your destiny to be an open grave.'

To which my husband retorted: 'Let the damn savage do as he will. Witchcraft will never work on me.'

My happy life was due to take a terrible fall – headlong into the deepest, steepest donga of doom. I was very worried when my husband related to me what the Chief had said, but what made me more worried was the fact that his father had always told him from a young age never to trust a savage and never to cross his path, because then you would be in serious trouble.

Chapter 15

Events gather momentum. Winnefred's child falls ill. They take her to Jessica, and then on her advice to Mtembu, who cures her. Benjy's cattle are struck by lightning. Mtembu embarks on a mysterious journey. The priest from Nongoma Mission. Mtembu returns and treats Winnefred's family.

A MONTH WENT BY but everything seemed to be wrong after the incident. I was nervous and frightened. One night Juliana, who was almost six months, cried so bitterly she refused to suck the breast. She screamed and screamed. I tried to look for an injury, perhaps on her head or body, thinking maybe her maid had let her fall by mistake when trying to strap her on her back. But Juliana wasn't even feverish and there was no mark on her body. It was not until after the first cock-crow, which is three o'clock in the morning, that she fell asleep.

I was so tired the next day. In the evening I burnt duiwelsdrek and doepa, and told my husband when he came back from work about her not sleeping. Worse was to begin. That night all my children couldn't sleep. Jessica was screaming and saying there was a short man trying to choke her. Next thing the child started gasping for breath and I ran to the adjoining room to wake my husband. 'Oh Benjy, come quickly.'

But when he came to her bed she was blue, gasping, till she lay motionless, frothing from her mouth and nostrils.

Oh God! Oh God! I screamed and all the children were screaming. The paraffin lamp blew out on its own. My husband lit it up again and again. It blew out. I had my child clutched to my heart and was crying to God to please not let her die. My husband grabbed the child away from me and kicked the door open to stand with her so she could get fresh air and he shouted aloud, saying: 'Winnefred, take the children to my parents' rondavel and light the big lamp.'

Meanwhile I was shouting and saying: 'Oh God, in your name I ask you to cast out this evil in my home. Save my child's life.'

I felt very strong, and determined to fight for my children's lives, so I flew in the dark to the old people's rondavel with my children, all of them screaming and holding on to my long nightdress. I fumbled to find the lamp in the pitch darkness and a match to light it. I banged the door behind me and ran back. My husband was on his knees, with his child in his arms. He was praying aloud but he said to me: 'Go back to the children. She is breathing, she'll be all right.'

Dinah was called early that morning and was told by my husband about what had happened. Sibiya was speaking to my husband with tears freely running down his cheeks, saying: 'Nkhosana, I warned you of this thing. Now it is too late. Your only protection against these things is the white people's Unseen One, which your father and mine always told us about. But everyone knows how strong and cunning and dangerous the Chief is. So take this child at once to be treated by Jessica, though I doubt if she will be able to help it.'

Auntie Jessie's homestead seemed to be further than it was. All the way there I was praying, running behind my husband – who was far ahead of me, also running, carrying his dying child to the only doctor we knew. We came to the crossing at the Bululwane River. He shouted to me to cross carefully – he was on the other side already – but I just threw myself in and swam across, soaking wet and half choked with swallowing some of the water in my haste to cross as fast as I could.

We ran up the stretch to the homestead, my husband shouting at the top of his voice: 'Jessica, Jessica, my child is dying. Help, come quickly.'

Jessica was prepared with smelling salts and took the limp little half-bluish-faced Juliana in her own arms, saying: 'Oh God, my goodness gracious me. What have you all done to her?'

The child sneezed as she sniffed the salts and Jessica gave her some duiwelsdrek drops to drink. She hiccupped and yawned, while Jessica undressed her and rubbed her little body with some herbal oil, saying to us: 'This is beyond me. This poor child has been attacked by a tokoloshe. You have to go back at once and pass by the inyanga Mtembu, who might be able to drive this evil spirit back to where it belongs. It's only by God's mercy that she is still alive.'

Juliana drank a little sugar water. Straight away my husband bundled her up, with me practically running behind him – to cross the river yet again, back in the direction we had just come from. We reached Mtembu's kraal just at milking time. Now my husband was very quiet as we neared the kraal, and said to me: 'Winnefred, I don't know if this is the right thing to do, but to save our child's life we've got to trust God to take over now.'

I couldn't talk, I just nodded and walked on.

The dogs barked as we waited outside the fence made of tall overgrown aloes and then someone shouted at the dogs to be quiet and ushered us into a huge round hut which was quite dark and eerie. My husband cried to Mtembu who was squatting on a mat in the corner: 'Please great Mtembu, my child has a tokoloshe, please help us quickly.'

Mtembu never said a word, but leapt up and took the child and turned it upside down, hitting it on the little backside. Then he spoke some words which made no sense to me. He grabbed one of his many little gourds and let the child's head fall back while he put a pinch of powdered muthi into its mouth, making sure it went into the throat. The child coughed and coughed, and vomited a blackish liquid full of phlegm. On the hearth there were dying embers. He put another pinch of something else into the fire which gave out a smell and smoke, and he passed the child over the smoke three times.

Juliana started crying, to the delight of both Benjy and I. I silently cried, thanking God. My husband's tears rolled down freely as he said: 'Oh Mtembu, you've saved our child.'

The old wizard had a wry smile, saying he didn't understand how she had survived this terrible terrible umkhuba. But we had come just in time or else it would have possessed the child altogether; then it would have been very difficult to take it out.

He ordered one of his wives to bring a little gourd of fresh milk from the kraal. Again he took some powder from the little gourd around his neck and poured it into the milk. He forced the child to drink it by opening her mouth with a small wooden spoon. Then he told me to put her over my lap and give her an enema. I had to take a mouthful of the milk mixture, hold it in my mouth and squirt it through the bamboo syringe into the child's backside. In this way the child would excrete all the dirty evil that was already forming little black bumps inside the stomach.

I listened and did as he said, half believing but with the Christian soul inside of me having doubts as to how this could possibly be. He sensed my doubting spirit and said to me: 'Please do as I tell you.'

My husband said: 'Don't be afraid, Winnie, just do it.'

I squirted a mouthful into my child; then Mtembu said: 'Now turn her and hold her with her head facing down, and hold her buttocks together so the milk can stay inside. It will curdle the poison and bring it out.'

Juliana cried and started pressing, letting out a stinking blackish liquid on to a heap of cow-dung which had been specially brought inside.

Mtembu said: 'Leave her to let some more out,' which she did. This time it was mixed with little black dots that resembled a rabbit's droppings. The stink was unbearable and I wiped it off his floor, feeling quite embarrassed.

I said: 'I am so sorry for all this mess, I should have taken her outside.'

And he shook his head saying: 'Then you would never have seen the seeds of evil: they cannot stand the sun or light of any kind.'

Last he shouted for a piece of broken clay pot and stacked the coals, putting the half moon of broken clay on to the fire. When it was red hot, he told us to come nearer the fireplace. Pouring some other watery stuff on to the hot clay, he said we must touch it up to our mouths with our fingertips as quickly as we could.

My husband urged me to be brave and obey. I was sobbing by now and feeling very cold. When it was over, Mtembu called his wife and told her to bring me a blanket to wrap myself up in, and left the hut crawling on all fours looking like a baboon. As I took off my wet clothes, my husband held the child and her eyes opened wide while she cried.

We could hear Mtembu outside his hut, praising his ancestors. He came back inside and said not to worry, the child was healed and he would come with us to bind the evil spirits, as they would surely try again. An evil man never gives up. Full well he knew it. His grandfather was the only sangoma that Chaka spared, because he told him the truth about the sprinkling of the blood around his own hut and was not afraid to die for the truth.

We got ready to walk through Mahalahaleni together with Mtembu, with all his skins wrapped around his many hanging gourds and the beaded little bottles dangling around his neck. I wrapped my blanket tighter around my naked body as my husband carried our child who was alive. No one spoke even when we walked through the bush. I thought of the wild pigs and shivered even more, crying softly with relief. Even the wild pigs didn't really scare me as much as the terrible nightmare of almost losing my child.

Mtembu never uttered a word. As we came into our yard I could see a huge fire with big logs burning on the hearth outside and the hot-water drum steaming away. I needed a bath, but my first thoughts were for my children. I ran to the rondavel to find them fast asleep on their grandparents' huge bed. Both Nyawo and Dinah were waiting for us and nodded silently when they saw Mtembu. He flew like a fox to the fire and started throwing powder into it which made a green flame and smelt like mphepo. Then he disappeared to the back of the yard, sprinkling powder as far as the cattle kraal and the grave, all around the fruit trees, and even on the roof of all the rondavels. And then he dug little holes with a small sharp spear and buried powder in each hole, talking to himself in his own tongue.

We had finished bathing when he finally finished his work. All he said to us was: 'You will sleep well, as I've sent the evil back to its owner. Son of the Great White Chief, you must come back to see me after a month.' Then he was gone into the pitch dark night.

After that we slept in the old people's rondavel with our children. My husband was moody and uneasy. He made sure to come home every day, not staying at work overnight, until one day at the month's end he said he was resigning. He felt I was not safe alone, even during the day.

We lived in constant fear as the days went by, but my husband did not go to see Mtembu again.

Just one week after the month ended, in broad daylight, with no clouds indicating the coming of a storm, lightning shot from the sky. Then I heard a terrible resounding sharp peal of thunder, as if the sky was cracking open. I ducked under the high bed, listening for more; all was quiet, but I still thought it would be coming again. These electric storms go like that. Just when you think they're over, another peal comes, even sharper than the first. But there was silence. I got up thinking: Where are my children? I ran to the kitchen to find them playing with the maid.

Just as I was coming out of the door Sibiya ran into me, saying: 'Where is my brother? All his cattle are lying dead in the field, struck by lightning.'

Oh God, now what? Is my husband also dead? That's what I thought, as I screamed and screamed. My husband came running from the mealie shed where he had been packing some new heads of mabela.

'What's wrong, Winnefred? Is it the child again? Has she taken a bad turn again?'

Only for Sibiya to scream: 'Oh my brother, I don't know what is going on in the house of Rorke. Your cattle all lie dead, hit by lightning.'

'What do you mean, Sibiya? Are you crazy? There was barely a storm. It was just a passing peal of thunder, bringing the winter in – how can what you say be true? Where are they?'

Benjy grabbed Sibiya's hand and pulled him to look down on the first field next to the kraal. Everyone in the yard ran down to the kraal to see. There the cattle lay, already starting to swell up.

My poor husband went to sit on top of his father's grave and held the marble cross, weeping uncontrollably. I was so scared I trembled.

Nyawo had got up early to go and feza – look for wood – after the storm. There were always fallen dry branches then. But she had no idea what had happened. Even the herdboys didn't tell her, for fear of being heard by the grass and the wind which might carry the message back to whoever was responsible for this terrible thing.

When she heard the news about the cattle, she said to me: 'Oh child of Dambuza George Nunn. What on earth have you and your husband done? What is this evil?'

She immediately went to the grave where my husband was crying for his father, and comforted him saying: 'My son, your father never believed in black magic. It is his faith in his white God which protected your whole household from the evil. It was not a natural storm that hit the cattle. Therefore stop weeping and hurry down to Mtembu. Get up, my son, and go like the wind. Take your horse. Dead cattle can be replaced but dead children cannot.'

Mtembu was so angry he shouted for all his ancestors, praising Chaka for sparing his grandfather, and ran outside to his kraal. He told my husband to sit right in the middle of the kraal and hold the little spear toward the sky and pray to the Unseen One whom Chaka had feared and respected, and ask for protection for his family. He then gave my husband some powdered incense to burn around the yard and to bath all his family in, saying it was indeed a hard thing to fight fire with fire. He would have to go on a distant dangerous journey to ask for advice what to do. But meanwhile my husband was to slaugh-

ter a white goat, for him to present the gall bladder and so appease the
spirits of those he was visiting.

'By tomorrow you must have the white goat ready to slaughter. I
have many white goats, which I use for various cures; and as you know
you will only pay me when you are fully cured. I am afraid there's still
more trouble to come, and this time I have to warn you it could be
fatal, unless I go quickly to curb the worst of it. I cannot promise to
stop this man as he has many eyes and ears and heads and hands, and
you have none.'

He then ordered two herdboys to drive the white goat home with
me, and told me not to say a word until the goat was slaughtered. I
was not to allow the herdboys to eat the flesh, nor even the dogs; but
to bury the whole carcass, skin and all, in the kraal, scraping even the
blood off the ground and making sure to bury it together with the rest.
He should give the herdboys the gall bladder, wrapped up in cow-
dung. And he told my husband he'd be back in one month's time.

I asked my husband after that to please let us shift and go and live
next to Walter or Jessica, but he said if he had to die it would be here
where he was born.

'Winnefred, my dear wife, we've been through such a lot of pain,
we will overcome this together with God on our side. We will not die,
and nor will our children, by the hand of a man who did not create us.
He will soon be dead, as he is growing older with evil every day.'

Then he sent word to Jessica and Walter, and asked Jessica to send
her husband to the Mission Hospital in Nongoma to ask for a priest
to come down to bless our homestead.

The priest arrived about three weeks later. His name was Father Jacob; he was a small wiry little man with twinkling eyes and bandy
legs. He told us he had sometimes been to Jessica's homestead to talk
about herbs and their different uses, as he was also a herbalist. He
said we must not hesitate to use whatever the old inyanga Mtembu
told us to use, as he knew full well that you could not fight those evil
happenings with herbs only. And in a smattering of broken Zulu he
told us not to be afraid, he would give us holy water to sprinkle and
some incense to burn which he had brought from the Black Forest in
Germany. We gave him some lunch; then he was off on his donkey,
looking very satisfied with himself.

Later Mtembu came to our home to tell us he had accomplished his journey. He summoned my husband to bring each child, then scraped some saliva from their tongues and took a few threads of hair from each of our heads. He wrapped these up in a mixture of herbs. He put incense on to some hot coals; both Benjy and I had to put our urine into the mixture, and we all had to inhale the smoke very very deeply.

Then he darted like a fox into the kraal and ordered my husband to dig with his bare hands about a foot into the grave of the dead goat. Then he poured the mixture inside and my husband buried it again. Mtembu spoke in his own language, mostly to the ancestors, and asked us for a gourd of water. Without saying goodbye, he rushed away into the darkness, heading for his home.

I comforted myself with the words of the priest who had said: 'Don't be afraid, do as he tells you,' but I shyly asked my husband: 'Where did Mtembu go to?'

He said: 'Right near where you were born, across the Jozini River to Tongaland. It is said the Tongas are the best inyangas and wizards and witches. That is where he practised being a good inyanga.'

Chapter 16

Down at the river, Winnefred hears laughter. A beautiful bird sits on her shoulder, then disappears. Her rosary breaks. More laughter down at the river – and dizziness and sleep. Her dream.

THERE WAS PEACE FOR ABOUT A MONTH. I was down at the river by myself doing some washing when I felt very uneasy as though someone was looking at me from behind the rocks, but I thought that I was imagining things. Then I felt cold and distinctly heard laughter, as though children were taking turns laughing at something. I thought nothing of it, but it made me shiver and feel frightened. Maybe it was the bush babies having a good time eating berries, or just jumping from tree to tree. Ah, but bush babies don't cry in the daytime. They only cry at night and not quite like that.

I carried on washing, but hurriedly; and suddenly the laughter started again. This time I listened carefully. Those were real children, not bush babies. Maybe it was the children from Zulu's kraal, which wasn't far from the river. But it really puzzled me. What would small children be doing in the bush alone?

I started shouting, asking who was there. 'What are you doing all by yourselves in the bush?'

It was silent. I waited for an answer. There was none. Why was it that they couldn't hear me and I could hear them so clearly?

So I finished rinsing the clothes and hurriedly walked out on to the sunlit pathway to go home. My heart was beating very fast. As I walked I could hear them laughing again. I felt dizzy with every step. As I walked into the yard, I collapsed. All I could remember was the laughing children.

My husband asked me: 'What's wrong? Oh my God. Winnefred, don't tell me you're pregnant again.'

I felt foolish and didn't want to add to his misery, so I laughed and said: 'It's just a headache, I'm not pregnant.'

I really loved doing our clothes down at the river. The water was plentiful and there was a huge flat rock as big as the floor of a whole room. You could wash blankets so conveniently and rinse at the same time, as the spring water flowed merrily and silently down to where there were huge rocks and dense thickets.

That was where I had heard the laughter coming from. I'd never gone so far. It looked too dark and dangerous, as though the rocks got bigger and went down steeply towards a dangerous precipice. Sibiya never allowed the cattle to go near there as he said many had fallen deep down to their end and no one had been able to reach them or even see where the carcasses lay.

So I said nothing about the laughing children, not even to the maid. I dismissed the incident. I had enough far more important things on my mind.

I wore my rosary even at night. I clung to it and touched it almost as though my very life depended on it. I prayed from morning till night, saying the rosary and asking Mother Mary to protect my family. I sprinkled the holy water from Father Jacob, and burnt the incense that he had given us – rather than the one Mtembu had given us because Mtembu's one had such a terrible smell. It smelt like dead animals and it even looked as if it was mixed out of tiny birds' feet and skins and bits of bone and pieces of toe-nails of some animals. It really had a stink.

There was peace for a while, until one day a beautiful bird sat right on the clothesline. I went closer to admire it. It just sat still and didn't fly away, but jumped and sat on my shoulder. Oh, I was thrilled and I called my maid to see it. As she came running, the bird just noiseless-ly disappeared.

'Where is it? Hawu Nkhosikazi, I can see no bird and I saw no bird flying off your shoulder. You are making it up just so I can be near you. I know you have become very frightened.'

'Oh, but it really was sitting on my shoulder. Do you think a big woman like me would lie to you? You are really losing respect calling me a liar like that.'

She walked away like a dog with its tail between its legs and shyly looked back to see if the bird really was there. But of course it was gone, because even when I tried to feel my shoulder there was no bird. Oh well, it must have dropped down in the long grass, birds have a way of just flying off silently.

I came into the kitchen to prepare the children's lunch. My husband had gone to the Loefflers' store, and he was going to pass by Jessica's home for some more rubbing herbs for the baby as she still cried a lot, even in the daytime. She hardly slept except on the back of the maid, who had her tightly strapped even now.

I gave my children their food and I had a cup of tea. Meanwhile my children fought to lick the bowl in which I had been mixing some honey cakes – for my husband to have with his tea when he came back from the store.

All of a sudden I wanted to go down to the river and have a nice bath. My children begged me to take them with me, clinging on to my apron, but I simply pushed them away and refused. My husband had said to me the children must not go further than the yard. So what if some-thing happened to them on the way to the spring?

My beloved children kept asking to go with me. Little Agnes, who was so plump and so pretty with her flat nose and curly red hair. Jessi-ca, who really was the prettiest, had dark curls, and rolling black eyes. She was skinny and taller than Agnes, whereas Juliana was bandy-legged like me and had straight black hair. Her slit eyes were like a Chinese person's and she had a broad mouth with two protruding front teeth. She looked sick and tired, but otherwise she had recovered completely from her terrible ordeal.

I told the maid to lock the door to the rondavel and play with the older ones in front of the kitchen. Agnes, who was about six years old, always acted like a little mother, and she matter-of-factly asked me: 'Mama, when will you come back? You must come back quickly.' I sensed a quiver in her voice and knew she wanted to cry. 'Mama, you must come back quickly. I am very frightened.'

I touched her hair. It was always in a bush. If I plaited it, it would get loose again in no time. She never liked standing at the mirror to admire herself; she was always running around and doing chores, like a boy, very domineering and demanding. Nyawo loved to taunt her by the name Sibiya had given her: Mbodla, the wild-cat. When she was angry her eyes would open up and twitch, she would frown, and her hair turned a tawny red like a real wild-cat.

Sibiya's wife was sweeping the yard with her children all round her as I shouted to her and said: 'Look after them. I'll soon be back. I just need to have a bath. It's so hot and I'm feeling very hot and bothered.' She shouted back to ask what she should put on the stove for supper and I said: 'Boil the mealies for amasi and grind them ready for Khosana to eat when he comes back.'

As I spoke I ran back to my room to fetch my piece of lavender soap. I swung around while grabbing the soap in the soap dish, but my rosary hooked on to the washstand and snapped so sharply that all the beads rolled right under the bed, and some right to the door. I was angry and thought: Oh my, anything to keep me from going to bath. I wanted to smell nice for my husband when he came home so I decided that I would pick the beads up when I came back. I heard my children crying behind the house but I thought, they'll soon be over it and find something else to do.

I felt as though I had run away from home. As I walked hurriedly toward the river, I giggled and thought it wouldn't be a bad idea. I was sick and tired of all these mysteries. Seeing a bird with my own eyes, ha! khosi yami, and it disappears without a sound. Oh well, I'll never tell my husband, he'll think I'm stupid. He always says I am so stupid, anyone can bluff me into believing something not true.

'You are so silly – can't you think? Don't you know what to do? Must I always teach you?'

Like the day I covered the newborn calf. It was raining and cold, so I brought the calf inside the old rondavel and covered it with an old blanket.

'This is not one of your babies, this is an animal, you're so stupid,' he had said to me.

And yet I saw him covering the calf that first winter I came to be his wife. Even if I'd told him about the laughing children he'd have said:

'You're so stupid, what would small children like that be doing down at the river on their own?'

I really wanted to be alone with all my thoughts. I felt so angry with the life I was living. With what was happening. Witchcraft worked for the Zulus, not for us. Could this really be happening because of witchcraft? Maybe it was just a normal bad stretch. Perhaps just a time in one's life when everything changes in different directions.

As I neared the river, getting into the opening in the trees, I felt ice-cold and shivered. I stood still for a second and felt my heart beating. It lurched as though wanting to come out of my chest. I felt giddy for a split second. I wanted to turn back and go home, but then I thought: A cold bath will fix me up.

I washed the few clothes first and felt a little better. Maybe it was the feel of cold water. Then a sharp, taunting, high-pitched laugh pierced my ears and my heart. The next one followed, followed by many more. I stood up to see if I could see anyone as the laughter seemed to be right above me. There was nothing. Luckily I hadn't started bathing, so I decided I had to find these children. Did they also think I was a fool? What were they laughing at me for? When I found them, I'd show them who was a fool.

I tiptoed stealthily, peering left, right and centre in case they were hiding right under my nose. If I picked a stick to hit them with, the cracking branch would scare them away. So I'd pick up a stone. No, I'd hurt them if I threw it at them. As I clambered up the first rock, another burst of shrieking, piercing, mocking laughter rang through the whole bush, followed by many more.

Only now it seemed the laughter was further down by the huge high rocks, full of twining foliage. I was hot and perspiring, dripping with sweat. But so angry and hurt at not knowing why the children were laughing at me. I was desperate to find them. I'll get you all, bloody rude damn savages.

I was now on the top of the precipice and fuming with rage. This time the laugh mocked me with pity and as I peered, trying to clear away some heavy twining foliage, I slipped and fell. I tried to cling on to the thick wild creeper, but it seemed as though someone pushed me from the back and I lost my grip. I felt numb and dizzy but I landed on a very soft spot where I fell off to sleep immediately with the smell of some kind of incense lulling me and making me feel amazingly relaxed. Then I seemed to dream many unusual dreams.

I dreamt I was falling through a long dark hole and many children were holding me as though protecting me. They floated along with me. But these children were not mine and they were all black and very ugly. Some had no teeth, or had rotten black stumps for teeth, as they grinned at me, nodding their heads from side to side. Even their hands were ugly and rough with long black fingernails, some broken and with soil in them as though they had been ploughing and had not had a chance to wash. Some had cows' hair stuck between their fingers as though they had been eating the heads of cows or oxen. The head was cooked with the skin still on it, so their hands had an oily look, but they were not old and rugged and I knew that they were the hands of young herd-boys. I noticed their feet were full of open cracks and long curved-in toenails. Their feet were very big for their short bodies. Some had long grey beards and some were bald-headed and had black rings around their heads, with fierce red eyes. But I didn't feel threatened or afraid of them as they seemed to be very concerned about helping me to land comfortably.

I eventually landed on a comfortable heap of soft skins and carried on dreaming that I was bathing down at the river and using my lavender soap, thinking I must smell nice for my husband. As I bathed and rubbed my body, I started having very strong desires for my husband. I loved him so much. I could almost feel him close to me on the heap of skins. I felt the urge to turn around and touch him. I could feel his hairy chest and wondered why the curls felt so tight, but it really didn't matter. I carried on caressing his face and felt his sideburns and beard. The curls did feel a bit tight, but it never really mattered as my desire grew stronger. I gave myself completely to him.

Deep down in my heart all I had was my sincere unending love for my husband – and I wanted to please him for all the past months when we could not be intimate. I felt that he was feeling the same way too. He had been starved too long, that was why he prolonged the procedure.

I carried on dreaming of falling through tunnels, long dark pathways in some far-off land, and half walking, half falling, down steep precipices and dongas. And at every dark corner faces peered at me, black ugly faces, gesturing as if they were pointing towards some far-off mountains, and laughing so hauntingly. I could see my home, and my children standing in the yard crying and calling me, and me talking to them – but they just kept on crying and Juliana was getting blue in the face. In my mind I knew I had to go to her rescue and give her some smelling salts, but I couldn't reach her. Voices hummed and spoke inaudible messages, pointing fingers at my husband who stood shivering and naked in the middle of the cattle kraal. I wanted to run toward him to cover him up, but I was numb. I couldn't even move a foot. I tried to call my mother, whom I could see standing in our garden at home with her hands in the sky, praying and beckoning me to come to her. I could see Nkamana Mission, where I schooled, but it seemed as though it were floating against a black forest or passing me by very fast, as I shouted for the nuns, who were laughing at me and waving their arms in total despair. I carried on screaming and trying to get their attention and sympathy, but I couldn't move to wave my hands.

Looking around me, trying to find something or someone to hold on to, I saw big rosary beads, all scattered around me, but they were all black and slippery. As I tried to grab them, they kept on circling in front of my eyes and disappeared into a black hole. Then I tried to call Mother Mary to please help me, but the eerie sarcastic laughter of the children made me so angry I screamed and screamed, telling them to stop laughing at me.

But it seemed the sound of my voice had gone. I probed for my inner self and tried in vain to reach it to feel some response, but black swirling smoke would choke me and my mind would go pitch dark, and blank as a white sheet. It carried on swirling inside the black tunnel until, at the far opening, my husband stood there. I knew it was my husband but I couldn't really see his face. But I saw clearly the beautiful bird sitting on his shoulder, and I was so happy. I ran toward him and wanted to catch the bird, but he grabbed me into his arms – and I was so happy as we rolled on to the heap of skins and made passionate love. Our passion was beyond imagination. In my deepest heart I knew I was pregnant and that thought made me happy.

I started feeling very tired but kept on thinking: At least my husband is safe besides me. And as I went back to float in the black tunnel I had a feeling of being watched by many eyes – just eyes, rolling everywhere I turned; they turned with me into the black tunnel. Now I knew I was dead.

Everything became very still and very dark.

Chapter 17

Benjy tells Mtembu of Winnefred's disappearance. Assisted by Benjy and witnessed by Sibiya, Mtembu recalls her.

MY HUSBAND SAT ON HIS HAUNCHES in Mtembu's huge dark hut and told him I'd been gone for two days. At first he thought I'd gone to see Sibiya's baby, which I had helped to deliver. But eventually he summoned everyone in the homestead and launched an extensive search. All my things had been left on the rocks by the river, which meant I hadn't been trying to run away. The whole of Ngome and Ntendeka was alerted by herdboys on foot and women and children, all dumbfounded by what had happened.

Benjy's first wife had died very young and now the second had disappeared like a zombie into thin air. This was the talk of the entire village. But Sibiya had other thoughts for he knew well enough what might have happened and he had to act very quickly before the third day for by then I would be very dead.

Sibiya ran like a demented witch, calling for my husband; but he was nowhere to be seen. So he ran down the Mahalahaleni valley, across the small Esikwebezi, straight into the dogs barking at Mtembu's kraal, to find my husband kneeling totally at the mercy of Mtembu himself. Sibiya had no words, but huffing and panting, perspiration dripping like water, he screamed at the top of his voice: 'O Nkhosi yamaKhosi, great healer of all nations, come to the aid of this poor man's wife. The tokoloshe have taken her. It will be three days tomorrow, and you know as well as I do she will be dead if not found in three days. Oh Makhosi amakhulu, please I beg you consult the ancestral powers of the iZulu himself, the only great king there ever was, and ever will be, of the House of Zulu.'

My husband was crying freely and openly. Thank God, Sibiya came in time. Mtembu leapt up like an eagle, grabbed an old dilapidated skin bag, and ran out into the middle of the kraal crying and shouting, calling his ancestors. He then took his spear and started cutting his half-naked body while my husband ran to beg him not to kill himself and think it was his fault. But he pushed my husband toward the entrance of the kraal. He ordered him to drink something from the gourd that his old wife handed to him and also beckoned to him to strip and join him.

Then Mtembu made a leap toward my husband, who was trying to hide his private parts with his hand, and pulled him close to make a very small incision on his chest, right under his heart. Scraping the blood, he mixed it with some of his own and called for coals to burn the blood mixed with incense. While this mixture sent a clear white smoke straight up to the sky like a river flowing upside down, he grabbed a huge horn and blew on it.

It made a sound that was overwhelming. Sibiya says the kraal was like a graveyard. Just as everyone was always made still by hearing some wild animal such as a roaring leopard, when they heard it even the dogs shuddered and crept away to hide.

Mtembu then took a long black twisted horn which was very sharp and blew some kind of powder into it, calling for the wife of the friend of Chaka, who was a white warrior and Chief, who loved the land of the Zulu. 'Show us where she has been taken to.'

And he groaned and cried, weeping like a broken man, groaning and crying, talking and shouting, and then he was as if in a trance. He became a heap of skins and horns and all manner of little bottles all over his limp, lame, dead body.

My husband ran to him thinking he was really dying, but Mtembu's faithful old wife told him very sharply not to go a single step further. 'He is not dead, only in a trance talking to the spirit world of the ancestors to beg and plead for help.'

Whilst he lay motionless, she beckoned to my husband to call his wife's proper name and her ancestors, both the white and the Swazi.

Sibiya says that he hid away so he need not fear or see how his brother wept and called the mother of his children. 'Oh God, why do you punish me so much? Take me, but not the mother of my children. You've taken the first one, who also had to leave her children. Now, oh God, must all my children be motherless? Why, why, my God, do you punish me so severely? Take me, but not the mother of my children. Please, dear God, bring her back to her children. Don't let this evil carry on. Stop it my Lord, in your Holy name.'

Mtembu started stirring slowly. He was stuttering in some language that Sibiya says he himself couldn't understand.

Somewhere deep inside my mind I heard a faint echo. It grew a little louder as I tried groping through my mind, and willing my senses to focus; but visions kept recurring and smokescreens arose, blocking out any clear picture or sound. I groped, fighting against defeat and holding on to the will to listen to the faint sound. I knew that it was there, somewhere in my mind, but how could I harness it so that I could hear it again?

Somewhere I heard the echo again, and now I fought and willed my mind to listen more intently. As I listened I heard it again, this time a little clearer. It was coming from a distance, as though it was someone calling my name.

My senses were alerted and they became sharper. Could it really be my name? What was my name anyway? Everything became blank and dark again. I preferred to be left alone in the blankness of my mind as I really felt I couldn't struggle any longer. But as I let go of all thought, suddenly I heard the sound in my mind, sharper and clearer. I struggled again; this time I felt an intense will to hear it clearly. Slowly the shifting shadows and visions and smoky screens cleared and allowed me to see into my mind, thus enabling me to grasp the sound, and then it was a voice unknown to me, calling my name.

Whose was this voice? Groping for a clearer sound I heard my name, my father's name, and my mother's voice, clearly calling me: 'Winnefred, Winnie my child, come to Mama.'

And while I listened to that voice I heard another voice, my husband's: 'Winnefred my wife, come back to your children, please don't die. Come back, Winnefred, come back.'

But I also heard the sound of a horn, loud and clear in my head, and wondered who had taken a new girl to be his wife. It was customary that when a girl said yes to her suitor a large horn was sounded in thanks to the ancestors. It was sounded in the cattle kraal for a whole week so that everyone knew not to propose to her as she had already been promised to the owner of the homestead where the horn sounded.

I shouted to my husband to say: 'I am not dead, come and fetch me I am here,' but not a sound came out of my mouth. Not even my tongue could move. I tried to open my eyes but it was as though I had no eyes at all. Where was I, why couldn't I talk? I tried to move my hand to feel my eyes, but my hand couldn't move either.

Only then did I pray. Oh Mother Mary help me. My whole body ached. I felt as though I had been inspanned and had pulled the plough by myself, getting whipped on my back and legs and arms. Even my hands were aching, but I couldn't move, talk or see. Why couldn't my husband come for me? Did he know where I was?

By now I could hear forest birds of all sorts and I could smell the forest. I could even smell the spring and hear the tinkle of flowing spring water. If only I could move. I was so thirsty and pangs of hunger made me even more dizzy. I had a splitting headache. I wanted to feel my face. If I could just raise my arm. Please, dear God, help me. It seemed like an eternity.

Now I willed my senses to smell and search for familiar smells. The crickets and tree beetles and frogs made a deafening noise as if trying to tell me: 'Yes, yes, yes, you are down at the river.' I couldn't hear whether it was the lark or the frogs that seemed to be saying: 'W-i-n-n-i-freddy,' and the echo sounded back so clearly in my ears. Thank God, I could hear – and smell. Someone was definitely calling me. 'W-i-n-n-i-e-e.' I tried to scream so they could hear me, but no voice would come out of my throat, not even a croaking sound. Tears, hot tears, rolled down my cheeks.

There were voices coming nearer. I could make out my husband's voice: 'Winnefred, where are you?' And Sibiya's voice: 'Awoo Nkho-sikazi, please answer, don't die. Your children are crying and so is your husband. Please tell us where you are.'

And then there was a less familiar voice, a man's voice sounding old and cracking as it spoke in desperate tones, saying in ancient Zulu some words that were new to me, saying: 'Come out of the belly of darkness, child of light.'

I could hear the heavy thud of nearby footsteps but they sounded somewhere far above as if on a steep donga or precipice, and then I heard someone coming down, with stones falling and someone scream-ing for help. I heard my husband saying: 'Sibiya, hold on. I am com-ing. I am coming. Hold on to the thick creeper which I am bringing down to you. There, Sibiya, catch it with one hand. Catch it. Hold on, hold on, Sibiya.'

My heart was bursting with excitement, but my mind was strangled with frustration. I couldn't bring my voice out of my vocal cords. I knew the third voice was Mtembu's and thanked God over and over for all three. But how were they going to find me when I couldn't scream? Sibiya was helping my husband to clamber down. There were rocks and stones rolling down under my husband's weight, especially as he had Mtembu on his shoulders with all his paraphernalia all stuffed into an old skin bag. Sibiya says he looked like an old baboon carrying his own baby on his shoulders.

I could hear them landing. They seemed so close but couldn't see me. Then where was I? Was I in some spirit world? I was not dead. I am not dead. I know I am not dead. Please find me, I am not dead. I tried to take a deep breath to smell again, but all I could smell were the familiar smells down at the river, and old incense that made me cough and cough and cough.

I could faintly hear them saying: 'Oh God, Oh God, what is this?'

Mtembu croaked: 'Don't touch her, please don't touch her, please.'

I felt him feeling my neck for a pulse and then my arms for broken bones, and then my legs, and I felt him trying to open my eyes and I heard him croak: 'Oh aah, aaa, Makhosi amakhulu, she is alive. Bring my bag, get some twigs and start a little fire. I have to burn incense, incense with the heart and eyes of the black eagle – who sees a rat right inside a hole, just as she is inside this cave, left to die there by the umthakathi.'

Sibiya says all he could do was hold my husband, who was crying uncontrollably, and cry together with him. They sat down to watch the old inyanga feverishly pinching a hint of powder from one or the other of his sacred black dried-up little gourds, which he fished up from deep inside the tattered skin bag, pulling them out of yet another little bag made of pure untreated crocodile skin. Deep, deep in my heart I thanked my father-in-law for shooting the leopard, and the boys who sold some of the precious parts to the Chief and some to Mtembu. I knew Mtembu was using these. Did my father-in-law know from his grave that his misfortune – in killing a leopard he would rather have left alive – had been instrumental in bringing me back to life again?

I still couldn't talk. My tongue felt as though it was getting longer and thicker. I smelt the incense. It had a horrible smell. Mtembu urged me on, begging me not to give in, saying I'd soon be eating meat with my husband and children. That the vultures would not eat my flesh but would soon eat the flesh of the evil one who had done this wicked umkhuba.

When he noticed my tongue almost hanging out, he screamed hoarsely and painfully, saying: 'Hawu Nkhosi yamaKhosi. He was coming back to turn her into a zombie. Hawu. He must have gone back to fetch the heart and liver of the tortoise so that she will never grow, but walk with short legs and always stretch her neck out to peep into corners and spy out the enemy. He has already treated her tongue with dog's saliva to draw it out to lick those of his enemies he will send her to.'

Mtembu pushed back my tongue, using something liquid that tasted violently bitter. I coughed again and felt as if I had almost swallowed my own tongue.

He turned to the others, saying: 'It is plain to see that he has prepared this hide-out specially to do this crime. He has many other such caves where he performs his operations, turning dead people into zombies. This is where he brought the zombies to call her by enticing her with laughter. He would then have had a precious white zombie to add to the vast collection which he took over from his wicked father. But I swear, by my mother the great elephant, I will make him eat soil.'

I could hear everything and became even more confused and terrified when I heard his words. Especially about turning me into a zombie. Oh God, could it really work? But I'd heard so many such stories it scared me to death. Why in God's name didn't he just kill me? Then my husband and children would mourn. Finally they'd forget and life would carry on. But to know that their mother had been made a zombie, and was still a zombie roaming the dongas and bushes and choking people in the night! I'd rather be dead.

My Mother Superior at school taught us never to underestimate the devil's power. Witchcraft had all the power of evil and it can happen. It's not a lie, it does happen, because the devil has power over evil. It's as though I could hear her now. Oh my God, please have mercy on me. It can't happen to me! I believe in God, I am a Catholic, not a heathen.

I was crying bitterly but couldn't hear my voice. I could feel hot tears coming from my tightly shut eyes and I cried with sheer fright. Mtembu pulled me out of the cave by my legs while saying the others must not come inside the cave, in case they too got very sick. The cave, he said, was full of evil satanic things and they were not strong enough or covered with the necessary muthis involved in forming a protection against such evil.

They dragged me on to the rock and into the spring, which felt so good. Mtembu said he had to bathe me with many mixtures before carrying me right outside of the cave's area. My husband and Sibiya were sighing and weeping softly.

At last Mtembu heaved a sigh of sheer relief, with his hands in the air gesturing toward the cave, and called on his ancestors to burn up the evil. 'Burn the evil, raze it to the ground. Let it sink to the bottomless pit that it be no more.'

Sibiya says a black cloud of stinking smoke came out of the trees

like a black mamba, twitching and twirling through the huge green
sea of forest as though it arose from deep in the stomach of the earth.
The heap of skins and gourds and muthis were all burnt. After a while
Sibiya and Benjy could hear rocks falling, covering the mouth of that
cave forever.

It is still buried there at Ngome and we still did our washing and
drank water from the crystal-clear spring above the cave area. The area
was given the name: 'It is done.' In Zulu the word is Emsenzweni:
where it happened. Mtembu named the place and it carries the name
till today, but it has also kept a mysterious, eerie atmosphere, which
you feel when you go there.

Chapter 18

*Winnefred's convalescence. Unpleasant memories, self-loathing,
depression. The happening is explained by Mtembu's wife. The
return home. The Chief sends his induna to inquire after Winnefred's health. Benjy's anger.*

I STAYED AT MTEMBU'S KRAAL FOR ONE WEEK. Every day I went
through a different ritual, bathing in hot scourging muthis mixed
from various herbs and drinking many different concoctions, vomiting
out funny thick black evil-smelling phlegm.

My husband had told his family about the situation and they were
very helpful with the children. Agnes, the eldest, was due to start school.
Auntie Nettie took her to start in Durban; Jessica took little Jessica and
Juliana to stay in Bululwane; while my husband darted back and forth
between home and Mtembu's to see me.

I got my eyesight back, right in the middle of the kraal, after Mtembu rubbed my eyes with some sour liquid. As I blinked and focused I
could see blurry shadows which soon solidified as the old inyanga and
his dutiful wife. His wife came closer to inspect my eyes and said it
would take a few days for me to regain my clear eyesight. And I was
particularly lucky that her husband still had a little bit of liquid from
the big fish that swims in the deepest sea preserved in a tightly sealed
bottle to mix with the other herbs that helped to bring back my vision.
You see, fish never close their eyes and this kind of sickness required
the eyes of a fish.

Clearly this man had sent people far and wide to look for the best muthis. He beckoned my husband with one hand to come closer and have a look. I saw a scarecrow. Benjy looked like a wooden cross with old rags thrown around it. He was greyish, blackish, gaunt and his eyes were dull and black like those of a dead beast. Oh my God, I was sure he was going to die. Oh Mtembu, is this the father of my children? What has happened to him?

'If you could see your own face, then you would understand why he looks like that. But you must not worry, you'll both be well very soon.'

'Oh Mtembu,' said Benjy: 'you've brought the mother of my children back to life. What will I ever do for you in return? Oh Mtembu, you are indeed the wisest inyanga there ever was. I wish my father were alive to thank you personally.'

'Yes, Son of the White Chief. You have spoken well, but you forget that his spirit has been looking after your wife too. He has kept her alive through the Great White Spirit in whose home he has gone to dwell. Therefore, do not thank me but the Great Unseen One, as I really don't know how your wife is still breathing after all she's been through.'

I thought about dying and really sobbed, as my husband held me close and we both sighed: 'Thank you, dear great God.'

I thought of the one pound note that Jessie's husband had given me. It had been safely kept and I would give it to Mtembu. But then, he would want an ox. Maybe I could help to buy one as ours were all dead with lightning. Oh, oh, that's how it all started. All this madness. First the storm. No, no, first my baby, short little black men choking me. And children laughing at me. Then the colourful bird. And then I went away, very far away. I saw ugly people, queer people. But where did I go to? Why can't I remember? Was I dreaming?

I looked at Mtembu's wife and, thinking a woman is always sympathetic, I pulled her by the arm very gently, and said: 'Do you know where I've been? Let's sit there in the corner and you can explain it all to me. You know my husband is a man who cannot stand stupidity. If I ask him he'll be angry and tell me how stupid I am. Please tell me who pushed me down the Ntendeka.'

'My dear woman, I cannot tell you because I really do not know. What I do know, is that you've come back from the grave. And you have to do everything Mtembu tells you and stop trying to hurt your brain even more, as it is not yet healed. Just go home now and look after yourself and your children.'

This was really hurting my brain. Every time I tried to focus I felt dizzy. I was so weak I could hardly stand on my own. So I was given a walking-stick by Mtembu's wife, while my husband and he were in deep conversation in the corner of the kraal. She told me to sit down as she went up to her husband and knelt in front of the two men. You never stood in front of a man when spoken to, even if you met him on the road. I watched them talking and knew they were discussing something very important about me. I felt uneasy and very frightened as I hardly knew myself what had happened to me. Somehow, I expected to hear the worst. My husband looked at me and shook his head as though in disbelief, and became quiet; but his gaze was fixed on the mountains facing our home. I knew instantly that he was crying.

He got up abruptly and stood alone, and then Mtembu's wife walked up to me and told me not to be afraid about what she had to tell me. 'In one month's time you have to come back to Mtembu so that he can take out the evil dirty blood that the Chief has left in your womb. He only wanted to get your seed – because you are a fertile woman and you breed girls. He wanted you to spill your seed, mixed with his, so that he could make strong muthi to conceive girls, in order to obtain lobola. He got his semen mixed with your seed. That's why he had to leave you to run to his kraal to conceal the seed while it was still alive. There he could mix it up with other muthis and use it on his young wife, who of course cannot conceive a girl child. Every time she loses her girls to the strong evil that is in her womb. And of course it is the tokoloshes who are this evil.'

'Do you mean I slept with a tokoloshe?'

I froze and felt faint all over again when she said: 'No, in actual fact the Chief slept with you, but urged on by the evil power of the tokoloshes. He had to get your seed mixed with his semen. So he put you in a trance through the evil that he used to lure you and put you in a deep sleep. He used the powers of the tokoloshes.'

Oh dear God. I remembered everything. 'I thought I was sleeping with my husband. At one time he was carrying the bird on his shoulders.'

'Oh Nkhosi yami. You poor woman. That was not your husband. You went to him because of the bird that enticed you. Sometimes you actually see a beautiful little baby and you pick it up to cuddle it and it turns into a man and you find yourself sleeping with someone you love very much. That is the power of evil. You are still lucky. Some people run at night to the kraal of the man who is bewitching them. A girl will find herself getting up in the middle of the night and running across mountains and rivers to the kraal, where she is being called by the owner who has put a spell on her. Sometimes the girl ends up mad or dead and she will always say she heard a voice calling her – so she runs in that direction till she reaches her destiny. That's if someone doesn't catch her in time and take her to a good honest inyanga to cure her.'

I think I had fainted. She thought I was sleeping but I heard everything she said as everything started making sense out of nonsense. I only knew I didn't want to live. I remembered the rosary. If it hadn't snapped maybe I would have been protected from all this evil. If only I had told someone about the laughing children. Sibiya or Nyawo would have known immediately what they really were. I was too embarrassed to tell my husband. I am sure he would have told Sibiya and this wouldn't have happened.

My husband will never treat me like a wife anymore. Surely not after this. I could hear Mtembu's wife saying they'd take the dirt out next month as I was too weak now, I might die. I could hear my own voice screaming: 'No, no, no, I want to die. What will my husband say, what about my children when they grow up? Everyone will think I am an evil woman, sleeping with tokoloshes.'

I ran, weak and frail as I was. I tried to run to the river to drown myself, but everyone seemed to come out of their huts to chase and catch me, and I lay motionless in the yard in the shadow of Mtembu's huge hut. I felt someone tie my legs together at the ankles so I couldn't run away, while they burnt incense and made me lick something very bitter. I must have dozed off.

When I awoke it was pitch dark. A flicker of dying embers on the rounded hearth and the hardness of the floor under the reed mats made me aware that I was in my hut together with Mtembu's wife, with her stinking skin skirt hanging right under my nose. She slept opposite me. As her snorting sounds made an unknown melody, I felt I needed to feel her. So I crept closer to her, right up to her backside as she let out a volume of air that sounded like deep thunder. But even that didn't bother me. I think I smiled as I cuddled closer and welcomed the stench. My sense of smell had long lost its edge. I was happy that I was not alone.

Somehow I was reminded of my mother. Oh Mama, Mama, I was

born to suffer. Everything is over. My life is finished. Oh my beloved husband. Now I've hurt him beyond repair. I cried myself to sleep and soon heard Mtembu's wife saying it's time to wake up.

Mtembu gave my husband all the necessary medication and instructions and my husband made sure I was securely strapped on the donkey to take me home. The journey seemed forever. As we reached the yard I cried silently. I wondered what my children were going to say – where had I been all this time?

Benjy unstrapped me before the household people could see me and carried me to the rondavel. And then he called for the children to come and see Mama. Aggie, the eldest, had already gone to start schooling in Durban with her Auntie Nettie. The other two children seemed scared of me. They were distant and looked me up and down, as though they didn't recognise me. But they were nice and fat, not thin and sickly. I could see they had been well looked after, but I felt so ashamed of myself. It was as though they sensed something evil in me. Yes, I feel so dirty. Yes, I feel unworthy. My own children were afraid of this evil woman, who slept with tokoloshes.

I tried to ask them if they had missed Mama but they just looked at me sadly. My heart had no space left over to take any more blows. I grabbed them both and pressed them to my bosom and cried: 'Thank you God, I am still alive, and my children are still alive too.'

The maid brought in the bath, steaming; and my husband told her to take the children outside to play, while he put the powder in the bath water for me to steam myself as Mtembu had said. After that she brought a tray of tea and buttered mealie bread, which was plentiful as it was harvest time. The smell was mouth-watering, so I took a large bite and chewed; but as I tried to swallow, it all came out. I had lived on very thin sour porridge and a little raw milk. I tried again, this time a little at a time, and welcomed the smell of Five Roses. Aah the aroma.

My husband said: 'Don't drink it too fast, you'll vomit it all out again.' But I caught a hint of sheer disgust in his tone.

He couldn't avoid saying: 'It's all through your stupidity. Now I've got to suffer for the rest of my life, because you didn't tell me about the laughing children.'

Half choking on the mealie bread I stammered: 'I am sorry, I am, I am. Oh please forgive me, I didn't know, I should have told you about them.'

He paused and said: 'I don't even know whether I am dreaming or this is true. I haven't come to terms with the whole situation. Please try and eat, so you can get stronger.'

He looked at me with such sadness in his eyes. They had a look of prolonged dismal pain; and yet even when he had that half-dead look he resembled an ox that had died with grace and dignity, like the ones that were struck by the mysterious lightning – they lay there grace-fully, like heroes, dignified even in defeat. His hollowed eyes and cheekbones bore the misery and confusion that he had endured from the time of Katrina's death up until now. I wondered just how much more he could endure. I'd hurt him so much by not telling him all from the start, even about the colourful bird. And now I could sense deep within me that there was some doubt in his heart. Somehow, I knew that this was the beginning of the end.

But I had to concentrate on getting stronger. I had to push these ugly tormenting thoughts to the back of my mind. At least until Father Ja-cob came to hear my confession and to bless me and my children and my husband and home. Maybe things would improve and I would know what to do next.

The women came to see me, even some of the Chief's wives whom I had taught to make stew and to bake scones. The custom was that you couldn't accuse anyone without evidence and a proper court case. When my husband saw the Chief's wives arriving he turned grey and said: 'Oh God, I hope the Chief doesn't decide to come personally. I will personally choke him to death.'

I was so scared. However, instead of coming himself, he sent his induna to say how sorry he was, but that he was very happy that the mother of the children was alive and he hoped that whichever umthakathi had done this terrible thing might soon be smelt out.

Sibiya sensed trouble, and knowing my husband's temper, quickly shouted for him: 'Nkhosana, come quickly, I have to show you this sick cow. Say farewell to the induna and the Chief's wives and then come along.'

Benjy's eyes were smouldering like a red hot mbawula. Sibiya said to me later: 'I saw flames flicker like sparks from his eyes as he screeched to a halt in front of me.'

Benjy said to Sibiya: 'He finds it amusing to mock me in my own home. He dares to make a fool of me by sending his induna to see what my reactions will be. He dares to test my anger. He knows full well who the damn umthakathi is. But he dares to provoke me. He has always said he'll cool my temper with cold water from the depth of the rain forest. So this is what he meant. He waits for my father to die to play with my life. He knew that my father would have shot him right through his savage brains. Oh Sibiya. I hate the savage.'

'Hawu, Nkhosi yami. Do you hear yourself? What you have said is making your father turn in his grave. I can see his heart even in the grave, bleeding for you and your family, but it is broken at your words. Go at once and kneel down by his side and say sorry, before you go too far.'

And Benjy ran down under the pine trees where his father rested, and oh my God, he started digging the grave and demanding that his father come out and shoot the savage. Sibiya ran after him. I watched frozen as Sibiya tried to hold him and comfort him. Then Benjy lost all control. He had pulled the whole tombstone out and thrown it to one side, when Sibiya stepped right in the middle of the grave, screaming: 'Stop, stop, you are crazy. Please, I beg you to stop.'

Yes, he stopped – in order to give Sibiya a generous healthy upper-cut directly on the face, which sent him back into the grave to sleep in peace for a while, while Benjy vented his anger on the poor young pear tree which he wanted to uproot. Failing in this he pulled every branch down, leaving the tree looking like an upside-down plucked ostrich.

I was feeling dizzy and knew I was going to collapse, so I quickly went to hide behind the house in the thicket of wild bramble bushes, together with my children and maid. I turned back to look at him one more time. My love for him urged me to run to him to help him with the great pain he was going through. It was all my fault.

I watched him running toward his parents' rondavel. He looked around frantically and picked up a huge boulder and hurtled it straight on to the rondavel window. That half of the wall collapsed on to the brass bed, and as if that wasn't enough he picked the boulder up again – it had sunk into the soft feather mattress – and with inhuman strength heaved it on to the next piece of mud brick wall which collapsed next to the door. He lunged for the boulder again, to hurl it with all his demonic strength on to the door frame, which groaned and released its hinges from the wood all in one go, falling outward.

I wanted to shout for him to stop at once. But my voice was caught in my throat. I shivered. The kids were screaming.

Luckily Sibiya was still alive. He pulled me by the arm and said: 'Run for safety with your kids. He is not himself, it's something they've done to him. They were sent to sprinkle dust on the ground where he would walk over it. He has to get some incense into his head now now now.' He hurried to the kitchen to ̗et some burning coals to throw powder on them, and at once the whole yard was full of smoke.

I watched from the bushes as Benjy started getting dizzy. He kept wiping his forehead and ripping clothes off, saying: 'Oh God, Oh God, help me. I am dying.'

And he toppled over, still trying to rip his clothes off. He lay motionless as I screamed running toward him, and then collapsed on top of him.

'Benjamin Rorke, please don't do this to me, you can't die. I am the one who should die. I am the cause of all this. Please, please dear God, don't let him die.'

Those were my thoughts as I lay on top of him, our children both having piled themselves on top of us. Sibiya knelt beside us and screamed with anguish.

My husband moved and said: 'Sibiya, yini, what is it, talk to me, what has happened, Sibiya? I thought I personally shot and killed the mad bull. Has it come back from the dead to do this terrible thing? My parents' rondavel. I treasured it. It has been like a shrine to me. Oh Sibiya, look at my father's pear tree. He was so proud of it. What's going on? What's gone wrong with this homestead ever since my father died?'

Chapter 19

Jessica and Benjy's mother arrive at the homestead, followed by Father Jacob and Mtembu. The three herbalists confer. The story of the tree of Life and Death. The cleansing of her womb. The birth of a fourth child.

M Y FIRST THOUGHT WAS THAT I WAS DREAMING, but now I could hear Auntie Jessica's voice screaming for her brother, and then another voice, his mother's, and finally Father Jacob's shouting in a mixture of English and Zulu. The old lady screamed for her an-

cestors and scolded her white husband for daring to lie there under
the trèes, not doing anything for her child.

Sibiya told them what had happened. As Father Jacob listened he
shook his head and said: 'Ne-ver, ne-ver say to yourself: "Where was
God, where was God?" The Satan got very happy, and he took his
soul; but he will repent now and all shall be well wit' him.' Father
Jacob prayed over Benjy in German and placed his huge wooden cross
and the rosary over him as my husband cried to God and pleaded
for his sanity and for his wife and children.

Jessica sobbed into her lacy handkerchief and said she had known
that something terrible was going on here at Ngome. She had had visions and very disturbing dreams so she had sent for Father Jacob and
had told Walter to let the old lady (meaning Benjy's mother) go to
Ngome to see her son, probably for the last time.

Right now his poor mother lay on a mat by the door of her beloved
rondavel, huffing and puffing with asthma and looking like she was
ready to join her husband under the trees. But she kept looking towards
his grave and talking to him as though he was standing right there.
'You gave him the leopard skin and you gave him strength to do this
to your own child. He had all the strong muthis, he even had the brains
of the leopard. Oh you white people will never believe what savages
can do. You always called me a stupid savage, but have you not seen
what stupid savages have been doing to your child? Can you still call
them stupid, you stupid fool? The ones who are stupid are you and
your son, for calling us stupid savages. But I, the daughter of the great
Chief Muhlahlela Nhlobozabafu, am going to do something drastic,
something I never thought I'd have to do. Sibiya, send one of the herdboys to Mtembu at once.'

I couldn't understand how Mtembu had heard my mother-in-law
telling the herdboy to run and call him from his kraal, and I still think
there was more than coincidence in his appearance at that moment.
I only know that suddenly he was standing right there with all of us.

Jessica, Father Jacob and Mtembu were all three very active doctors in their profession. They had healed and restored many people
and now they went into a long discussion on all the different herbs
and their use. Father Jacob spilled his bags of muthis from the Black
Forest in Germany. Jessica spilt hers from Ngome and Bululwane.
And Mtembu spilt his from Tembu-land and Tefuya-land, also from
Tonga-land.

As they spoke over tea, my husband's mother asked Mtembu if he had ever gone to where the early Chiefs from the house of Sobuza Dlamini, his father's tribe, took their baths down the most dangerous precipice of Mahamba near Mbabane. She had heard that that was where the tree of Life and Death stood. This tree was called the lamenting tree, because it cried like a lamb about to be slaughtered. The story went that in the old days it was a place where children were sacrificed, and it was their cries which could still be heard in the lamenting of the tree. When the tree lamented, she cried tears of blood, which fell under her and dried up. Those tear drops became dry lumps of Life or Death.

Everyone kept dead quiet as they listened to this woman's tale about the tree of Life and Death. Mtembu nodded his head at last and said: 'Yes, Great One, I have heard about that tree and have longed to get some tears from her. I want to stop this evil man once and for all.'

'Well now, Mtembu, we know how to stop him very effectively and very painlessly. This is enough. He is trying to finish my children. I swear, by my ancestors, I am going to stop him. Trust me: in one week's time I will have the lump of Death delivered to me right here in this home which I built for the white man's children. The Chief thinks the white man is dead, but the savage wife of the white man is very much alive.'

Father Jacob kept nudging Jessica, wanting to know what the old hag was saying now. In broken Zulu and half German, he got the whole story right and he became hysterical.

'I will ride on the donkey to get the blood my own self. Mtembu, I will go wit' him.'

My mother-in-law shrieked: 'Oh maSwati, no white man would ever survive. You white people are always putting your noses where only the savage nose can smell. You do not even know how to smell out a witch. You are too inquisitive. You want to know all about the use of herbs, but have never gone to learn how to live with them in their world. You do not know where to touch and feel, nor do you know how to taste and smell. Most of all, do you know how to talk to the herbs through their own spirits? Mfundisi, you must first learn all these things. Only then your herbs will be able to cure everyone who believes in them.'

Father Jacob told Mtembu that he was going straight up to the rain forest on his donkey with his piece of cheese and a piece of blood sausage and some dried figs. He was going to sleep there and talk to the plants and understand their language.

Mtembu said: 'Oh no no, Mfundisi, you don't take any food with you, and also no donkey. First I'll give you a bath with bark soap and you must sniff some powder for strength and braveness, and you'll have to take the only weapon you white people use, the stick that spits fire. Get up early together with the bird that never sleeps. Drink water in the spring together with the wild beasts and then start collecting every one of their first hot droppings. As you gather them, take a deep breath and inhale the smell. Close your heart and open your mind, and learn who the droppings belong to. Do likewise with the droppings of all the hundreds of different birds; but as for the largest bird, the red-beaked umkholwane, do not allow yourself to look at him. Shy away from him if you see him, but if you don't see him all the better for you. Lastly, when you know a herb pinch off a tiny bit of her with your fingernail and chew it and swallow it. Every one of them, even if you know they are poisonous. Just chew and swallow the juice, and as you do so tell them to be your friends, and tell them you have respect for them and will never ill-treat any one of them as long as you live.'

Father Jacob chuckled with enthusiasm and went bravely on his way up to the rain forest, without food or even a gun. He had only his tattered old sack slung across his back, eager to fill it up with more roots and bark and then present it all to Mtembu for final inspection on the next day, as Mtembu had instructed.

I had a chance to relate everything that happened to Jessica. She listened very intently, nodding and gesticulating with a puzzled look, hand on mouth, saying in a very down-to-earth angry tone: 'Oh my goodness gracious me. Oh my God. Goodness me. Oh you poor child. You had better not ever tell Nettie this story. She will start telling Mama off for being such an unworthy stupid savage. You know her big mouth. Benjamin is no better, sometimes I think they actually hate Mama.'

We spoke half the night about so many things that had happened since her father had died.

She spoke about her own life and said she feared for her husband's life as he was always away on duty. Right now, he was at Mtubatuba. She spoke about her daughter who was schooling in Pietermaritzburg and how happy she herself was, working very hard on renovations to her little hospital and of course of her patients, who came from as far away as Johannesburg.

My husband was awake very early to try and fix up the rondavel but his mother urged him to break the whole thing down. It was bad luck to rebuild something that was in that kind of condition. And she insisted on cooking a nice dinner for her son – his favourite: chicken and dumplings. But even that didn't melt his broken troubled heart. He just hugged her and stayed very aloof. She whispered to me and said she feared for his life and she was going to ask him to come and live with Walter or with Jessica. To which of course the answer was always: 'I'll die here rather than live anywhere else in the world.'

Jessica told Sibiya to meet Father Jacob halfway with his donkey as he would be carrying very heavily. But of course she wanted a few of his herbs as well, even though she sent her own boys to collect roots and bark from the rain forest almost every month. Father Jacob was in his glory. He said he had had such a wonderful experience and most of all he had overcome his fear of leopards and cobras. He said he had a great desire to live inside the bush from now on and he would write a long letter to his people in Germany and tell them of his experience. He had some of the chicken and dumpling which was his favourite too, while Jessica greedily ransacked his treasury of herbs. He reacted to this by saying: 'Fräulein Jessica, I have risked my life for those precious herbs, of which I have to send some to Germany. You live here under the rain forest. It is a mortal sin to steal herbs as they will heal some poor man, and I feel I am now a proper herbalist.'

He cackled like a proud mother hen protecting her new brood. At least we had a good laugh. He said goodbye and hopped on to the donkey, whistling some German tune. And talking and laughing with his donkey, and nudging its stomach with his little muscled bandy legs, he disappeared down the road.

Later on in the evening while we sat at the huge wooden table watching the round paraffin lamp making spooky patterns on the bare wooden ceiling, I thought of my wedding day. Oh, how happy I was then, and now I was dead inside of me. I hated myself. I didn't know if my husband would ever touch me again.

Jessie and my mother-in-law were ready to ride off in her chariot and horse. No more donkeys as she had said they were too slow. They had

morning tea as I came outside yawning and feeling very lost and confused. They both waved goodbye without a smile. Jessica pulled the
reins so violently, I felt even more guilty as I knew she must be disgusted by what I'd done. But my mother-in-law waved her bonnet at
me and the children till they disappeared.

Mtembu came the following week and told me Jessica had passed
by his kraal to ask all about this terrible umkhuba. He sighed painfully, saying that he had to see first whether I got a period or not, because if I didn't get a period that would mean I was carrying a very
dirty thing in my womb, even if it resembled a normal child. It would
look normal, but far from it. It would just be a tokoloshe, and there
were ways and means to destroy it, but I would have to wait for three
months by which time all the evil seed would have formed a live thing
so that nothing dirty got left behind. Sometimes inyangas made the
mistake of taking the first lump of dirty blood out, leaving the unfinished formation and by so doing causing endless problems for the
woman involved. She ends up barren or she dies, or she has an endless
pregnancy when there really is nothing inside of her except dirty blood.

The long summer days dragged by ominously. I hated myself every
day. I planned and plotted to kill myself. Dinah and Nyawo always
tried their best to reassure me and always told me not to give up.
'These things have happened to many women.'

As the time drew nearer to three months, I started to have some
hope. My life depended on Mtembu. Of course I prayed to God to
give me strength every day, and I knew that in the end He was the
only one who could help me. Father Jacob came on every alternate
Sunday to give me communion, and he was such a lively man he
seemed to think nothing at all about what had happened. He said that
as a priest he had experienced far worse things than this. I must thank
God that I was alive – and he would chuckle and smack his lips with
sheer satisfaction after having his chicken and dumplings.

My husband hardly spoke at table and frankly you could sense that
he wasn't amused by Father Jacob's jovial humour. He had lost all
interest in life. He looked like an old man, with a sagging jaw, flabby
muscles and greying hair. I looked little better. My eyes were swollen
and I had dark rings around my eyes. I looked like a spook, so I hardly ever looked in the mirror. If that was what my poor husband saw,
then I couldn't blame him for not wanting to look at me. Before all
this I used to powder my face every morning and sometimes even put

on some lipstick which Jessica gave me. I had 'Evening in Paris' and lavender soap, lacy nightdresses, but now I sometimes slept fully dressed and I'd often wish I'd never see the next day again.

Luckily for us it was summer. There wasn't much work to do in the fields. If it had been ploughing time, my husband's fields would have stood unploughed.

Then one day Mtembu appeared right in the middle of the yard as though from under the earth, looking like something inhuman. A piercing pain went through my heart. I was terrified of what I was about to go through, but he politely greeted us and said he had to go home first to do some work and he would be back before dark.

Poor Mtembu, his feet were so cracked, he looked so thin and tired but he never complained. He never ate just any food, only special food prepared by his wife with special herbs. He resembled pieces of dry biltong knitted together in the shape of a body suit. This man was truly a dedicated doctor.

I prepared what I had to prepare for my operation, shivering and dizzy. I knew I was going to die. As I wobbled along, half falling, unsteady on my feet, I tucked my children into bed and thought of the others, calling them all by their names. I said to them as I watched them sleeping: 'If Mama dies it will be for the man whom I loved, my husband. Don't cry too much for me, because I was given a second chance. I wanted to be loved as I had never been loved – the way I loved him. I'd die a happy woman knowing that at least I had been loved for a while.' And so many thoughts went through my mind. I babbled on like a mad woman, talking to myself, remembering the first time Benjy and I met, the wedding, the picnic, Nettie and the prince. Oh God, I even laughed like a witch about to be burnt to death. Everything seemed to have happened in another lifetime. And now another life had to begin.

My husband was deep in conversation with Mtembu in the kitchen. A dull fire on a black stove with a huge four gallon tin full of hissing water were their only company.

My husband said to me: 'Winnefred, my wife, I haven't forsaken you. This man's words are stronger than my heart. Don't be afraid. Drink all that muthi in the gourd. He says it's very bitter and bad. When you've finished he is going to bath you in front of me your husband and then I must syringe you. He says he'll have to stay right here in the kitchen by the fire as he has to burn incense right through the

night until the thing comes out. Sometimes it comes out in the shape
of a snake, sometimes a frog or even a pig. So when it comes out he
has to be there to see it and catch it and kill it with his strong muthis.
Because if it runs away then it will surely come back as a tokoloshe.'

My husband's face was blue like death when he said: 'I've got the
bright hunting torch to light up when she feels it's coming out.'

After inhaling the incense, I started to feel very sleepy. There were
all the mats and sheets to sleep on as Mtembu had said I must not
have a coloured blanket, I must use something white so he could see
everything that came out. I dreamt I was again in a dark tunnel, groping and looking for my children, who seemed to be lost. But just as I
thought I heard their voices, they seemed to be birds fluttering their
wings ready to fly. Every time I tried to catch one I lost sight of it. Finally I was so tired I tried desperately for the last time, but I could feel
my breath fading away. I saw the colourful bird looking so old and
bedraggled. I tried for it before it flew away, but it screamed like a
child and wanted to fly away quickly, away from me. I felt so sorry
for it, wondering who had ripped its beautiful feathers away. With
my last strength I heaved myself upward in the tunnel to try and grab
the bird, but it slowly turned into a child, wriggling in a pool of dirty
water. I tried to crawl toward the child, but all of a sudden it was
submerged in blood. There seemed to be blood all over the tunnel and
I knew I would drown in the blood if I didn't get out, but there was
no opening.

I screamed and screamed: 'Oh God help me. Help me dear God.'

I felt numb, my body was so heavy I couldn't move, and there right
in front of me was my father-in-law. He was as white as an angel.
He shone, with a long robe and a long beard. But I knew it was him.
He scooped me up and carried me to a river bed – so green, with
clear water bubbling merrily, and he said to me: 'Now wash your
hands and go to your husband and children. Don't ever come here
again.'

I jerked up to hold his hand as he seemed to be turning away, and
shouted: 'Daddy, don't leave me.'

I heard my husband saying: 'No, no, no. He won't leave you.'

But I felt this sharp pain like someone poking me through my stomach and I was reminded of what was going on and what was about
to happen.

I sat bolt upright and spewed out something tasting so terrible I thought it was my own urine. As I spewed I felt I had to push and two male voices urged me to push very hard.

I was so weak I knew I couldn't make it, but my husband, urged on by Mtembu, said: 'Lift her up quickly, before the thing goes back inside her.'

As he lifted me I felt something crawling out of me. Mtembu swore by his ancestors, saying to my husband: 'Look away, please look away, don't look this side. Close your eyes if you feel like turning your neck.'

I could hear continuous stabbing with some sort of dull object and the spattering of blood. But no sound of any crying, just Mtembu's murmuring, talking to his ancestors and thanking them for saving my life.

Deep in some beautiful green valley I could hear myself saying: 'Thank you dear God. The evil is out. Oh thank you God.'

Very faintly I could hear Mtembu saying: 'Go and get a hoe and dig a deep hole outside on the west side of the kraal. I'll follow you with this thing. I have to bury it and burn it to ashes, and when I have finished burning it, when its smoke goes up, the one who did this terrible thing, that one's heart will go down into the earth to burn forever together with this thing.'

The next day I awoke in my own bed, feeling very sick. I couldn't even turn myself. I lay there not knowing if I were ever going to make it. I heard my husband as if from far away, saying: 'Winnefred, drink some warm milk.' But he fed it to me as if I were a baby.

Father Jacob came to give me communion the following Sunday. I could walk with a walking stick that belonged to my father-in-law. I couldn't cook dumplings for him but my husband had tried and Father Jacob never complained. As we both told him the story he nodded and said Mtembu was right to stab the thing with a wooden stake. To kill anything that is demon-possessed you have to use a cross made of wood and he said I was very lucky that he didn't have to use the wooden stake on me while the evil was inside me.

Chapter 20

*More children are born. Benjamin draws away from Winne-
fred, and it is only much later that he makes some gestures
of reconciliation.*

THE DAYS FOLLOWED EACH OTHER in a dreary chain from autumn
to winter to spring then summer. My husband grew stronger but
also drew further away from me with each passing day. After a whole
year he came into my bedroom, more to release the pent-up frustration than to make me his wife. I fell pregnant. When I gave birth he
was there as usual to help me. As the baby came out I heard his voice
breaking and crying: 'Oh God, it's a kaffir. I knew it. I knew it. The
boy is so black, this can never be my child.' He stormed out to get on
his horse and ride to his brother's house and to his sister Jessica.

So everyone in his family got to hear I had a black child – yet he was
the spitting image of Benjy, just slightly tan. We named him Robert.
As the boy grew, Benjy began to realise his mistake, and he told Jessica to apologise for him to me. But he also asked her to tell me that
all the same he could never trust me again. And it was after the boy
had been born that he had started bashing me, swearing that the child
was not his, that I had cheated on him. The same with the children
who followed. He never came right until he was much older.

Father Jacob often talked to him about forgiveness, and reminded
him about the tragedy with the Chief, saying I could never have known,
that the Devil had his own deceitful ways of breaking people's lives.
Witchcraft was one of the strongest tools the Devil used to destroy
God's people. He would listen attentively, and then just as abruptly
start accusing Father Jacob of delving in the occult himself, because
he always came to fetch roots and bark from the rain forest. He would
accuse him of being a witch himself and ask what kind of a priest he
was, who uses muthis. He would also start accusing Jessica his sister
and say the same of her as of Father Jacob. Why did she defend me all
the time?

Jessica used to be very angry and ask him if he had ever gone to a
white doctor – all his life he had used herbs to cure colds and stomach
aches, herbs were used even to cure the cattle's illnesses.

Father Jacob started getting scarce. He would go straight to the forest and not pass by the homestead as my husband also started accus-

ing him of eating up his fowls! Jessica also got scarce, and so I was left alone, with my handsome Prince of Ngome Forest.

Whenever he beat me up, it was as though he beat new love into my being, for I loved him desperately. So whenever he invited me to his bed, I purred like a kitten lapping up milk, only to fall pregnant again – and again – till I had three others after my son whom he grew to love so much he even gave him his own name Benjamin as a second name. I tried to be a dutiful wife, but had no more support from Father Jacob or Jessica. Only my child Aggie stood by me through thick and thin.

All the helpers started fading away as he called them all abathakathi – and they were influencing his wife to marry the Chief! All of them were a bunch of savages. He hated them all.

Nyawo and Dinah still came quite often to help in the fields and just to help me around the house as I kept having babies. When Aggie went back to school I missed her so much, and wondered whom she'd marry. My prayers were always for her to find a good husband, but I never conversed about such deep matters with a child. Somehow deep in my troubled heart, I'd feel the need to send her far away where there'd be no men, perhaps in a mission, where she'd be protected from the outside world. I often thought of asking Father Jacob to take her to Nongoma to live in the hostel. But Father Jacob was himself becoming just a memory.

As my husband became more and more cruel and abusive toward me and my children, I started contemplating suicide, or at least running away from him. But my love for him was too strong. I couldn't leave him alone, what would become of him? Everyone feared him, even his own family.

I would look up at the Tendeka, and the silver waterfall, holding hands with my children, gazing at the forboding thick ominous dark forest, and I would shudder from sheer fright – the same feeling I had when I first saw it on horseback, coming from my wedding day at Nongoma. It seemed I never heeded the warning sign. How could I, when all I wanted was to fly over the mountains and start my new life with my Prince ...

As with the rain forest at times, there was no more beauty left in my heart. Instead a shroud of mist would envelop my senses, my whole being would seem to sink right there in the yard where I stood looking out with my children. The mist in my eyes would turn into a torrent

of rain, falling relentlessly on the rain forest and blurring its foreboding beauty from my memories forever. The birds had no more
songs, the insects had all lost their music instruments. Fate had stored
my pain into Agnes my child, who would in turn divide it with the
world ...

Mtembu died of old age after I had my third boy. He never ever told
me or my husband what had come out of my womb.

Agnes explains
... how hearing Winnefred's story changed her view of her
parents

I WAS SO ANGRY when I learnt about my mother's story. And so frustrated! Above all I was sorry that I had even gone so far as to hate my father! How could I bring them both back now, and take them in my arms to say sorry for all their pain? I had honestly had no idea about the terrible events in their lives: the quarrel with the Chief and his revenge, the frightening episode with the tokoloshe. I do remember quite vividly the dead oxen lying bloated in the field, and Mtembu appearing now and then in our yard, looking like a stray wolf.

But I knew there was something very wrong with my parents. I could never understand the total negativity and disrespect my father showed toward my mother. And I noticed a change in her. Sometimes she was very quiet and distant, though she never laughed or spoke much. I often wondered why she would do things repeatedly, like stoking the fire over and over again, putting more wood into the stove when there was enough wood. She would gaze as though in a trance right into the leaping flames, and never flinch; her eyes would start watering, but she would just carry on gazing into the fire with tears rolling down her cheeks. Sometimes she would throw a handful of dry grass or twigs into the flame to make the blaze higher, and bigger and brighter! As though she was burning away something inside of her, or rather giving herself up to a purification, burning away some evil memories ...

Sometimes she would cut herself while peeling vegetables, but she would never flinch or show any kind of pain. I found her very strange at times. I so wished to talk to her, or that she would talk to me! I was her eldest and I felt grown up, enough for her to confide in me; but of course in those days there was no such thing. A child is a child, and must never know big people's business. I would catch a few words sometimes, spoken in the company of one of the older women who came to help. She seemed most attached to Nyawo, her favourite. She would sit on her haunches taking snuff, and talk in gestures and mono-syllables. It was inaudible, as well as monotonous and depressing.

Once she threw her apron over her face, as though trying to ward off some evil omen. I heard her groan about my having to carry her womb; as I was the eldest, I would have to carry her pain and I would pass it on to my own eldest daughter.

I really didn't understand deep Zulu, but those words seemed to reverberate through the thick kitchen mud wall straight into my heart! So I slowly shifted away from the open window where I had stood straining every fibre of my young muscles to hear, standing on the grinding stone with my big toes stiff with cramps. I slid down the wall to sit on the grinding stone, aware while doing this that I had better not be caught. Sitting on the grinding stone was not only disrespectful but meant disregarding the foodstuff that was ground on it, rather like sitting on a plate.

My young mind would probe for answers: Why does she say I'll take her womb and in turn give it to my child? How long will I be able to keep that womb of hers?

The impact of that incident left me searching for answers for many years, until I met another old lady who told me the meaning of the saying. It means that you take after your mother; if she had hardships in her marriage, so will you – because you inherited them from the womb when she gave birth to you, and you in turn will pass them on to your first born.

When I was little, my home was a haven, a paradise ruled by the king and queen of my heart. I loved them both. So why this depres-sion and hopelessness?

At the time I remember once asking my friend Tobile if her parents ever fought, or had violent arguments like mine. She beamed, and gig-gled, rolling her round eyes at me, and said: 'Are you mad? How can I ask them such a thing? I never see them together, except I hear my mother screaming at night in his hut. The next morning she has both her eyes swollen or once she showed us two of her teeth and said she extracted them at night, while we were sleeping.'

We'd talk and laugh about other things and soon forget about our parents fighting.

I was destined to be present at my mother's death bed. She had refused to allow the doctor to remove her cancerous womb, as though protecting her secret inside, and cherishing the memory of how she had conceived from her Prince.

My father was not there to close her eyes, nor to hold her hand and say: 'Farewell Winnefred, we'll meet again!' He did witness her coffin being lowered. Standing there, he resembled two metres of parched river bed standing upside down. My heart bled for him even then, though I was only able to forgive him much later, when I knew their story whole.

PART TWO

Agnes

Agnes and Lemmy Lottering with Rhonda

Chapter 1

The Rorke home. Agnes and Jessie go to the mission school in Eshowe.

MY PARENTS' HOME AFTER THEIR MARRIAGE was near the Ngome rain forest, and that was where I grew up. Their homestead was close to my uncle Walter's, who had married my auntie Rosie, and there was much cooperation between the families. It was a lovely spot, but at the time my parents' marriage was not good. They did see to it that we had schooling, though – at a mission boarding school in Eshowe. It was called Little Flower School. I was nine and my sister Jessie was seven. The day we left, we had to get up at the first cock-crow. It was still dark and the air was fresh as always at Ngome at this time of the morning.

Our suitcases were packed and labelled and stood next to our rolled blankets and pillows and the basket with our padkos. My father had arranged that some young girls would go with us to the nearest bus stop at the forester's house and police station on the edge of the forest. They had to carry our things and also Jessie when she got tired of walking. The girls put our things on their heads and took turns to abba Jessie on their back. It was about four hours' walk to the bus stop.

We waited for a long time before we could see the cloud of red dust. By this time Jessie was hysterical to a point where she wee-wee'd herself. Not even a piece of chicken and mealie-bread or dumpling could pacify her. She was very scared of the bus, unlike myself, as I had already started schooling in Durban. The R.M.T. (Road Motor Transport) government-owned bus slowed down and came to a rumbling halt. There were two sections in this bus, the front section – Blankes – and the back section – Nie-blankes. Even though the section for Blankes was not full, people still had to get into the Nie-blankes, until the passengers were like sardines.

A timid-looking, red-faced Boer jumped out of his driver's seat to collect the busfares and hand out the tickets. All of a sudden he blurted out: 'Waar gaan jy met die bok, kaffer? Daar is nie plek in die bus vir 'n bok nie!'

To which the Beshu man in his traditional skin skirt pleaded that he was taking his wife back to her parents in Mahlabathini as she had been barren for three years. 'She has not conceived, that's the reason why I have to take this goat with me.'

The white driver burst out in laughter, peals of laughter, saying: 'Okay! Go in with the goat, but make sure to keep the goat between your legs.' With his poor wife silently sobbing behind him and the goat pulling back, the man moved forward. Our turn came and the driver asked: 'Where are you going to?'

I feebly replied: 'Eshowe.'

At Ngome postbags were loaded and some were off-loaded. It being January, the air was stifling hot. The odour of fat smeared on the isi-dwabas of the sangoma who sat directly in front of us, coupled with the smell coming from the recently inflated animal gall bladders hanging from her head, made it difficult for us to breathe. The sangoma kept snuffing and humming her ancestral songs. I asked in fluent Zulu for the windows to be opened.

The man had wedged the goat tightly between his legs and was talking at the top of his voice, telling his neighbour just what he was going to say to his in-laws in Mahlabathini. The goat was under strain and as soon as the bus jerked forward, it became more distressed and started to pee and make droppings. Just then Jessie wanted something to eat. I opened the basket with padkos, took out the mealie-bread and dumplings and broke off a piece of fowl with my hand. The bus suddenly swerved and caught brakes, causing Jessie to lose her balance. She dropped the mealie-bread, dumplings and fowl in the goat's droppings and urine. Wasting no time, I was down on my knees to save our delicious food. We ate in silence, even though the bread and chicken tasted extra salty with the goat's urine.

The man eventually ushered his goat out as we stopped in Mahla-bathini. Still cursing his wife!

Arriving at Eshowe stop, Brother Quicksilver was there to meet us. We travelled through the little village until we could see the gum trees that surrounded the hostel and the school buildings. Sister Timotha showed us around to the dormitory and bathroom, and I was relieved that Class One and Standard One shared the same dormitory. This meant Jessie would be close to me.

After the long journey we were told to take a bath. The baths were nothing but square concrete tubs in a row, almost three feet deep and filled with soapy water from the dirty washing! As we were still small, bigger girls had to help get us in and out the bath. I found this way of bathing very dirty, as we were used to bathing in springs, in running water from the rain forests of Ngome.

The next morning we were lined up outside our classrooms. The teacher asked everyone for their names and where we lived. 'What is your name, my girl …?'

I tried to reply in English, the way I had been taught while I was stay-ing in Durban with my father's sister Nettie. I said it was Agnes Lorke. My home was Ngome forest and my sister was called Jessie Lorke. (I couldn't say 'r'.)

He asked: 'Do you live with the monkeys and baboons?'

To which I replied with wide eyes: 'Yes, teacher!'

I was quite happy to learn to read and write. My favourite was writ-ing compositions and telling stories and anything to do with what was happening around me and in the world.

The games we enjoyed playing were hide-and-seek, five stones and hopscotch. I never liked to lose, but I felt sorry for the others, as they could never beat me to come first. I was hopeless in sports, except swimming, because I liked swimming in the rivers back home and climbing trees.

We were treated like prisoners by the German nuns and priests and brothers at the Little Flower School. There were occasions when we had excitement, bewilderment – some very disturbing moments. Like the time when we had Brother Vincento, who must have been Italian judging by his name. He loved to play with the bigger girls – to grab them by their buttocks or squeeze their breasts, especially when we went into the cellar where they kept the smoked ham and the huge barrels of lard and the preserved fruit and cabbage soaked in vinegar, salted and stuffed into vats. When you opened the barrel the smell was terrible, and worms would float all over the surface. Brother Vincento loved to scoop them up with his bare hands and push them down one of the bigger girl's breasts so that she would scream and wriggle and half-tear her blouse off. Then he would come closer and mumble something in his own language, and look so sorry while he tried to comfort her. At the same time he'd be fondling her breasts, huffing and puffing like a dog with his tongue practically hanging out of his mouth – and turning red as a turkey too. Sometimes he would corner one of the big girls and tell the rest of us to sort out the rotten potatoes outside. We would try to peep, but the cellar was so gloomy and dark that we never really knew what happened inside. When the girl came out she would run past us upstairs to the dormitory without saying anything. In any case the bigger girls never told us their secrets, but we had our own ideas, and we would just giggle to ourselves, and carry on with our work.

Then there was Brother Heribert, who had deep-set eyes that looked like a squirrel's. The girls were really terrified to work with him. His nickname was Goatie-Boy, as he had a little beard like a goat's. He spoke like a goat too, and he even moved like a billy-goat, hopping and skipping when he saw the girls. His beady blue eyes shone at every passing girl, and he couldn't keep his hands off their buttocks. He would whistle a little tune of his own composing, just for the girls to hear. Maybe he had been a dancer once, for he had such swift movements; but he had bandy legs and was quite a stumpy man. Maybe he had killed many people in the German war, perhaps in the concentration camps, and then had joined the brothers to escape.

We would never know. Those people lived a very private, secret life. They were cruel and heartless, and we believed they actually hated us, for they called us 'animals' and 'bastards'.

This Brother Goatie-Boy used to be the carpenter and handyman. There was nothing that he couldn't fix, and there was plenty that needed fixing, for in those days there was no outside supply of electricity – we just had lights on the walls, and when there was a storm all the lights would fail as they were run by a huge generator somewhere in the bowels of the building. Brother Goatie used to come to fix up the damage, and sometimes for no reason at all the lights would just cut off in the dormitory. Today I think he used to tamper with the generator, to give himself an excuse to come up to the dormitory. He would climb into the girls' beds and start fondling girls' private parts. You would hear the big girls screaming from our dorm, as theirs was adjacent to ours. One big girl ran out once to the Mother Superior's rooms in her bloomers. No one wore panties or bras in those days: you either slept naked, or you slept in your bloomers – that is, of course, if you didn't have a nice nightdress or pyjamas from home.

We were grateful for the education and the Christian upbringing we got, but there were many things that we couldn't understand. For instance, they treated us as though they were forced to educate us, and had to teach us to work very hard. It really seemed as though they didn't enjoy what they were doing. They were full of colour prejudice. We never ate what they ate, for instance – we always had scraps. They showed us no love or understanding.

The brothers and the priests were just having a good time with us young innocent girls. As for the boys, they got such severe punishment that sometimes they would run away from the school.

The sisters treated us girls with utter hatred; they would take our clothes away if they were at all pretty. You were not allowed to question a sister, let alone answer back. If you did you would be severely punished – and I am talking about locking up a girl in a closet for one whole day and night, with no water to drink. That was cruelty surely – and if you dared to be cheeky you were given stale old porridge with worms afloat in it. Or if you couldn't do your needlework in class you were pricked with a needle on your hand until you bled.

Sister Timothea was the Dragon. She hissed fire out of her mouth when she spoke to you. She used to call us bastards. We would never see the Kingdom of God, she said, because no bastards are allowed in heaven, so we would all burn in hell.

Then there was Father Felix, a real glamour boy, handsome and tall. He wore glasses over big green eyes with thick eyelashes. He was much admired by the big girls, and everyone wanted to go to confession to him on a Friday afternoon. He was noted for loving to hear if you had committed fornication; you had to tell him in full detail.

I once went to him to confess about my first love Pieter. Pieter and I had at this stage done nothing more than kiss.

'Father, I kissed a boy.'

'How many times?'

'Only once, Father.'

'Are you sure you are not lying to Our Lady? She will not bless you if you are lying! Tell me how many times, and what did it feel like?'

'I felt a bit dizzy.'

Then the chair would screech as he pulled himself closer, and pressed his right ear against the grille of the confession box, and whispered hoarsely: 'And what did he do then? Did he pull down his trousers? Did he pull out something looking like a sausage? Did he do that, girl? You must tell the truth! You must make the Virgin Mary happy! You know that she was a virgin and that you must follow in her footsteps and then she will bless and protect you always.'

At the end I said: 'Yes, Father, he did do it to me.'

And then in a husky voice he said: 'How many times, girl, did he do it to you – and did you enjoy it? Because if you did then you sinned willingly, and for your penance you must say twelve Hail Marys and twelve Decades of the Holy Rosary. And you are not to see this boy again, or even think about him, for it is a mortal sin to think about boys, and you will be punished by the Virgin Mary, and you will burn in hell. Now go in peace, my child, and say your penance diligently, and sin no more!'

He thoroughly enjoyed being told about fornication, and he practically forced you to confess to something you didn't do. We were so scared of Mother Mary and hell, that we owned up for fear of burning in hell. Many a girl in our school who had been to Father Felix's confession box confessed to things she didn't do, and therefore made a mockery of confession. Sometimes the girls would crack such jokes about confession that it became like a weekend movie. You waited for Friday to confess a nice juicy piece of fornication, because you knew Father Felix just loved that.

These are some of the many things that confused us as kids. Until today I wonder what kind of religion that was. Of course it still goes on, but when we were young we were totally at their mercy, and we believed with all our little hearts and minds that what the Father said was the way and the truth and the light.

Father Felix, who must be in his nineties now, is still alive. But he is so full of hate that he chases away anybody that comes into his yard. He had some pear trees in his yard which he ordered to be chopped down because people kept pestering him, asking for fruit. I went to see him last year, and he looked like Dracula – miserable and haggard. He unleashed the dogs on us and told the old gardener with whom he lives to tell us to leave him alone and get out of his yard, or else he'd call the police. I felt sorry for him, and even said a prayer for him in my heart.

The nun we called the Dragon died at Little Flower School, and the younger generation say she still spooks till today: you can see a blue flame darting back and forth from her bedroom to the chapel at certain times of the month.

She was a terror. We farm children used to feel sorry for the Durban kids, as they were not used to such a hard life. Furthermore, they knew nothing about samp and beans and boiled mealies and boiled sweet potatoes and madumbies. They used to cry when it was time for lunch or supper. So often Sister used to push the food into their mouths until they vomited, and she would push it back, vomit and all – oh, it was terrible to watch her when she was in one of those moods, when the kids refused to eat what she had so painstakingly prepared. She did work very hard in the kitchen: she was the head cook. Of course she had the bigger girls to help her, and they often had ugly burns on their arms or their faces where she had thrown something hot at them when she got angry. She once pushed a girl headlong onto the fire for stealing a piece of meat, which of course was prepared solely for the sisters and brothers. The girl ended up with a head only half full of hair, and we teased her and called her Ikhanda – which means 'head'.

In spite of everything, we were carefree and happy, sad and glad. I had one good friend, Lily Thompson, and we spent many a happy moment giggling or whispering our secrets to each other. It was better to be at the boarding school than at home, although being the eldest I cried every night, wondering if Mama was still alive; whether I would still find her at home when we went for holidays, and wondering how many nights she had had to sleep in the cattle kraal. She would say to me that she found the dry cow-dung warm when her husband chased her out. When at home we used to go to sleep with her, snugly against the cows, and she would cover us with dry, fresh-smelling dung. I'll never forget that smell. Sometimes when I am lonely and I cry myself to sleep, I press the blanket up against my nose and think I smell the cow-dung, and call Mama's name. Oh Mama, where are you?

Chapter 2

Agnes is courted by the white farmer's son Pieter. Meanwhile her schooling comes to an end (together with her tomboy existence) by paternal decree.

D URING THE WAR, in 1944, when I was seven years old, I can first remember these white farmers coming to our farm. They came in July to buy cattle from my father. There were two brothers, sons of one of the farmers: one called Pieter and the other Jannie. I started noticing Pieter when I was fourteen.

He looked at me with eyes that were deep and dark, like the fire when Mama cooked our meals outside. When the embers seemed to die off and the coals were stoked again, there was a glow that was not quite red but topaz, almost reddish-black yet at the same time glittering and colourless – that was how his eyes looked at me. They made me feel warm and reminded me somehow that I was fourteen years old and starting to be a woman.

The thought frightened me because I thought of becoming like my mother. Oh God, please, I must have a good husband! I didn't want to live on a farm, I had the dreams that all young girls have – I wanted the town! Who wanted to be a farmer's wife – and a white man's at that? I'd be just another slave like Mama, ploughing and harvesting and seeing to the milking and making butter. But oh! I wanted so badly to put on high heels and wear lipstick like the film stars we used to hear about.

One day in December they came again to buy cattle.

As usual I was called to make the tea and to serve it outside on the grass near the cattle kraal. As I handed Pieter his cup he looked at me again. I shyly looked back and our eyes caught. I tried to be steady but the cup of tea spilt all over his khaki trousers and I turned red as a tomato.

'I am sorry,' I mumbled, but his hand was over mine, trying to wipe his trousers, and he flashed a look at me. I felt flushed and frightened, but he squeezed my small hand in his big hairy one. I walked away fast with the empty cup in my hand.

The next day he sent a herdboy from his farm with a note: 'Meet me down by the river after lunchtime.'

I went to the river, feeling all excited but scared at the same time.

His horse was waiting, tied to a nearby tree, and he sat on a stone. He beckoned to me to come closer, and gave me a bunch of wild flowers. I took them, trembling.

He touched my cheek and said: 'Don't be afraid, I won't harm you. I am in love with you. I want you to be my girlfriend and I'll be your boyfriend. Do you like me a little, just a little?'

He said those words in such a simple way that I laughed.

'My father will kill me, and you too,' I said.

'No one will tell your father, and no one will tell my father. When we're both grown up we'll run away and go to Swaziland, and get married and have a lot of children.'

I listened, but I had nothing to say. I knew that my father would find out somehow. Then I said I was too young, and I had to get back as I had come down to the river with a bucket to fetch water, and Mama would be waiting. He said he would see me again before I went back to boarding school.

Three days before going back to school he sent the herdboy to tell my girlfriends that he wanted to see me. We were neighbours; their names were Tobile and Kanji, and we were almost of one age group. Their father Sibiya had been my father's friend for years and we girls had grown up together and been friends from when we were very small.

We did a lot of things together, like gathering wood for fire and playing with our dolls, which were made of clay, and making mud cakes. I had a doll that was sewn by Mama with rags, which I loved, but she was so ragged that Tobile didn't like her. She made me dolls out of clay.

Tobile came running to find me. 'Umlungu wants to see you down by the river,' she whispered into my ear as I was on my knees polishing the verandah floor with cow-dung. She helped me finish and I washed my hands but forgot to wash my knees. I was trembling with excitement and so scared of my father. He might just be near the river, and perhaps catch sight of the horse. I kept asking Tobile where he was, and saying she should peep to see if he wasn't anywhere in sight.

I ran down to hide in the thicket until I came face to face with Pieter. I almost bumped into him. My heart was beating so fast, I said: 'What do you want so near the river? You'll be seen by my father.'

'Come here, you little wild buck, you worry too much. Don't be afraid.' He held my hand and smiled. His teeth were like a cob of mealies – so well set and square and white, as if they were put there one by one.

His eyes twinkled mischievously. He caught me in his arms. I felt like I was squashed between two granite rocks, ready to be pulped.

His breath smelt like mealie fields, his armpit smelt like fallen leaves in the forest, and I realised that my own knees smelt of cow-dung. As if he sensed it, he said I smelt like a baby calf. He whispered, only it wasn't a whisper, it sounded like Nkunzi's rumbles when he wanted a wife. Nkunzi was our bull, and we were all terrified of him. Only when he said: 'I love you', I knew it wasn't Nkunzi.

Inside my childish mind I couldn't really grasp the true meaning of love, but I sort of yelped: 'I love you too.' I knew it sounded like a cricket, but his grip tightened. I could hardly breathe. His lips were on mine, pressing as if he would swallow me up.

I tried to wriggle out of his grip and push him away, but he kissed me even harder. I had never been kissed by a boy before, and I had been told not to because I would fall pregnant. Mama had told me so many times; how could I disobey her? What was I doing?

I got scared and he sensed it, and said nothing would happen – he loved me too much, that's why he kissed me, because when a boy loves a girl he kisses her, to show his love for her.

I broke away and ran home to tell Tobile. At that time I was mainly interested in cows and calves and horses and ploughing and inspanning the oxen when it was ploughing season – that I was more like a boy than a girl. I never took care of how I dressed. I loved to wear a bhayi, which was just a piece of cloth tied around your breasts. I never wore shoes – my feet were full of cracks. I would swim and go hunting for honey and rabbits, and I knew how to set the best traps for birds.

But now Tobile said that I was ready to fall in love, as I was going to be an intombi. I already had breasts and I had menstruated. She told me that white people's customs were not like theirs, because they did not have lobola – you just fell in love and got married and had children – so why was I afraid to fall in love? I laughed because Tobile was so serious.

I had my birthday on Christmas Day. I was fifteen, and yet I didn't feel any different. I shuddered at the thought of what Tobile had said to me. How do you show you've changed on the farm? I did want to wear high heels and lipstick and go to work in Durban, and bring my mother nice clothes and my brothers and sisters too. Yet thoughts of leaving Mama alone with so much work to do, and so many children to look after, just made me sad.

In January, we went back to boarding school. I was very lonely at school. I thought about Mama all the time, but I found I had thoughts about Pieter too. I could see him, I could smell him. He smelt like earth mixed with horse's perspiration – just like my father – he smelt of soil, and he was a fine big block of hard brown granite. But my thoughts of him were never clear. Sometimes I felt I hated him.

I told my cousin at school about him. She was sixteen and she told me she also had a boyfriend at home in Swaziland, but he was Coloured like herself. She was not pleased at all about what I had to tell her, so I studied hard and tried not to think too much about love, or Mama, or Pieter. I took my exams and knew I would pass.

My sisters Jessica and Julia knew about Pieter; Jessie always said she'd tell my father if I didn't give her my sweets or an extra piece of bread, or if I didn't carry her bucket of water or her pile of wood. I had to make her a clay doll and a string of beads for the doll; so I got my fair share of punishment from her. But we had our fun together. We laughed when we could and we cried a lot too, when things looked bleak and dreary at home.

Then it was holiday time. July came so fast, and I was thrilled I was going to see Pieter again, and my little brothers and sisters. I had missed them a lot. My father was waiting for us by the railway bus station with the horse and sledge, and in no time we were at home, greeted by Mama and the family, and a grinning Tobile and Kanji and the herdboys – and Gogo, my mother's helper, with the children. I loved Gogo very much. Her apron was so patched it looked more like patchwork. She had no teeth, and she loved to kiss our cheeks so hard that you could hear the smacking sound in the next room.

Back to all the chores again. July was reaping time, and everyone worked from dawn until dusk. That Sunday Jessica said she would go home and start the cooking, as she was thirteen – almost fourteen – so I could have time with Pieter.

I went up to him and stood motionless, as he had grown taller. He had new khaki clothes and he was so handsome. I didn't know if I should run into his arms, or run away. He grabbed me again, and I felt like I was squeezed between two rocks – only this time I didn't want to wriggle out. I was so happy. His arms seemed to squeeze all the pain out of me and a warmth I couldn't understand took its place. He kissed me and I responded – with the help of nature I seemed to have learned how to kiss. He said he missed me and we spoke for a while.

He said he'd come again the following Sunday, as he lived fifteen miles away, over the mountains on the other side of the Ngome Forest. The wild flowers he gave me had an extra-sweet smell; they were winter flowers from the bush, blossoms of wild apricot. I took them and crushed them against my chest. We kissed goodbye and his horse galloped away so fast – I almost thought I'd never see him again.

Father Jacob was at the house, where he came to give my mother and I Holy Communion. He loved to call me Saint Agnes, and this time I felt ashamed to be called that because I had just kissed a boy. I confessed my sins to him of anger and hurt, but I didn't tell him about the kiss. We received our Communion, and served him with chicken and dumplings, which was always prepared for him. He would devour every bit of it and not leave a taste for us. Of course he sat up at table with my father, and between them they would feast and leave us nothing. Then Mama would find something else for us to eat.

When Father Jacob had finished eating, he would get on his donkey and head for the forest, to collect bark from various trees, and herbs and roots, to make medicine for the hospital which was at Nongoma. From the forest he would take another route, which would get him to the Mission by night. He was such a jolly old priest. He loved my father because Father always gave him a chicken to take back to the Mission, as he had no money to put in the collection.

My father called for me, and his voice made me freeze. I thought: 'I am going to collapse!' I just knew why he was calling me – Jessie must have told him! Oh God, please help me!

I went up to him trembling, but he said to me in such a kind voice, I couldn't believe I was hearing right: 'My child, you are old enough to leave school now. Your mother is carrying high with another child, and she needs you here at home to help her. So you have to stay home from now on. A girl does not need to be educated. You will marry someone, and your duties will be to your husband and your home.'

I was still waiting for the next sentence, when he said: 'Run along now and make me some wild bush tea.' This was a favourite of his.

'Thank you, Papa,' I muttered, and ran to the bush nearby to pick fresh tea for him.

I took the cup to him and he asked me if I had made my mother some too. Is he getting soft, or is it old age? I thought. He was only in his early forties, and he was still strong and very handsome, with a thick mop of silver-grey curls. He really was a man, all six foot of him. I looked at him and wondered – maybe he still missed his first wife? Did my mother love him once the way I loved Pieter, or was it a duty, a commitment? What did they say to each other when they were alone?

'Call your mother here,' he said.

When Mama came up to sit next to him she was so small and humble, always obedient to him.

'Winnie,' he said almost softly. 'This child has grown up now, and she will not go back to school. You must teach her to be a woman.'

'Yes, my husband.'

'She has to learn to cook and bake and sew, and stop being a farm boy. No more climbing trees and milking cows and inspanning the oxen. No more hunting with the boys and swimming naked down at the river. Her place is at the house to help you with the children and the cooking. I know that she is going to find that very hard. You will fill two tins with beans to sell, so that she can have ten shillings to buy some material for clothes to go to church at Nongoma, and to go to the Post Office when necessary.'

'Yes, my husband. I understand. Thank you.'

My schooldays were over. At least I'd passed Standard Six, which was considered a high degree of education in those days. My sisters cried, as they would travel alone to boarding school now, and I cried with them and told them not to be frightened, as the bus driver always looked after us. We slept at the Mission at Nongoma to get the early bus going to Eshowe in the morning. That night was sad for my sisters and myself, but I was glad that my father had said I should leave school, because I could see Pieter more often. Most of all I was happy that he never mentioned anything about me seeing Pieter on the quiet, so I was saved from the lion's mouth!

Tobile was so happy – she had never gone anywhere near a school. Rural Zulus didn't in those days. They were meant to marry and have children – that was the custom.

My duties were no less than before. I found I was indoors half the day, and I hated it. I could sew on Mama's old Singer, and I could bake scones and cook dumplings. I was learning to bake a cake, but it just never seemed to come out right. The days dragged on.

My duties became even more tedious and more demanding. I learned all I could, I could sew a whole dress by myself without a pattern.

Mama was pleased with me and she said I must show my father what I could make. I showed him and he said I looked like a little lady, so I wore the dress to church.

It was ploughing season, springtime, when we went to the store with Tobile to buy sugar and Five Roses tea, and we saw Pieter at the crossroads, coming towards the forest. He stopped right in front of us and asked Tobile to go to the shop alone so that he could be with me. She had to come back and meet me there at this spot – at the crossroads, near the forest. She took the five shillings and went merrily along by herself, and gave me a mischievous glance. I knew what she was thinking.

I was so happy to see Pieter. He took off his riding coat and hung it on a nearby shrub, took the saddle off the horse to cool him and tied him near some green grass. Then he grabbed me by the arm as if he had never seen me before and said: 'You've grown up!' It was only a month since I had seen him. He held me tenderly and kissed me passionately, and then he said: 'Let's sit down among the wild flowers.'

The spring had brought many new blooms, and the air smelt of new pollen and fresh honey. The forest was alive with music from the birds and a multitude of insects, and distant cries from the baboons reminded me that we were very much in paradise. Oh, it was as though they were serenading our love.

We sat there locked in each other's arms, listening to our heartbeats, and he said softly: 'Do you love me?'

I said: 'Yes, I love you ...' again and again. He tilted my face, and said my skin looked like cream, soft like butter, and my lips were like red wild plums. His eyes had that glow like burning coal, his moustache felt rough against my cheek and neck.

I felt weak and delirious – I didn't understand why, but I felt frightened, and I pushed him away. He pressed me closer to him, and murmured in Afrikaans: 'Bruin meisie, ek is so lief vir jou.' He groaned so sorely I thought he was in pain, and then he said softly: 'O Here, help my.'

I still didn't understand. Only when his hand started caressing my thighs did I know what was going to happen. I was lost in a symphony of the wilds, and Mother Nature took her course. I heard a buzzing in my head – I didn't know if I was being transported to another world, but as long as we were together we would be all right. He was so gentle and he kept calling me 'my lieflinkie, my baba' and he panted like a tired calf that had run away from the stable.

I felt the same way too. I was so sorry for him, yet happy that he was so relaxed. We lay together oblivious of the world – only nature could see us, and spring heard our lovemaking. It's as though she hid the secret in her bosom, and in turn played us a lovesong, and sealed our love by giving us all she could give.

Your first love will always be your last love. You cannot capture those moments ever again.

Somehow I felt sad, and I cried softly on his chest. He lay motionless; his eyelids were like a baby calf's at sleep, but there were tears that looked like dewdrops on his cheeks. I kissed them off, and he kissed my eyelids and whispered: 'Don't cry, baby, God in heaven can see us, and nature gave us the right, because we love each other.' He said it so sincerely that my heart loved him.

We lay there listening to nature. We spoke about our parents, and I told him I'd finished with school. He said he knew, he had heard it from the herdboys; this was why he came to see me. He was going to learn farming at home, as his father was growing old. There was a nearby spring where we drank water and washed ourselves.

It was time to part. Tobile would soon appear at the crossroads. He said he would see me the following Sunday. We kissed, and he told me not to be scared as he would take care of me always. He would love me until death, and nothing must part us. If our parents found out, he'd steal his father's gun and shoot the two of us rather than let us be separated. 'No one will part us, we will always be together – only death can part us.'

These are the promises young people make so solemnly. I didn't know then that it would never last. It was too beautiful to last forever.

Chapter 3

Conversations with Tobile. Nettie. Agnes discovers she is pregnant. She tells Pieter. The fall. The baboons. The miscarriage.

As WE WALKED HOME TOGETHER through the thickets Tobile was so anxious to hear what happened between Pieter and me she could hardly keep a straight course, half-toppling over thick grass and off the path as I told her excitedly about Mlungu and how we made love.

She shrieked with laughter as she said that at last I was grown up. 'Don't you feel grown up?' she yelled, as if I were deaf. 'Don't tell anyone else, please don't tell Jessie, she'll tell everyone at home, and Nkhosana will hear and you'll be dead tomorrow morning!'

She ranted on and on about how she first made love with her boyfriend and how she missed him. He was working in Johannesburg in the gold mines to pay her lobola. I was lucky that Pieter had no lobola to pay. She said that he didn't deserve me, he should be made to pay lobola as his father had many cattle.

I was so happy then – I didn't care if the whole world knew what I had done. Tobile sang me a Zulu love song on her home-made violin, which every young Zulu girl had in those days.

But on my way to church I felt very guilty, unclean and not worthy. I cried and said I was sorry to Jesus, but I asked him to forgive me because I loved Pieter very much.

I saw him again the following Sunday. This time I couldn't wait to see him, I was so excited. My mother noticed the change in me. She said I seemed very happy these days. The cracks in my feet were gone; I rubbed in candle grease every evening, and my face was rosy. She said my eyes had the glow of a girl in love. Who could this be, as she never saw any young man come home? My cousins from Swaziland were the only ones who sometimes came to visit us with some boys.

I just laughed and said I was happy because of her baby, Robert, my new brother. I loved him – I loved to touch his little soft feet. I always carried him around the house.

I was hardly ever in the fields during this time when I was in love with Pieter, as my father had got another herdboy to help with the ploughing and other chores, and Gogo never seemed to get tired of fetching water and wood. Of course I still went with Tobile sometimes, but she noticed that I liked to wear my old school shoes now to keep my feet from cracking, and she laughed at me and made me feel I was really ready to go to Durban. Everyone in those days – perhaps even today – wanted to be in 'Durbs'.

We had an aunt who lived in Durban: Nettie, my father's sister. She used to visit us sometimes, dressed in the height of fashion, very saucy and modern. She worked at a beachfront hotel, where she met lots of people, and she told us about all the goings-on at this hotel. She would gabble and burst into shrieks of laughter, until my father got quite cross and told her to shut up and go to bed.

I remember the time she was trying to tell him about the Indian waiter who was caught in a bedroom with one of the chambermaids. My father got upset and said: 'Nettie, you are a bad influence on my children. I'll not have that kind of talk in my house, so go to bed at once.'

Nettie shrugged her shoulders and adjusted her low-cut blouse with her bosom half spilling out. This blouse she wore over a revealing tight skirt, cinched in at the waist with a wide figure belt, one of those elasticised ones. She had a pouting mouth thickly smeared with red lipstick – I saw her with it on from early in the morning until she went to bed, and after eating she would run to her bag and fumble for her lipstick and smear it on so thickly that her mouth looked like a messy watermelon. As children we all admired her, and wanted to be just like her when we grew up. Oh, we all wanted to go to Durban, to the bright lights.

My auntie was quite stingy, though she did bring us sweets and my mother a dress or two, but she would rather sell her old clothes to the Zulu girls who had become Christians and got rid of their amabhayi than hand them down to us.

We liked her because there was a bit of fun and laughter when she was around. She would scoff at my father and say he was too old-fashioned and 'carried on like General Smuts'. Then she would scandal and gossip about him to my mother at night, but Mama would just nod her head and pretend she was agreeable to all the insults. She knew full well that if she agreed verbally Nettie would repeat everything to my father, and then my poor mother would get a hiding. Oh, Nettie was a two-faced scandalmonger.

I did not notice that I had missed two months of my period. I just thought it would come again. Then I told Tobile – and she glared at me as if she hadn't heard what I said.

She snapped back: 'Yini, Nkhosi, why did you open your legs? A girl doesn't open her legs! The man must spill his sperm on your thighs, not inside you! Why did you allow him to penetrate, you fool? Do you know what you've done? Hayi Nkhosi yam'! Nkhosana is going to kill you, do you realise that? You are pregnant! You are going to have a baby!' She glared at me with eyes as round and as black as madonis.

I stood frozen – I couldn't utter a sound. My lips felt as if they were glued together. I sat down and felt sick. I was dizzy and weak and helpless.

'Oh Tobile, I didn't know that, but Pieter said it's all right, nothing would happen to me.'

Instantly I felt strong enough to defend him, for I loved him so much. How could it be wrong? He'd said he'd look after me, we'd run away to Swaziland and get married.

'Oh Tobile, what have I done? My father will kill me, I'd better run away straight away. You've got to help me run away. Please, Tobile,' I begged her, and sobbed bitterly.

'What about my poor mother?' I went on. 'What is she going to say? I have to tell her that I'm running away before my father finds out. Oh God! What have I done? Is this the punishment you get for love?'

The days went by. I got morning sickness sometimes. My mother began to question me. I was going on for four months in December, as I fell pregnant in early spring – September. I sent Tobile to ask our herd-boy to tell their herdboy at the dip to tell Pieter I wanted to see him. It was the first week of December when I made up my mind to tell him.

He came as quickly as possible. We met at the crossroads near the forest, on the same spot where we first made love. Summer was at her best – every shrub seemed to be in bloom. The forest was a silvery green, with darker shades of olive green and a black green further in. The wild lilies were all in bloom, the African violets in all their glory, flowers of all colours and shapes and sizes. The music of the forest was alive, all things playing their own tune.

Pieter gazed into my eyes, and he knew right away there was something wrong. 'Did your father find out?' he asked.

He held me so tight. His lips were burning on mine. I couldn't speak. We kissed as if for the last time. I felt his heart beating so fast. He moaned and groaned softly and kissed my mouth like he was going to tear my lips. A fire burned up inside of me, and we were together on the bed of flowers. Before we knew we had both dissolved into oblivion, only this time it was as if a volcano had erupted, hot lava seemed to be oozing from underneath us. The heat of summer helped us along; she played her part by lending us her cushioned bosom, warm and soft. We lay there perspiring and panting, both naked, and for the first time I saw him as a man. I was not afraid. He looked at my firm breasts and said they looked like dollops of cream with a raisin on top. We were like Adam and Eve in the Garden of Eden.

The air was quite still, not a breeze. It was as though the very silence in which we lay carried some prophecy of imminent doom. There are many things I'll never forget in my lifetime, and that was one of them.

We rolled away from each other, and there was a faint smell of crushed mushrooms. He grabbed some grass mixed with wild flowers and wiped me with them, leaving traces of crushed flowers and grass on my thighs. I cleaned him too, with the same grass and flowers all mixed up. We started playing, throwing grass and flowers on one another's naked bodies. He put flowers in my hair and I put flowers in his hair – only not the hair on our heads.

A storm seemed to be brewing, but we took no notice. We just carried on playing and laughing at our nakedness. Big drops of rain came down, beautiful warm raindrops on our naked bodies. Only when I stood up straight did he notice that my tummy was a bit fat.

'I see you are eating too much cream in your porridge,' he said.

I felt a shiver and sat down again. Then as the rain pelted down I held him and clung to him like a baby, and whispered: 'I'm going to have a baby. That's why I'm getting fat.'

'Wat! 'n Baba! Ons baba – my baba?'

'Ja,' I said. 'Ons baba.'

'Does your mother know?' he asked.

I said I hadn't told her yet as I wanted to tell him first before I ran away, because I was sure my father would kill me.

'Nee, nee – you're not going to run away. I'll take you now – on horseback – to an old uncle of mine who's living in Swaziland with a Coloured woman – she'll look after you till we can get married. Don't run away with my child, please – whatever you do. I'll die if I don't see you and my child. Let's go now – don't go back home. Come with me now!'

And he held me close and kissed me again and again on my naked body, and as the rain fell we made love again. There are things in this world that one doesn't understand, and feelings that one cannot put on paper, moments you just can't describe. This was one of them.

Our clothes were wet, and as the storm subsided we spread them out on the rocks to dry. The hot summer rain seemed to have made the rocks even hotter. Our clothes were dry in no time.

While they were drying we clung to each other. We spoke about our baby: would it be a boy? He said he wanted a son, and I wanted a son too, because I had never had a big brother.

We put on our clothes and walked along the side of the forest to the spring, where there was a huge fig tree. It was covered with ripe figs. I climbed up to get some, while Pieter was tying his horse to the next tree.

But before I could eat even one fig, I slipped and fell, because the tree was still wet and slippery from the rain. I remember landing on my backside right on a rock. I fell so fast that I didn't feel any pain then, and I realised that Pieter had not seen me falling as he was tying up his horse. I didn't want him to know that I had fallen out of the tree – he would just tease me.

While I was having these thoughts I felt a pain so sharp I had to scream. For a moment I couldn't move with the pain. I screamed again and the horse took fright and broke loose and galloped off into the bush.

I slid on the carpet of fallen leaves and lay still for a while. Then I seemed to feel something hot coming down my leg. I didn't know what it was, I put my hand there to feel and there was blood on my hand. I screamed again for Pieter. Instead I heard a troop of baboons calling nearer me, and I got so scared that I just kept yelling. I felt as if something wanted to come out of me, and I felt the urge to push. My hand went to feel what it was, and I took my panties off to see – only as I reached for my panties a big baboon mother hovered over me. She had breasts so I knew she was a mother, and she smelt terrible. I froze over with fright. I must have fainted, because all I remember is that big mother baboon hovering over me.

The next thing I remember is seeing Pieter with beads of perspiration running down his face. I thought the baboon was still there, and screamed again. I could hear the baboons crying from a distance. Pieter knelt down by me and cradled me in his arms and asked me what had happened. I didn't really know. I was half choking with tears and pain. The mother baboon had taken my baby. I had to run and chase the baboons to get my baby back.

'Pieter! Pieter! Run and catch the baboons – take the horse – they've got our baby!'

Pieter was speechless. He just couldn't understand what was happening. I tried to run. I fell, caught in the thicket of the forest. Right then I hated the bush and thought if it were not for all these huge trees like castles, the baboons would have no place to run.

'My baba, my kind – Pieter, help me!' I cried.

First he just grabbed me and fastened a grip tight around me. We fell together and I sobbed with pain and misery. It was growing dusk as I tried to tell him what had happened; and he said to me, crying and trying his best not to let me see: 'Don't cry now, the baboons can't have taken your baby. Maybe you're going to lose it, but lieflinkie, it's not yet a baby, it's still just like a thick clot of blood.'

'They did! That big mother baboon took our baby!' I screamed.

He said: 'Haven't you sometimes seen the sheep get a miscarriage and it's not like a lamb yet, it's not yet fully grown? I've seen it on the farm. Please don't cry, my lieflinkie, bly nou stil asseblief.'

We clung together and cried softly. Then he put me on his horse and I sat crossing my legs, not riding the horse with my legs astride its back. He had taken his vest off and made me use it as a napkin, and covered me with his shirt as I was all messed in blood.

'Where are we going?' I asked, afraid that he was taking me to Swaziland as he had said.

'Your mother has to look after you for a few days. You need to be strong so I'm taking you home.'

He rode the horse very slowly until we reached my home at about seven o'clock. It was summer so it really was not so dark. He left the horse down by the river and tied it securely and carried me the short distance home. The dogs were barking so viciously that he had to leave me with a very short goodbye.

As he kissed me he was shaking and he whispered: 'I'll love you till I die. I'll never forget what I've done to you. What happened to us to-day is written in heaven.' Somehow he always referred to things that happened to us in a sort of godly fashion – he seemed to believe in the things of God as much as he believed in nature.

I walked slowly straight to my mother's room. My father had a separate rondavel outside in the yard, so there was no way he would notice that I had been missing. He ate his supper at five o'clock, and by six every night he was in bed, to get up at four o'clock every morn-ing – even on Sundays he never slept late.

I plucked up my courage and told my mother by the dim light of the paraffin lamp everything that had happened. She just sighed and gave me a mild mixture of permanganate of potash; she said it would kill the germs. I had a hard time falling off to sleep as I kept crying and thinking about my baby and Pieter, even though Mama also tried very gently to explain to me that it was not yet a full-grown baby, and that what had happened to me was maybe the beginning of a miscarriage.

But somewhere in my heart I wouldn't believe that. I knew the baboons had taken my baby. I had seen the breasts on the mother baboon and nothing in the world would convince me that she wasn't suckling my child. This meant that it was alive. The thoughts turned around in my young mind.

I tossed and turned on the grass mattress till I fell off to sleep, but I woke up screaming. This time I was in real pain, and I had dreamt that the baboons were all around my baby, and they were tearing it apart. Oh! It was terrible. I was shaking – and delirious, as I kept calling for Pieter to ride after the baboons and get the baby back. I was bleeding a lot and having what seemed like bad period pains, and in my child's mind I thought another baby was coming, so I went to my mother's bed and woke her up. My mother got up. Her own baby was crying, and Jessie woke up to help with it while my mother saw to my needs. Jessie kept asking me what was wrong. My mother told her I was getting the flu.

Early next morning I woke feeling better, though I was still bleeding. Mama convinced me it was just the dirty blood coming out.

'I'll go get Gogo to make you some muthi to drink, to take all the dirty blood out,' she said.

She helped me clean myself and put old rags round me for a napkin, and told me to sleep.

I awoke again when the sun was shining already, but I was fine. I went down to the river to fetch water, and Gogo went with me. My mother had told her so she dug some roots, and back at the house she boiled them, and gave me muthi to drink. Mama told me I had to forget about what happened, because my father would kill her and me if he ever found out. No one must ever know about this because we could all go to jail. As Pieter was a white man, he wouldn't go to jail, but we would. She went on and on, and said that I had sinned, and I must go to confession in Nongoma on Sunday.

I went to Nongoma, for I was strong enough – I was a very strong, healthy girl. But I never confessed about Pieter and me and the baby. I just sat there in the church and cried silently and asked God to please keep my baby alive till I found it. Then I thought of telling Father Jacob to look for my baby when he went to the forest to get medicines for the hospital.

When I got home that evening Tobile was waiting for me. She wanted to know everything. Tobile made me believe that my baby could be alive: another young girl had given birth to a half-baboon child because the man who paid lobola for her was to marry another whom he loved more than her. Her parents had made muthi for her to give birth to a half-baboon. They destroyed the child at once. It was the Zulu custom to destroy a baby that was abnormal straight away, at birth. In a strange way this story made me feel that my baby was still alive. Together we were going to look for it in the bush.

The next day we went to gather wood, and we went right into the forest. I heard the baboons crying, and it was as if they were saying: 'Bo bo bo bo bo, come and take your baby.' I started crying, and Tobile was so sorry for me that she cried with me, and said: 'Let's go home. The baboons will never give you back the baby.'

We were both young and foolish. She also believed that the baboons took my baby, and I believed her. Why? Because in my heart I wanted to believe that it was alive.

Chapter 4

Pieter's plans for the two of them. He speaks to Agnes's father and departs. Agnes's father's reaction. The beating. Agnes's dream. The news of Pieter's death. Agnes leaves for Vryheid.

PIETER CAME TO SEE ME two weeks later on a Sunday, at our usual place in the forest. He seemed a little thin and more mature. Oh, he was so handsome! He jumped off his horse as if he resented it and pulled the reins so fiercely I thought they would snap. He came to me with his arms outstretched, and I fell into them. I felt as if the world stood still. All my thoughts were swallowed up in this white man's strong arms; all my pains and fears melted away. We were from different worlds, but right now we breathed with one heart.

The hush of the bush and the birds singing directly on top of a little shrub made us aware that we were alive and two separate beings.

He whispered hoarsely: 'My lieflinkie, how are you feeling?'

His voice was sad, and I sensed pain in his eyes that I'd never seen before. I felt so hurt for him. I loved him even more than before. What had happened to us bound us together for ever.

'I'm going to your father to tell him about us. I'm taking you with me to Swaziland at the end of this month. We'll get married in Swaziland and be happy. There are no apartheid rules there.'

Was I hearing this or dreaming it? I pulled away abruptly and said: 'You can't do such a thing – your father will shoot you, and mine will kill me – and my mother. Please don't even think of such a thing.'

Pieter said he didn't care any more. There were many white people who married Coloureds and lived in Swaziland. He said he was not afraid of my father. He got on his horse so fast that he left me standing breathless.

My legs felt weak – I couldn't walk properly. But he was gone in the direction of my home. 'Oh my God, he's going right now to my father!'

I tried to run and stop him, and I called his name, but he went like the wind. The horse seemed to be flying in mid-air as he headed for the homestead. As I sat down I somehow got courage and knew in my heart he was doing the right thing.

I followed slowly. By the time I reached home he was talking to my father by the cattle kraal. I ran to look for Mama to tell her; she was in a corner of the kitchen with the baby on her back, trembling and crying. 'What is going to happen to me? Oh God, child, what have you done? Where will I go to with my children? Why did you tell the white man to speak to your father?'

I was so scared that I stood like a zombie in one corner, waiting for the lion to growl. The hooves of the white man's horse thundered past into the bush; he was gone.

'Oh God, what's next?' my mother whimpered like a little puppy. She was praying: 'Holy Mary, Mother of God, help us! One thing, you must never let your father know that – what happened. He will kill me – and you too!'

My father came into the dining room – he looked like a rhino about to stampede. He grabbed a chair, almost jerking it off its legs, and sat down. The chair squeaked into place under the weight of his heavy bones. He took out his snuff-box, took a deep pull, and called Mama and me to come and sit down. My poor Mama was motionless. I could hear my heart beat as if it was going to come out. I held my chest with both hands and sat down trembling next to my ashen-faced mother, who was still mumbling: 'Hail Mary, full of grace ...'

'Winnie, the white man wants to marry our daughter. Did you know about this business? Have you been hiding it from me? As always, I'm the last to know anything that goes on in my house! Answer me, woman!'

'Papa, please Papa, listen to me! Mama knows nothing about it! When the white farmers came to buy cattle from you, Pieter told me he wanted to marry me. I've never told Mama because I was scared. I beg you, my Father, please to understand. Mama knows nothing about this at all. You can kill me, but please don't kill Mama. No, Father, don't hit her! It's me you must hit, not my mother! Please, Father, please!'

It was as if God heard our prayers. Father simply told Mama to go out and see to the cooking. Then he told me to bring a sjambok, and he started lashing at me. He said a marriage with a white man would never work out. General Smuts was dead and buried! Did I know what I was doing? Did I think I was old enough to do as I pleased in his home? Bringing such disgrace! He loved me and thought I would marry someone suitable – but not a white man. 'He will use you and never marry you, even though he says he will take you to Swaziland! His father will kill him before he crosses the Pongola River.' Oh what a fool I had made of him! With each stroke of the sjambok I got weaker, until my mother ran in screaming.

'Please Benjy, stop! Benjamin Rorke, please stop! You will kill your own child!' she pleaded, and got in between us. She got a few lashes herself, and I ran outside and crawled into the nearby bushes to hide. I could hear him lashing my mother, and I prayed for him to stop. Finally it was silent, and only the baby cried.

I wept softly so that he wouldn't hear me. I cried myself to sleep, wondering if I'd ever see Pieter again, and hating my father and thinking of my baby with the baboons. All these thoughts raced through my mind. I slept right there in the thicket.

When I woke up I was feeling sore all over, and I was cold, so I crawled up to the house and knocked on Mama's window. She opened it and helped me jump in. She never said much, but I could see a few blue marks on her arms. I was black and blue myself. I crawled into bed, and as I fell off to sleep she whispered: 'My child, you'll have to run away. This white man really loves you. To have the courage to approach your father and ask if you can go with him to Swaziland and live there for good!

'Look, my father was a white man and your father's father was a white man, and they both married black women. I don't know why your father is so against your marrying a white man. As soon as you are strong you've got to get to Swaziland.'

'Mama, I can't leave you and the children here! I'd worry too much, and I'd miss you too much.'

'My child, I made my bed and I have to lie in it. You are not responsible for me. You have your own life to live. You must go with Pieter.'

I had dreams about my baby and Pieter. I was in pain: my body ached all over and I had a headache. Finally I cried myself to sleep. When you are young and strong, physical pain never lasts long, and wounds heal fast; but the pain in your heart, and memories: they never quite heal.

Pieter was coming for me at the month's end. My father kept his distance and became very sad. He spoke very little, only what he needed to say. I felt sorry for him somehow, for he was after all my father. There was always that bond that no one can take away. Maybe he did love me, in his own way.

I looked after my mother and told her I would come back with nice clothes for her when I was married. I helped her to sew for the children.

Life was hard and painful at home; it was almost like being in prison. All the same there were times when I got scared and did not want to go to Swaziland. What if I died there? What if Mama died all alone here? All these unpleasant, scary thoughts crossed my mind.

Then the week before the month's end I had a terrible dream. I was in a faraway place with rugged mountains and big rocks all around. I was surrounded by boulders and I couldn't find my way out. I knew that I was in Swaziland. I said to myself: 'I told Mama I didn't want to go to Swaziland.' I tried to hold on to a big rock to climb up. I saw my baby lying deep down in a donga, and I wanted to fetch the baby, but it was too deep and dangerous. The rock seemed to shift with me on it, and I looked to see if my baby was still there. But instead it was Pieter lying there and waiting for me, in the same spot where we had first made love. It was so real, so real ... I couldn't get him and I shouted to him to come and get me. But he just lay down and smiled up at me. I wanted to touch him so badly, but I couldn't reach him. The rock I was holding on to seemed to go higher, and higher, and he just went further down, down, down ... I shrieked for him to come back up, but he just went on smiling at me.

I woke up screaming. Mama said I had to get a grip on myself. 'Stop thinking about the baby. It's dead; there is no baby. If you stop thinking, then you will stop dreaming these dreams. You're getting thinner and thinner – you never eat properly. You've got to stop this nonsense.'

But I wasn't dreaming only about the baby, it was Pieter too I was screaming for. I got up the next morning and tried very hard to go about my duties, but I felt a heaviness in my heart that I couldn't understand. I told Tobile about my dreams and again I told her what had happened when the baboons took my baby. We had covered the spot with sand and dead leaves until it looked like a little grave, and we had put ferns and wild flowers on the little grave. She gazed at me and said: 'Why did you do that? There was no one in that grave. You made bad luck for yourself.'

'Oh Tobile, I feel so sad, and my body aches as if I am going to get the flu.' Immediately she told me that I needed to drink some strong herbs, and she would go to dig some roots out and prepare them for me.

While she was gone, Gogo came to see me. She asked me how I felt, and she looked so old – her face seemed like biltong, and her little beady eyes were misty and grey. She always made me laugh, but I couldn't laugh now because she looked so sad. She said: 'My child, I hear you are leaving us to marry a white man. Go with God, my child, and be blessed with many children.' She kissed both my cheeks, as she loved to kiss me. She always smelled of snuff and smoke.

As she went to her hut, a boy on horseback came into the yard, and Gogo said in the traditional Zulu way: 'Sawubona mfana. Yini na?'

The boy got off the horse and said he had a message to give to Mamatjie, meaning me. He spoke to Gogo for a long time. I heard very little of what was said and continued with my chores. Then the boy rode off as fast as he had come. My father was in the fields as usual.

Gogo called my mother with such a broken voice, it occurred to me she was crying. I carried on washing dishes, but I could see her face from the window, and she said something to Mama in Zulu – we all spoke Zulu around the homestead – but Mama answered in English, and in anguish she cried: 'Holy Mary, Mother of God, help us! Oh my poor child!'

I knew immediately something was very, very wrong. I ran outside wondering if something had happened to the herdboy, or even my father in the fields – perhaps a mamba had bitten him.

'Gogo, yini indaba?' I asked. My mother ran behind the house to hide away from me.

Gogo held me tight in her flabby old arms, and said: 'My child, your white man is dead. The boy came to tell us that he fell off a mountain, a long way away. He had gone to climb with the other whites from Vryheid.'

All I said was: 'Who saw him? How do they know it's him? It can't be him! Maybe they heard wrong. No, Gogo, it's not him.'

I ran to find mother, who was praying on her knees behind the house. She got up and made the sign of the cross so solemnly, tears running down her cheeks. Crying and praying, she said: 'My child, you will meet him one day in heaven. Your love was not to be on earth – it wasn't meant to happen.' I knew my mother well enough to understand that she was in pain. She held me close to her bosom, and said: 'God bless you and make you strong to be able to accept this thing that has happened.'

All I said was: 'No, Mama, it's not him, they are mistaken – they did not see him. It's someone else, not Pieter.'

Tobile came running with the herbs in one hand, screaming: 'Oh Nkhosi yam'! I knew this was going to happen! Oh Nkhosi yam'!'

My dreams of the previous night came flooding back. Could he really be dead? Oh no! Dear, dear God, no! I was numb. I couldn't cry, I couldn't think, I just gazed into empty space. I saw no one. I couldn't hear anything.

My father came home from the fields and he was told the news. I started feeling sick and I had a running stomach. I spewed all over the place, and I remember my father carrying me to the toilet, which was right behind the house. I must have fainted, for when I came to the next day, I didn't know if I had dreamt that Pieter was dead. I asked my mother in a whisper, and she answered me and said that he was waiting for me in heaven.

I did not speak again, I just lay awake. In my heart I couldn't accept that he was dead, and yet I was frightened that he was. What is death? I had never seen anyone dead. How do you die? How do they know he's dead? Why didn't he tell me he was going to die? My young mind simply couldn't grasp the meaning of death.

That night I knelt down to pray, and I started crying. Mama, who knew the whole story, came to hug me. She held me very tight. 'My child, you've got to go away. It will help you to forget. And we can't keep this thing a secret, and you know your father will kill both of us when he finds out, so in the morning you must pack your things and go to Vryheid, or to Swaziland to your relations.'

We made plans, but all I had was two shillings. That would only take me to Vryheid, so I had to think of who I could stay with there. And on the way I would be able to find out more about Pieter. No, Pieter was not dead. I knew his farm, so I would go straight there.

I finally fell asleep, to be awakened by a voice I knew was my father's. My mother was busy in the garden.

'What's the matter with you, Greta?' (This was short for Margaret, for my father never called me by my first name Agnes. He called me 'Gomey' when he was being really friendly, but when he wanted me to read a letter for him, or had something serious on his mind, he would call me 'Greta'.)

I knew by the thunderous sound of his voice that I was in trouble. 'I don't see much of you these days,' he said. 'Are you just plain lazy, or getting too big for your boots?' That was his favourite taunt. I did not answer, and as I crawled out of bed he helped me along with a kick from his boot that sent me sprawling back onto the brass bed with its solid iron legs. I was stunned as he landed a slap. 'Is this the time a girl wakes up? The sun is shining outside, and you are still asleep? Perhaps you're pregnant? That wouldn't surprise me – with this white man who wanted to marry you!'

I knew then that I had to go – because he was suspicious, and might bully my mother into telling him what had happened, and about the baby. I got up crawling, got dressed, took the drum for water, and walked slowly down to the river. My side was aching and my back hurt where I had got bumped on the leg of the iron bed. But my heart, most of all my heart was aching, for Pieter.

I couldn't run away that morning. I had to wait till I felt a bit better. The days went by, and my mother began to be on at me about going away. She was also getting frightened. So one day I packed a few things and took my two shillings, and walked off through the forest.

As I came to the bus station a group of Zulus stood waiting for the bus as well, and they were speaking about how the Big Baas had gone to Bloemfontein to fetch his son's body. They had been climbing the mountain, and two of them fell and died – Pieter was one of them. They were saying how distraught the Old Baas was, because he wanted Piet to run the farm, and the Ou Nooi hadn't eaten a thing since she heard the news of her son's death. Their farm was not far from the bus stop. You could see it down in the valley. These were some of their farm labourers.

I felt numb inside, and when the bus came I almost went underneath the wheels – not because I meant to, but just because I couldn't think straight. I got in so fast I never paid. I just sat there staring. The man asked for the money – it was in my hand, two shillings to Vryheid, Price's Motor Service.

How does one write pain on paper? How do you write despair? Yes, writers do, but it can never be the same as feeling it. Time has a way of churning pain and misery and the past in its big machine.

Chapter 5

Agnes's arrival in Vryheid. She meets her future husband Lemmy. Living at Mrs Field's. Lemmy and she become lovers.

I MET MY HUSBAND ON MY VERY FIRST DAY IN VRYHEID. I sat trembling and half-crying in a dingy little eating-house where my school friend Lily Thomson worked for her parents. I was anxiously waiting for her to come on duty, for the woman who was cleaning the tables had told me she would be coming in at one o'clock. I gazed out of the door watching out for her with a heart that was neither mine nor somebody else's.

I was scared. Some of the farm Africans might notice me, as Vryheid was the main shopping centre for all the neighbouring farmers, but no one spoke to me. I felt relieved, for I was a bundle of nerves.

I was so mixed up inside. It seemed as if some part of me wanted to cave in. I couldn't even move. I just sat there, gaping at the door. Where will I sleep? I wondered. What will I wear? What will I eat? If my friend's parents found out I had run away from home, maybe they'd even call the police, and I'd go to jail! All these thoughts raced through my mind, and I felt sick and giddy. My stomach ached with hunger and sheer tiredness. I was only a child – not yet quite sixteen years old. I prayed the only prayer I had been taught – Hail Mary, Mother of God, please help me!

As I looked up at the doorway, two Coloured men walked in. One was quite old, but the young one looked very cheeky and strong. He wore shorts and a skipper, and the muscles rippled on his arms and legs. I got even more scared as he came up to my corner table and said a cool 'Hello'.

A sound came out of my throat that sounded like a mouse squeaking, and I saw that he noticed I was trembling.

'Can I join you, or are you waiting for your parents?' I nodded and looked down at the faded old pattern on the plastic tablecloth.

'Did you come to do some shopping, or are you looking for a job? What is your name? I can see you are new in town. My name is Lemmy Lottering. I live just behind the tea-room with my family, and I am on my lunch hour. I work at the Vryheid Gazette. Please tell me your name, I won't bite you, don't be afraid.'

While all this came out I still didn't look up, as I knew my eyes were red from crying. I said softly: 'My name is Agnes Margaret Rorke, and I am from the farm of Ngome. I'm waiting for my friend Lily Thomson. I went to school with her at Little Flower in Eshowe.'

'Oh! She isn't here today, she has gone to Durban with her mother. They'll be back on Monday, but I'll ask my mother if you can stay with us for a while to do your shopping.'

'Oh no!' I almost screamed. 'No! I know Miss Field, our teacher at Little Flower, her mother lives here in Vryheid and if you could tell me where she lives, I'd be happy to go there.'

'Okay,' he said. 'I know her very well. You'll have to sit here till half past four, though. When I knock off, I'll take you there. In the meantime, let me buy you a meal and a cool drink. I must go now – I'm late already.' With that he rushed out.

The other man had gone already. When the meal was served, I was so grateful to him. I thanked Mother Mary, and ate fast – I was hungry.

Half past four took a long time to come. People walked in and out, and I knew none of them. I was forced to get up and ask for the use of a toilet, and the man behind the counter looked at me with perplexed eyes. He asked me who I was, and I quickly said I was from Swaziland, and my parents would be picking me up – they had gone to buy parts for the farm tractors. Then he wanted to know my surname. I just said I was Miss Henwood, as this was a well known surname in Swaziland. He showed me the toilet, and made me sit nearer at a table, and offered me tea and scones. He said he would soon be going home, as he knocked off duty at three. To my relief he was not going to stay in the tea-room any later.

Mrs Field's house was not far away, and Lemmy was as punctual as Punch. He strode in front of me like a soldier, the muscles of his legs rippling, as though to show off to me. I was embarrassed by the clothes I was wearing: I had on a faded little dress with yellow, red and blue daisies on it, and shoes that looked as if they were my great grand-mother's. One strap was sewn on with raw leather strips – polished over with charcoal to make them look black. My hair was tied in two thick plaits, with a broken hair comb fastened on one side. He could just see I was a wild farm girl. I really felt awkward walking with him, but I was even more scared of where I was going with this sprightly little man.

We got to Mrs Field's tumbledown brick and iron house, which was in fact a renovated garage. Inside it was beautiful and clean; there was a row of old chairs in the small dining-room, and a round table covered with glasses on a tray, with a pretty embroidered cloth. A big coal stove shone in the kitchen, and a mouth-watering aroma roused my stomach with hunger.

Just then a tall, stately middle-aged lady came in. 'Hello Lemmy, what are you having today?' she said. Then she looked at me, and her eyes sort of popped. 'Where did you pick her up? She looks very tired and hungry. In need of clothes, too! Who is she, Lemmy?'

She took me by the arm and ushered me into her bedroom, which was beautiful – a big double bed and a pretty porcelain water jug and basin, and she whispered to ask me what size shoes I wore. I had to say I didn't know – I had never had new shoes bought for me. She was so kind.

She said softly: 'I know you've run away. I also ran away from the farm years ago. Do you know anyone in Vryheid?'

I said: 'Only Lily at the tea-room. I went to school with her at Little Flower. And of course I know Miss Field, who was my teacher – that's why I asked Lemmy to bring me to you.'

'So – we'll have to find you a job as quickly as possible. You can't stay here long, there are too many men coming in and out – it's not good for a young girl to stay with me. But Lemmy is a good man – he'll look after you. Don't be afraid of him.'

So I stayed with this lady who dressed in furs and high heels – she looked like a film star. She was very refined. The next day she took me to town wearing something she had given me, and some shoes, and told me to do my hair in a beehive. She bought me a dress and underwear and a bottle of 'Evening in Paris' perfume, and Pond's face cream, a facecloth and towel, and some handkerchiefs.

Oh! I was so excited and so grateful, I'd never had a pair of bought panties. Mama used to make them out of flour bags, and we would sew our own little handkerchiefs. Now I really felt like a little lady.

Lemmy came to see me every afternoon after working at the Vryheid Gazette, where he was a printer. He told me not to talk to the other men if they spoke to me. I must just keep quiet and not answer. I wondered why so many men came in and out, and they were always drinking from bottles. One day Mrs Field told me that she sold liquor for a living, and that's why I couldn't stay there too long. It was a shebeen ...

I helped her cook sometimes, but she had several African girls doing all her household chores. When Lemmy came she allowed me to sit and talk to him in her bedroom. Of course the door was always left open – she was a very strict lady. She really had old-fashioned values, and I loved her like a mother. She told me that Lemmy was a good man because he worked. He was sporty and played football. He was decent and he never drank too much. He didn't in those days. When he took me to the bioscope on a Friday evening, she made sure I looked smart. Lemmy was kind to me; he bought me a box of Black Magic chocolates, and when we sat in the bioscope he would sit close to me and hold my hand. But all this time he hadn't said anything to me about being his girl.

I did get in touch with Lily, but she didn't prove very friendly. I found out later that she had had her eye on Lemmy too. But she did give me some clothes.

One day after bioscope Lemmy took me to my workplace, as far as the gate, and he said to me very seriously: 'I want you to be my girlfriend, baby. I've got a soft spot for you in my heart.'

And then and there I humbly agreed to a relationship. But really I had no understanding of it, and no feelings of love for him. The only man I thought I loved was Pieter; the love I knew for Pieter was so real and at the same time so unreal – it seemed to me as though nature had waved a magic wand, and somehow all the beautiful sweet scents of the wilderness had intermingled to create that love.

But my love life had ended there in the wilderness, for I had already grown old with grief and pain. I really didn't understand love at all. What I felt for this man Lemmy was a great sense of gratitude. He had found me when I was lost. I felt no heartbeats, I never saw anything that made me want to hold him and tell him I loved him too. So I just said: 'Yes, I'll be your girlfriend.'

From then on I did everything he asked me to. I was sometimes very scared of him. Eventually I fell pregnant, and that's how I came to marry him. Tobile used to tell me that in their customs a man was never questioned; you were his slave as long as you lived. You had to obey him and respect him. And from that day when Lemmy said that he had a soft spot in his heart for me, and kissed me to seal the agreement, I did my best by him.

Chapter 6

Lemmy asks for Agnes's hand in marriage. The wedding.

IN THOSE DAYS A MAN HAD TO ASK for house consent to marry the daughter of a farmer. You had to show yourself to her parents for final approval. So Lemmy hired Joe, who worked with him, to drive us to Ngome to meet with my father and ask for his daughter's hand in holy matrimony.

The little hunchback Ford V8 lumbered away, groaning and huffing and puffing like a dung beetle carrying a heavy load on her back, leaving a thick mist of red dust behind. Lemmy was swearing at those farm roads. 'How the hell am I supposed to make an impression on those farmers when my white shirt is red with dust? Oh hell, Joe, close the damn window.'

Joe snorted back: 'You want my car to topple over into the donga? Hey, ek sê, ek is nie mal nie. Dis jy wat die plaasskapie wil trou, nie my Ford nie. So shut up and show me the way. I've never travelled on this God-forsaken gravel road before and I'm telling you now, if my carburettor is ruined, jy sal my mooi kyk.'

I sat in the back, scrunched up, protecting my stomach, and wondering what my father was going to do to me. Nobody knew we were coming. My father would probably say my mother planned all this behind his back. Oh God, please help me.

Joe dropped us at the police station. We were to walk the rest of the way. As the V8 left with a hiss, Lemmy stood swearing, rubbing his shirt with a handkerchief soaked in dust. I was wiping my eyes and blowing my nose with my small handmade handkerchief. Never mind, I thought, there's plenty water in the forest to wash our faces. You'd better lead the way into this terrifying place, Miss Rorke.

As we ventured into the thick, gloomy woodland, Lemmy grabbed my hand, and held it even tighter when we heard voices behind us. When we were greeted by a group of woman and young girls coming from the store, carrying sacks of mealies on their heads, I felt relieved, and so did Lemmy, because he loosened his grip on me. As we neared the opening of the last bush where I had been with Pieter, an urge crept into my heart and soul to run deeper into the forest to find my baby. Fear crept into my womb. I couldn't take a step further. So I sat flat onto the carpet of fallen leaves, pretending to be urinating. I thought I was going to lose this baby I was carrying and prayed for strength to carry on.

We passed the spot where Pieter had had his horse tied to a huge tree. My heart thudded so loudly I thought Lemmy could hear it. I felt cold sweat on my brow. I held on to a vine for balance as hot tears rolled freely down my cheeks, and a lump as heavy as a stone filled my heart. I could smell Pieter's perspiration. I could see him walking in front of me. I knew he was here with me.

My father sat in his place at the head of the table, my mother on the side near me and Lemmy on my father's left. He was staring at the wooden frame of grandfather's picture on the wall.

There was absolute silence, then the bull bellowed.

'What is your name and surname, boy? State your purpose and make yourself clear.'

I shuddered and prayed silently.

'And you, Greta, have you forgotten how to write a letter, warning us that you are coming with a man to my home? Speak up, my boy, I've got work to do in my fields.'

Lemmy's voice came from deep inside an empty chasm as he quivered and grimaced.

'Excuse me, Mr Rorke. I've come to ask for your daughter's hand in marriage.' He was shaking, his top lip quivering like an arrow. 'She is carrying my child.'

My father looked impossibly handsome as his sun-bronzed face and brilliant dark eyes seemed to pierce right through Lemmy, who was left weak and appalled, shifting his gaze towards the door, making it quite clear that he wanted to run out and never look back. His hopes of meeting a feeble and humble old farmer, tottering around, scared of strangers, had vanished completely. This was something else.

'You have yet to tell me your name and surname, boy. Who are your parents? Why have you come alone?'

'My name is Lemuel Abraham Lottering, sir. I have no father. He passed away two years ago together with my eldest brother in a train crash. That's why I've come alone.'

I was surprised by my father's mild response. 'I admire a man of courage; walking through the forest full of leopards is quite frightening for a city dweller.' But then the explosion came. 'You have had the audacity to spoil my daughter. Did you perhaps want to make sure that she wouldn't be a barren woman or is it merely a law pertaining to the Bushman tribes of the Karoo or Kalahari? Did your father put your mother in the family way first before he married her? Or maybe it is the modern ways of the city? I, Benjamin William Rorke, am not in the habit of giving my children away to cave men. Your twisted hair, your flat nose and yellow complexion tell me you are a descendant of a yellow race. Go back to your home. My daughter can have ten different children before I will give her to you. I have nothing further to say to you, Mr Lottering. Kindly excuse me, I have to finish my ploughing. As for you, Greta, you have broken my heart.'

His voice broke with genuine sadness, as he gazed at me. The fierce, penetrating glow from his eyes became clouded, almost like that a dead ox. I couldn't bear to look at him. I got up to run outside as he bellowed: 'Greta, I am not yet finished with you. I've not excused you from the table. Sit down at once and stop crying. You've brought shame to the house of Rorke. Your sister Ivy has married into a genuine Coloured family from Mangete, John Dunn's decendants, and so did my sister Sarah. Winnefred, has this child been writing to you about this Bushman? Maybe you've been hiding things from me?'

'Benjamin, I swear by Holy Mary, Greta has never written to me concerning this man, or that he was coming to ask for consent.'

'He will be gone at the first cockcrow and will come back again at the end of the month in time for me to confer with my people.'

'Thank you, Benjamin,' my mother sniffed, wiping at her tears.

As my father abruptly lifted his massive structure off the creaking chair, I thought he would topple the table on top of us. He took three strides across the veranda in the direction of his fields. I knew he was weeping and what better place to weep than his fields. Alone with nature talking to the soil, to the wind and sky, bearing all his pain and misery as these were his true friends.

'What have you done to your father? How could you hurt him? You've broken my heart as well.' My mother and I clung together and sobbed bitterly.

Lemmy sprouted up like a mushroom after a thunderstorm and retorted in those fast tones of his: 'Agnes, why didn't you tell me your father's a raw uncivilised farmer? Didn't he go to school? How can he say things to me like that? I am not a Bushman, ek is nie 'n hotnot nie, hey, die toppie moenie met my speel nie.' He spat the words out, laced with venom, his eyes shifting back and forth as though he was in the Kalahari, hunting for gemsbok. His round face twitched at the forehead and his flat nose perspired.

I was taking all this in and getting quite scared. After what my father had said, it became clear to me that Lemmy was indeed different. But I had no idea what a Bushman was. I had truly thought Lemmy was a Coloured like myself.

By daybreak, Lemmy had disappeared. A week later I received a letter from him. 'I will be coming back for you at the month end. I am determined to break your father's pride. I'll prove myself a good man for you. Please, babe, don't change your mind. You are carrying my child, you are my wife.'

I was surprised and a little apprehensive at receiving his letter, after his departure without a goodbye. In fact, I felt a little angry and degraded. My father avoided me like the plague. He hadn't spoken a word to me since Lemmy's departure. I kept wishing that Lemmy would never come back.

On the morning of the big indaba, when Lemmy was due to arrive, auntie Jessica arrived first, followed by uncle Walter on horseback. They were in deep conversation with my father in his rondavel when I brought in the tea. The three of them looked so alike. Such striking beauty, such strength and dignity.

I loved Jessica. She always smelt of lavender and wore pretty voile floral dresses that made her look like a queen. She patted me on my back and asked how the baby was. As uncle Walter shifted his gaze onto my belly I knew what his reactions would be.

'Don't pamper her, Jessie, she is a disobedient, headstrong woman.

My girl, you have disgraced your family. You ran away from home to come back with a huge belly and a Bushman coming to ask for your hand in marriage. You need a good sjambok.'

'I am sorry, uncle Walter.'

'Sorries are always too late. You're going to marry this man because you gave in to him. The child cannot be born a bastard. I've made that clear to my brother, so has Jessica. You made your bed, so lie on it. I am riding back home. I do not want to have an encounter with a Bushman, lest I lose my head.'

He galloped off in sheer disgust, shouting: 'Benjy, take care, boy.'

Jessica tried her best to pacify my father. 'Benjy, no man will take her as a wife after she carried another's child. Hawoo, Benjy, it's a disgrace to our family. The child will be born a bastard. Please, my brother, let her marry before she gives birth.'

'She can have ten children from ten different men, before I will throw my child away to a Bushman. He thinks because he has made her in the family way, now he can have her for a wife, just like that!'

'Oh, Benjy, just cool your temper. Don't be so angry. There, have another piece of braai.'

Mama and I were busy preparing food in the kitchen. 'Winnefred, I'd like a cup of strong Five Roses, my head is very hot,' Mama had mumbled.

I was dreading Lemmy's arrival. Oh God, I hope he gets sick or just backs off.

'Agnes, my child, you've got to stop worrying. At least you'll be married. He might turn out to be a good man. Do you want to be like your mother who had two children out of wedlock? People will say I influenced you.'

As we spoke in hushed voices, there was Lemmy right in the middle of the yard, as spritely and alert as only a Bushman can be. He was dressed in a dark green three-piece suit, matching Stetson, shirt and tie, and crocodile-skin shoes.

The herdboy that had been to fetch him at the bus stop to walk with him through the forest presented him to my father, and Lemmy politely took a few shillings out of his pocket to give to the boy. He made sure to make an impression. As he thanked the boy he took off his Stetson to greet my father as well.

At that moment auntie Jessica chirped in a very English, high-pitched voice: 'Oh my goodness gracious me. What brings an English gentleman to these parts of the world? Pray sire, are you lost? Whom do you seek? A damsel in distress, or a dragon to fight to the death? Draw your sword at once.'

My father sounded just like a dragon as he bellowed and charged forward, going straight for Lemmy's neck.

'Oh hawoo, Benjy, my brother, are you mad?'

But Lemmy jumped clean over the old wooden bench that was behind my father and in true Bushman style evaded my father's grip.

'I'll kill him, Jessica. My child will never marry this Bushman. I'll break his bones and give them to the vultures. Who does he think he is, strolling into my home with a three-piece suit? I am not a child. I am not easily bluffed. That suit is covering a wicked man underneath. You dare to give him compliments in my yard. You are already falling for his tricks. He can fool you, Jessica, but not me. Not me, Benjamin Rorke!'

Jessica tried her best to explain. 'I was only trying to make him feel welcome.'

'Oh, welcome in my home, so he will be welcome to do as he likes to my child!'

Lemmy was already disappearing beyond the hill, heading for the forest, with one shoe on. The other one was lodged between the seats of the old rugged bench. The herdboy grabbed it quickly, before my father could see it, and held it behind his back.

'Jessica, did you see how he runs, faster than a gemsbok? That's how the Bushmen are; they run faster than their prey.'

Everyone had deserted the yard. Even the maid had run off with the children down to the spring with a bundle of washing. I came out of my corner behind the kitchen where I had been hiding, witnessing everything, and the boy gave me Lemmy's shoe. As I took it, I started shaking all over, and the shoe dropped. I bent to pick it up, but my father got to it first.

'Oh Greta. Do you love him so much that you are keeping his shoe as remembrance? Oh, what a silly girl you are. There are far better-looking men in the world, my girl. You will have your baby and look for a proper man. Your mother found a man who gave her children and a home. There's no need to throw your life away on this low-class Bushman.'

'No, Benjamin Rorke, my dear brother, please stop this nonsense now,' Jessica was pleading. 'If he came tattered and torn, you'd have said he was a tramp.'

'Tramp or gentleman, it makes no difference. He's not getting my child. Does he know how to plough or to milk a cow? No, I bet you he can't even hammer a nail into a plank. His hands are too soft and feeble. He must be working in an office like a woman.'

They carried on and on arguing until lunch was ready. When provoked, my father's appetite was enormous. Like an angry lion he devoured the whole platter of meat, demanded fresh milk for a wash down, and headed straight for the fields.

'Oh Jessica,' said my mother, 'thank you for coming. What would have happened to us if you weren't here. I am terrified of your brother when he is in that state. I hope to God everything will work out for the best. I say my rosary every night for guidance and peace. Oh Holy Mary, Mother of God. If he caught that poor man's throat, he'd be dead. But I must admit I've never in my life seen a human being running so fast. Hey wena, he flew like a springbok.'

Auntie Jessica was laughing out loud. This was the first time I had ever heard her laughing hilariously. Mama joined in. I eventually laughed myself sick, but only because daddy had gone to the fields. We wouldn't have dared to laugh like that in his presence.

Once we finally calmed down, Jessica said that I should go to Vryheid to stay with my uncle Henry and his beautiful wife, auntie Elizabeth. Henry Strijdom was a stepson to auntie Jessica and he had married a Miss Barns from the Cape Province. They had bought a house in Vryheid, not far from Lemmy's home.

'Don't worry, Winnefred,' said auntie Jessica. 'I will persuade Benjy to come up to Vryheid to sign the marriage licence. I will be going there myself next month to see my new grandchild.'

Auntie Jessica gave me ten shillings to get to Vryheid. 'Use the change to buy some georgette to make a wedding dress,' she said, 'but as you are spoiled, you can't wear a white dress.'

'Oh Jessica,' Mama interrupted, 'I've kept my wedding dress for so long. I always thought my eldest daughter will use it one day at her wedding.'

'Winnefred, it wouldn't get over her arm. You were so thin, almost a size 32.'

'Auntie Jessica, could you not take a piece to add on to the waist?' I asked eagerly. 'Maybe I can still squeeze into it?' I used to look at that dress, longing to wear it to my own wedding one day. It used to fit me well when I was seven or eight years old.

My mother and I never spoke another word to my father about Lemmy. We were very close and the time went by quickly. My mother hardly had to teach me about changing napkins and bathing a baby as I had learnt from her own babies.

When the day came, I arrived in Vryheid at almost lunchtime, as if fate was repeating its work. I was heading for the Strijdoms' house when I suddenly met Lemmy, coming out of a narrow little lane. He looked up and said: 'I am sure I am not dreaming. Agnes, is it really you? When did you come, how are you, how is the baby? Oh Agnes, I thought I'd never see you again.' He held my hand and kissed me. I sensed he was trembling.

'Oh, babe, I was so scared your father would kill you. If he got me that day he would have killed me.'

'No, no. My father wouldn't have killed you. He was just very angry. Maybe he would have choked you a little, but he would have let go again. You see, I really broke his heart and he thought you were just a show-off.'

'I've never been so scared in my life. Did you find my shoe?'

'Yes, I have brought it to town with me.'

'I am going to wear the same shoes for the wedding. I hope he agreed at last?'

'I think auntie Jessica persuaded him to let us go to court and get married.'

'When?'

'As soon as she finishes my dress. I have no dress to wear. I am going to buy material tomorrow.'

'I must go back to work. Can I visit you this evening?'

'I don't know. I'll ask auntie Jessica first.'

'Okay, I'll see you.' And he walked briskly away towards his home.

Walking through the forest with my big stomach had made me so tired. I slumped into the chair in the Strijdoms' kitchen and heaved a sigh. Hot tears rolled down my cheeks. I missed home already. This was not my home. These people were wealthy; they had hot and cold water, a bathroom, big windows. I felt lost and confused.

Then auntie Jessica held me tight in her arms and led me to the bathroom to wash my face. She introduced me to this beautiful woman with long brown hair, all piled up on her head, big eyes, brown eyelashes like a calf's and the most beautiful smile showing off milk-white teeth. She was carrying the loveliest little baby boy who looked at me with such love that my heart twisted. I asked to hold him and she put him in my arms. He was wrapped in pretty blankets and smelt so sweetly of powder. My baby brothers and sisters had never had such pretty clothes. 'I wish he was mine.'

'Oh, but you'll soon have your own,' the pretty lady said, 'and I'll keep all his small things for your baby.'

After this conversation I felt a bit better. That evening Lemmy came to visit me. Auntie Jessica welcomed him and told him my father would come to sign the marriage certificate as soon as we let him know the date. My father had agreed to sign but said he would have nothing to do with me after the marriage. I would have to look after myself.

Lemmy came to visit me again on the Friday evening. He knocked so loudly that auntie Elizabeth came to the door and reprimanded him. Her husband followed to see what was happening. 'Did you have to knock like a policeman, Lemmy?'

'I want to see Agnes.'

'She is still busy fitting on her dress, just a minute and she'll be with you. Come inside, take a seat.'

My auntie turned around, thinking he was following her. But he stayed where he was and violently retorted: 'I never asked for a seat, I asked for Agnes. Is she here, yes or no?'

'Yes,' said auntie Elizabeth, surprised, 'but I asked you to come inside and have a seat.'

'Do you think I am hard-up for your chairs, because you all are larnies and I am your boy?'

That was too much for uncle Henry. He was a tall man and very powerful. He gave Lemmy one clout, and Lemmy flew right out into the garden. When he sprang up, heading for uncle Henry, a second one knocked him out for a second, sprawled between the flowers.

'Agnes, my girl, I am afraid you cannot stay in this house any longer. You have made your bed with this animal. Please follow him. I cannot accept such behaviour in my home and in front of my wife.'

Jessica humbly tried to apologise to her stepson on my behalf, but Lemmy was wide awake by now, loudly demanding that I come with him. My auntie had tears in her eyes as she handed me my little belongings. My wedding dress was folded up, neatly pinned up here and there, as it was not quite finished. Confused beyond all measure, I walked away following Lemmy to his mother's house, where I stayed until I got married the following week.

My wedding itself, if you could call it that, was a nightmare. My father had been called to give me away, as I was still under age. He came to the court in Vryheid wearing gumboots and ploughing gear. He had come on a tractor, not his own, but one he got a lift on from one of the neighbouring farmers. He stormed into the courthouse, called the sweeper as a witness, and signed his name right across the form. He said he had no time for fun, he had to finish ploughing before the sun set! So I never had a wedding cake. There was no wedding dress – I did not have the heart to complete the half-made dress and never wore it. There was no reception, no photograph.

Chapter 7

The birth of Agnes's first three children. 'Running home' – weekends at the farm.

MY MARRIAGE WAS A TOTAL DISASTER. I was never happy. My dreams haunted me year in and year out.

Trouble started soon after our wedding, when we first moved into our own house. Lemmy would swear at me, calling me all the dirty names he could think of. 'I married a bitch, a whore, an old cow! Now she dreams of her lovers! She's too tired to make love with me, her own husband. When she pretends to she lies there like a dead cow, dreaming of other men. Then she gets up screaming and tells me she's having a nightmare. Get out of my house!'

He would drag me out, half kicking me to death, blow after blow. I'd be begging him to stop, but a violent kick would send me sprawling outside, and the final bang of the door would make me understand that I'd better stay out.

My heart would break, because I didn't know what wrong I had done. I was not satisfying him sexually, but then I never could enjoy sex with him: either he had been hitting me and swearing at me, or I was bleeding from my nose, or I was thinking of Pieter. How could I ever enjoy sex with a man like Lemmy? The only times I tried were if I thought of Pieter and imagined it was him in the wilderness. I think that's when I used to fall pregnant.

We lived out of town then, in the backyard of a white family who were retired farmers. We were lucky to get that tin shanty. It was the first place we had on our own. We had been living with Lemmy's mother since the time we got married. But after he one day nearly killed her, she called the police to have him thrown out of her house.

She was a tall, dark-skinned woman, and she could drink and swear very violently. Her nickname was Ouma Moor. She swore at everyone when she was drunk, and the people around were frightened of her. I too was scared of her – I never knew women could drink and use such ugly words, as my parents never got drunk. She spoke Afrikaans as she was from the Cape. I felt sorry for her at times, because she worked hard keeping her offspring alive. Her daughters worked in Durban and Jo'burg. They all had children. And they would just come home to give birth and then leave their children with their mother. They never gave her a cent. Lemmy's father had died in a train accident together with his eldest brother, so she had no income other than the few pennies my husband gave her, and her pension money.

She used to curse me and call me 'die wit kaffir' because I was from the farm. Sometimes I used to feel sorry for her, and think of my own mother. Actually my mother-in-law's case was worse, as she only had three rooms and she had to look after her dead sister's children as well, and they used to drink and fight all the time. I often cried, telling my husband I wanted to go home, but by that time my father had practically disowned me. I had to work hard keeping the house clean and washing and ironing for all these people, even while I was heavily pregnant.

When we got that first place of our own I shifted what little I had and walked down the road to the shanty we had taken. Ou Nooi and Ou Baas, the white couple we rented from, were very old and lived alone, but they still had a few chickens and cows. They had about two acres of land, and we lived in an old two-room tin shanty on the other side of their house. They could hear the noise when my husband was beating me, and many times Ou Nooi would phone the police and he would be arrested – for one night. The next day I'd be getting bashed all over again.

Sometimes Ou Nooi would call me to wash for her, and in return give me some milk for my kids – never money – and she would say: 'Hoekom het jy so 'n slegte Hotnot getrou? Jy moet wegloop van hom, eendag sal hy vir jou doodmaak!'

What I hadn't known was that when my husband was eighteen years old he had murdered a man and had been to juvenile jail in East London. When I married him I had no idea of this, as I came from the farm. I just met him and got married so fast – I didn't really know him.

They say that history repeats itself. Well, my life was just like my mother's. Perhaps she married my father because she felt like an outcast, like a wounded animal that needed shelter and love.

When my little girl was born, at the local hospital, I was all alone.

Giving birth comes differently each time. The birth of Rhonda, my first-born, was painful – perhaps not knowing what to expect makes a difference. You scream and rant and rage, until finally someone says push, push, harder, harder.

'No man nurse. I can't push. I've got no more strength to push anything. Please help me.'

'I can't help you to push your own baby out. Weh Mama, it was nice when you were holding him tight, and saying push it in deeper, deeper. Eh, eh, push the baby out, and stop screaming.'

I had my wedding ring off as my hands were swollen; I think she thought I was a young unmarried girl. She hadn't even read my chart, she just came on duty and heard me screaming. She was a huge middle-aged midwife with big rolling bloodshot eyes from lack of sleep. She hovered over me. A flashing memory crossed my mind: the baboon that took my baby.

The nurse had sideburns, a slight beard, thick reddish lips and a big flat nose. But it was her ears that I saw first. They actually had hair growing from inside. Nostrils flaring, she repeated: 'Hey wena, do you want to kill your child? I said push, p-u-s-h!'

I had the urge to push even harder and felt something coming out but my senses went back to the baboons and my baby. 'My baby, Pieter, my baby.'

'There's no Pieter here. He left the baby inside and disappeared. I don't think you'll ever see him again. That's what happens to young girls who want men straight after their first period. You don't even know how to wear a pad but you wanted the men. Ahena, nazonke, you've got a girl! Oh, she's so lovely. We hope your father Pieter comes to see how beautiful you are ... Now push again, push, push.'

Plonk, something came out. 'Oh Mama, I've got two babies. How will I look after them?'

'It's not a baby, it's the afterbirth.'

'How long will I have to keep the afterbirth?'

'Hebinja baba,' she looked up at me, her mouth gaping, showing two very long protruding brownish teeth. Her laugh sounded like the train that was passing not so far from the hospital behind us.

She was real – my baby – the baboons didn't get her! I held her close and suckled her, but when I did that it felt like I had suckled before – my first baby, Pieter's baby. Oh, I was so confused. Please, dear God, this is a real baby – the baboons never took her after all! Oh Pieter! Where are you to see this baby of ours! I would gaze at the entrance to the ward and half expect him to stride in, tall and handsome, to see his child. I'd gaze until my eyes were sore and visiting hours were over, but still no Pieter. No Lemmy either.

I think the nurses sensed my anxiety, and they would ask me where my husband was. He did come one evening to see the baby. He just stood and looked at her and smiled, and asked me if I was all right. Then he said I must come home tomorrow, as there was no one to cook for him. No clothes for the baby or things that I needed, nor even the least concern for my welfare. A frightening thought crossed my mind – maybe he'd kill my baby! Must I run away from the hospital and go back home to face my father? But then I knew that was futile. I could never go home – I just had to carry on.

But when I came home my husband's attitude changed; he seemed to love the baby and he even bought some napkins and a few things like baby powder, Vaseline and soap. He was very kind for a few weeks and he would even carry the baby. He really showed concern and I thought maybe he would change. It didn't last long.

By the time the second little girl was born my father had at least grudgingly forgiven me, and so I went home to have the baby. It was an easy birth. My father was the midwife himself and Mama helped too. Beryl was a lovely little girl and I needed no doctors and no medicine – everything went well. But two nights afterwards I heard a bush baby crying and I got so frightened. It sounded just like a baby – my baby! I started crying and held Beryl so tight. Mama knew what the matter was – she held me and my baby and told me to forget about what had happened. 'God has given you other children, my child, you must let the past go, stop torturing yourself.'

I went back to my shack, and things were worse now that there were two children. Lemmy resented the kids.

'When I come from work, I can't even have a decent cup of tea, let alone proper supper. You are busy bathing the kids or feeding them, or breastfeeding the one, whilst the other is screaming her lungs out. Oh, the child is teething, she's got a cold, she has a running tummy. Where it's running to I've no idea. Every day I am told to bring a bottle of verkrampdruppels, or duiwelsdrek. All the f... shit from Lennon's products, there's a whole chemist in this house. Still the children scream. What the hell is going on? There's no peace when I come home. I work the whole f... day. You can't manage with only two children. My mother manages with so many. Then you sleep like a dead dog. You're always too tired.'

He would eventually quieten down and eat, and go to bed, waiting for me. Then he'd start getting fidgety, and pull me abruptly towards him. 'I want some Pepsi.' He never ever used the word sex in those days. The men used many other terms, such as 'koekie' or 'snoekie'.

I pulled away and said I was still bleeding. Beryl was not quite three months yet.

'Oh shit, don't tell me that. I kept away long enough with our first-born.'

He went ahead, forcing me to succumb. I never thought a man could be so violent, especially Lemmy. He was not a sex maniac. But he tore everything I had on and forcibly penetrated me. I tried pulling away. He choked me till I was almost out of breath. I tried to say: 'I am still bleeding'. He went on like a raging bull. Finally he pulled away from me, and I rolled over to get up but he was back on top of me, huffing and puffing. I was so scared. He'd never done this to me before.

Then he said: 'Change these bloody sheets and go and sleep with your precious babies.'

The stark realisation came to me – he was actually jealous of his own children.

From that day on I started cooking early, bathing the children early, and eventually getting a young Zulu girl called Layila to help me with the children.

I was scared of my husband. If ever he wanted me at night I wouldn't say a word lest he choked me. But I did tell Dr Simon, our family doctor, what happened because I thought I'd get sick having sex while I was bleeding. My mother said I must not have anything to do with my husband while my baby is breastfeeding. He had kept away for nine months with my eldest daughter, but the doctor assured me nothing would happen. Those were old woman's fables. I was so embarrassed when I was relating the incident to the doctor, I started crying. Dr Simon was Jewish, and very caring.

'Mrs Lottering, it seems your husband would love many children. I don't blame him, you are young, beautiful and very strong. You could have a dozen of them.'

In due time this very doctor closed me up after the fifth child was born by caesarean birth. He said five children were more than enough.

By then he knew what a hard life Lemmy had given me because of the many times he had administered calming pills for him and stitched him up after a violent fight in the bar. Often when swearing at me, Lemmy would shout: 'I am the law within the law. Do you understand, woman? This is not the plaas here where you look at cows and goats. This is Lemmy Lottering. Ek is die man!'

One day on a Saturday, when Lemmy was working, some Coloured neighbours called the Naudés invited my girls to come to their child's birthday party. This family lived across the park from our little shack. Even though they did not like Lemmy, they felt sorry for my kids. I took them to their house in the afternoon. Rhonda and Beryl were so happy, seeing cakes and sweets, balloons, and just being with other children, something they were not used to. We hadn't even been here half an hour, though, when Lemmy came charging in like a bull.

'Where is this f… woman? There's no food cooked at home. I'm working my ass off and she roams around having parties!'

The man of the house came out when he heard Lemmy's voice. He quickly ushered me out the back door, but while he was helping me with the children, Lemmy gave him an uppercut. The man went flying onto the veranda, smashing all the pot plants. His wife and mother-in-law came out to see the commotion.

'What are you doing, Lemmy? You'll hurt the children. Don't drag the woman while she's carrying the baby. Oh Lemmy, my God. Run Agnes, leave the kids. I'll see to them.'

But I was down, Lemmy had me by my leg. All my clothes were pulled up my back and he was dragging me by the leg in the gravel road toward my shack.

'Phone the police, he's going to kill her.'

My girls were screaming, trying to run after me: 'Mummy, Mummy!'

'Don't you know where you live? What are you doing in other people's houses on a Saturday afternoon? I came home, no woman, no food cooked. What do you take me for – a dog?' He dragged me right to my door. 'This is where you live, bastard.'

Just then the van screeched to a halt. The police had come for him. He ran and jumped right over the fence. The police shot a bullet into the air and he stood while they handcuffed him. I was so bruised and bleeding that they took me in the police van to hospital. The neighbours looked after my children till I came out of hospital. Lemmy slept in the cell that night and paid a fine of R10. I was too afraid to lay a charge against him so the abuse just carried on and on.

Charles and Maureen and Mrs Naudé, Evelyn was her name, are still alive and living in Escourt. We met not so long ago at a friend's funeral and Charles told me he still remembers that day.

Then the third baby came – a boy we called Butch – and my husband was so thrilled. He seemed to change again. He really was excited to have a boy. This baby was born at home, early in the morning at six o'clock, just before my husband went to work. He had a son – he was so happy! He came back early from the Gazette and he came to see me in the hospital. I had gone there with Mrs Carlson, an American missionary. She had been with me on the previous night when I complained about having birth pains. Mrs Carlson had been a midwife in America and she said I was going to give birth any time. So she came to my shack early next morning, just in time for me to give birth. She acted as midwife, and right after the baby was born she drove me to the hospital, and they saw to me and sent me home soon after, as everything was fine.

Mr and Mrs Carlson were elderly people who had all their children in high school, so they had enough time to visit the poor amongst the Coloured community. As most of the people were Catholics, very few attended their services, but I sent my kids to their Sunday school. I never attended the Catholic Church as I felt I was an outcast. The Carlsons used to help me a lot with my children. They even gave them clothes.

When my son was born my husband started attending their services, and he stopped drinking. He was happy to have a boy, and he brought home two little pups when my little boy was six months old. He even bought a pram – and that pram lasted right up to the last little girl who was born. For a full three years he stopped drinking, and we even taught Sunday school. I taught the little girls and he taught the boys. Life was so different. He bought me a bedroom suite, a coat and nice shoes and dresses, and a hat for church, and we shifted into a little two-bedroomed cottage on the other side of the graveyard. There were fruit trees and a little verandah, though there were no lights.

I loved my little cottage. I worked even harder at planting. The missionaries often came to my home to take us to church, and sometimes they would even take me and my husband for picnics. I had never been on a proper picnic before, so I was excited; but Lemmy was always aloof. He never spoke much, and I was always uncertain as to what he really felt or thought. I just lived from day to day. I had another son, Rocky. The dogs – Boxer and Tiger – grew up together with him, and he loved them. But after a few weeks Tiger was knocked down by a car. I was sad, as I had really grown to love them. My girls used to play with them after school, feeding them and taking turns bathing them.

Home seemed a little happier. Here was peace – only my husband never really laughed or played with his children. But I tried.

One day I made a gingerbread boy, a little man with arms, legs, a big mouth, and eyes made from raisins. Oh my boys were so thrilled when I said to them: 'Close the door and the window, he might decide to run away.' Butch put the chair against the door, little Rocky climbed up on another chair, carrying a peach stick to hit him if he decided to jump through the window. I laid the gingerbread boy on the table to cool him off. Rhonda and Beryl were all wide-eyed, looking at him closely.

'Mummy, his eyes opened. I saw them just now, Mummy,' Beryl said. 'Mummy, he wants to say hello to us. Mummy, he can speak, I saw his mouth moving.'

The excitement. The children had never seen anything like that. I always made scones, but never before anything like this.

Butch said: 'Mummy he's feeling cold.' He darted to the wardrobe to look for clothes for the gingerbread boy to wear. He came back with his old little trousers and his shirt and cap.

I was giggling with pleasure to see my kids so happy. Then Rhonda said: 'Oh Mummy, Daddy's going to hit him if he comes.'

Beryl said: 'Let's hide him under the table.'

Boxer, the dog, was wagging his tail as though listening to the conversation and also giving his opinion.

When the gingerbread boy was cool and ready to eat, I asked them to sit still. 'Now it's time to eat him up!'

'No, no, Mummy. Keep him for always. Don't eat him up.'

They refused point blank to eat any of him. They started crying. I was so moved, I cried too.

On another occasion, one Easter time, I had made my own Easter eggs. I had my own fowl-run in the yard. I boiled a lot of eggs and painted them with colouring chalk. I'd work at night till Lemmy came home.

The next day there was a little problem. I had hidden the eggs in a basket in the fowl-run. Early in the morning the hens had turned the basket over and the eggs were lying all over, very dirty. I tried my best to pick up every one of them and hide them away from the children. When Lemmy saw me wiping them up and colouring them all over again, he started helping me. To my amazement, he had bought the children some chocolate eggs as well. We hid them in the grass behind the house in little nests, where there was an empty acre belonging to Ou Nooi.

We told the kids to start looking for Easter eggs as the Easter Bunny had come last night. My children were beyond themselves with excitement.

'I found a nest!'

'I've got a red and yellow one!'

They were running like little rabbits themselves, finding nests. I heard Lemmy saying to Butch: 'Open it up and eat it, son.'

Lemmy was running with Butch and Rocky; Rhonda and Beryl were at the far end of the fence, flying like real rabbits, screaming with delight. 'Mummy, Mummy I found a chocolate egg!'

I couldn't understand Lemmy's mood. He was like a little boy, laughing and running with his sons, and Boxer barking away. I think that was my happiest day since I became Mrs Lottering. My children never forgot the gingerbread boy and the Easter eggs.

For a while I thought Lemmy was a changed man. I was wrong. After about three years the drinking began again – and all the other problems with it. My husband worked: he was never a loafer, and did well as a printer, but all his money went on liquor and gambling. The bashings started again.

One Monday he came home at lunch-time. He had bought himself

a scooter, so he often came home for lunch. He loved to give his sons
a ride. The carrier of his scooter was just big enough for both of them.
'Daddy, Daddy, I am first,' Butch would call, leaving Rocky to stum-
ble after them with his little fat round feet.

I prepared lunch for Lemmy quickly, as time was running out for
him to get back to work. As if he sensed it, he said: 'No need to rush,
I'll get half brown and maas, I'll be fine. But ... er ... er ... Mr Large
is hosting the King Kong show on Friday and Saturday. We've sold
200 tickets already. He wants us to print some more as people are
coming from Ladysmith, Dundee, Glencoe, let alone Vryheid Districts.
I wanted you to come as Miriam Makeba will be singing with them.
I hear she sings like a lark. Here's R10, buy material and shoes. Make
use of your Singer I bought for you. I want to see if you can sew a
dress for yourself instead of sewing stupid doll's dresses for your
children. But please don't sew a farmer's dress with long sleeves and
big bows all over. I want you to look smart.'

I was shocked but excited. I'd never seen a live show, though he'd
taken me to the bioscope when we were still courting.

I remembered the first time I wore a dress auntie Jessica had made.
It had long sleeves and I did my hair in a hairnet and high kiss-me
curls in front. But after he had married me he said it looked like I
was carrying a black clay pot on my head. Now he even gave me a
peck on my cheek. I felt quite thrilled.

The next morning I was at Gibbons Fashion Centre, feeling like Mrs
Lottering.

'Oh, I like that one,' I said, pointing to a mustard Chinese silk
with dragons on it. The fashion then was Chinese collars.

'No, no, no,' the fat rosy lady said. 'Take this blue Chinese, with a
silver background and black dragons and trees with beautiful birds in
a darker blue. This blue will suit your colour. You are quite fair, but
don't make a Chinese collar as don't have a long neck line. Do it
in a Marilyn Monroe low-cut style and put a silver band across your
forehead. Are you going to the King Kong show?'

'Yes, my husband is taking me.'

I said it so fast, it sounded like someone else had spoken.

'O wêreld, everyone is going. There is no more red satin – it's all
sold out. Some of the farmers from Swaziland and Pongolo are coming too, you know. Ag tog. Mr Large is maar'n goeie Engelsman – a
good Englishman. He always makes sure we see the latest films and

now, foeitog, he's made sure to bring die hele klomp Hottentots van die Kaap af. O haai, van so ver af. How many yards will you have, mevrou?'

'I'll take two yards, if it's going to be low-cut and no sleeves.'

'Okay, that will be R2,30 and 60 cents for your silver band, and black ankle straps R3,99.'

I still had money to buy something to cook, some sweets and chips for my children. I knew I still had a bit of 'Evening in Paris' and lipstick, a blood red. That was in fashion, Marilyn Monroe style.

I practically ran home. When my two girls came back from school I showed them my material.

'Oh Mummy, can we come too?'

Friday couldn't come quick enough. I sewed and stood in front of the mirror every time to see if the fit was right, as I had no pattern. Oh boy, I was really getting civilised. Friday morning I did my hair with the hot comb and used tight donkies – iron rollers for kroes hair. I did my chores with a zing.

I got dressed by five o'clock because Lemmy had said I must be ready early so that we could get nice seats. As soon as he arrived, we left. My children took us halfway up the road, commenting on how lovely Mummy looked. I walked in my old shoes as far as town, then changed into my new shoes, putting on my perfume only when I was near the door of the theatre. I slipped my old shoes inside the black dirt-bin near the theatre. It was clean inside as the dirt was collected on Fridays.

The theatre was made to house about three hundred people. White people downstairs, about a hundred people upstairs in a small space – only coloureds; no natives and no Indians.

As we arrived even Mr Large complimented me. 'Lemmy, your wife looks dazzling.' Lemmy and I walked hand in hand. I felt so good. He sat me down like a real gentleman and kissed me, still holding my hand. During interval, he excused himself and came back with Black Magic and ice cream.

Then the main show began. I was so excited at what I saw on stage. 'Oh my word. Look at that man Majiet Omar. He is dancing so well. He's so flexible. Look at his waist. He moves like Elvis Presley.'

Lemmy gave me a violent push. I nearly fell over. Luckily the chairs were close together and I just bumped back. I screamed. I thought someone else was pushing me.

'Ja, go to him!' he shouted.

Another push.

'Go to him now! You bloody farm skapie. I work my ass off trying to make you a lady! I even bought myself a new suit. I got no compliments. Your eyes are looking at another man's movement. Fokof, go to him!'

The bouncer came to order us out. Lemmy tried to push me down the stairs. The bouncer gave him a clout. I walked out heading for my flat shoes in the bin. He pushed me right into the bin from behind. Oh my God. My face inside this stinking bin. He was rolling the bin, with me half hanging out, when the bouncer floored him with a violent kick into the drain in the street.

As Lemmy sprang up from the drain, he caught the strap of my dress, which ripped right off my shoulder. That's when I ran with my ankle straps to the police station, with half my breasts showing. My hair was matted with dirt from the bin; my lipstick was smudged, my eyes popping out. I ran straight to the fat, tall, red-faced police officer's arms and held him tightly by his belt. 'He's going to kill me, help me please.'

'Die Hotnot is dronk.' He pushed me away from him. I went on the floor in a heap, sobbing. Trying to sit in a decent position, hiding my breast with one hand, I crawled under the counter, as the black policeman said to the white one: 'No sir, this is Lemmy's wife. You know that boesman from East Street, Ouma Moor's son. He's always hitting this poor woman.'

I could hear Lemmy telling them lies. 'She ran away from the theatre. She said she was scared of the people. She thought King Kong was a big gorilla.'

I was sitting on the bench now with an old coat over my shoulders.

'Ja, Hotnot, wat gaan aan?'

'Meneer, die plaas skapie is bang vir King Kong. She ran out of the theatre. I tried to chase after her but she tripped. She's not used to high heels. She ran like a mad woman, straight into the charge office. Hey man Sarge, I've been living with her now for almost ten years. I've got five children from her. The first time I take the vrou out, she disgraces me like this. You can't take the bush out of these farm skapies.'

I was dumb. I couldn't say anything as clearly. You could sense they were falling hook, line and sinker for his lies. I just cried softly, defenceless.

'Agnes, it's late. The kids are alone at home.'

I got up still with the old coat over my shoulders. He put his arm around me as we walked out of the police station. As soon as we were out of earshot, he let me have it. 'So, you were running to your boy-friend? You've even got his raincoat. Why didn't you run to Majiet Omar, maybe he would take you to Cape Town?' He swore at me all the way home. 'Next time don't go paying other men compliments when I am with you. I am your husband, you hear.'

I was terrified of my husband. Even my kids were terrified – when he came home they would cower in a corner and keep still. The little Zulu girl who helped me look after them used sometimes to take them quickly outside to hide in the long grass, where we had a special old green blanket and an old overcoat to cover us with. Sometimes we would sleep outside the whole night. Layile was only twelve years old but I depended on her so much, and she always reminded me of To-bile. Layila once said if we feared God the way we feared my husband, then surely we would all go to heaven!

Things got so bad at home that I used to run away to the farm with my children for weekends, as the two girls were now going to school. The idea of running home made me happy in itself. I used to go past the spot where Pieter and I made love for the first time, but not once did I go to the place where I thought I had buried my baby. I would feel frightened – a cold shiver would run through my body when we walked near it. But still I would ask around if it were true about Pieter's death. Tobile had married and moved away to Paul-pietersburg, so I had no more friends to talk to. Gogo was gone too, and her little grave was so forlorn. I'd go and sit by it, and talk to her and ask her if Pieter had really died. Did you see him, Gogo? I'd ask in Zulu. You are on the other side now, haven't you seen him? Tell me, Gogo!

I find it very hard to write this story, but I've got to put it to rest once and for all. If I read it in a book, then I'll feel as if it happened to someone else. After all, it is just a story, though it's more than that too: it's the story of my life.

But how do you write pain? How do you write love? It is some-thing that blends together in a mysterious way. God created human beings to feel pain and to love, and even wild animals protect their young, so we have to accept it as God's way of sometimes talking to his creation. We reach out through love, and then we are touched, and learn to understand through pain. The two are almost inseparable. No human being has escaped such moments; they are inevitable. Everyone has tasted of this thing. These two feelings make you a stronger and sometimes a wiser person.

Chapter 8

Lemmy continues to be incorrigible. Trouble with the authorities. A visit from George Nunn, Agnes's grandfather. She takes her daughters to a Home in Durban. The trip back. Agnes's thoughts on the train. The return. Birth of the last baby.

LIFE WENT ON MUCH THE SAME in my little home, except that I found employment. I started work with my husband at the printing press. He was a printer by trade and he taught me a lot, but he was so violent and demanded so much of me that sometimes I felt quite hopeless. I felt very lonely, as I had no friends to talk to. I used to cry much of the time.

I worked hard but still he was never happy – he bashed me even at work many times – I'd go home bleeding and with stitches on my head or my arms. But I couldn't leave him; my husband was feared by the community as he was a murderer, and no one wanted to befriend a murderer's wife. I was a social outcast. My father didn't know about my husband going to jail and I never even told Mama.

Then my sister Juliana came to live in Vryheid, as she had also run away from home; so I felt a bit better. At least I had a friend, but we hardly saw one another as she worked for white people and stayed with them.

One Saturday afternoon she came to visit me, and my husband was drunk and fighting with me. She tried to stop him and he took a chopper and hit her on the head. She was taken to hospital by ambulance – Ou Nooi phoned for one when my daughter ran to tell her that she thought my sister was dead. She was in fact unconscious and had to have nine stitches on her head – and I had five stitches on mine as I also got hit with the chopper.

That was enough: the welfare people were called in and my husband was jailed for one week. For that week there was peace in the house, but when he came out I was so scared that he'd kill me that I told the welfare lady that I'd have to go to the farm for the weekend.

When I got home to the farm with my kids, my stepsister Ivy was there. I had never really got to know her well. When she visited the farm, she would sit with my father and chat with him, and never say anything to us. She would bring my father nice things from Durban like sweets and clothes, but she never brought us a thing. But we didn't mind, because we didn't even know who she was – she was just a Durban lady who came to visit, and she would have chicken and dumplings. She always had the best and never shared it with us, but then we had other activities to occupy our minds.

After the weekend I went back home to my shack and my husband was very nice to me – but only because he had been told he would be sent away to a rehabilitation centre if he didn't stop drinking. The next weekend he started his nonsense again and beat me up and swore at me, saying I went to the farm to meet my men, and that's why I wanted him sent away. He would kill me if I allowed the welfare to send him away. And of course we ran off to sleep in the long grass with Layila, but this time he caught us and kicked Layila hard, and me too. Butch, who was seven years old, tried to protect me, but he kicked the child so hard that we were screaming. When a police van passed by and the men inside heard the screams, they came to our rescue. This time they took him away and booked him in properly. He was ranting and raging and swearing. They forced him into the van and he was gone to jail again.

I was going crazy with worry, wondering when all this would stop, but at the same time I was strong and young and determined to make a home for my children.

The welfare lady came again the following week and told me she had found a place in Durban for my two girls as by then they were schooling, though some days they couldn't go because of the problems at home. She spoke to me about my life with my husband; how it was affecting my children, and that therefore they should go to an institution, and I agreed. I knew they would at least get three square meals a day, and an education. Never mind how much I'd miss them, it would be for their own good.

Then, one morning while the girls were still at home, I saw a tall but half-bent white man coming up to my door. He reminded me that I was his grandchild! This was my mother's father, George Nunn. I had seen him before, but he was much older now. I was amazed to see him. I held him tight and I could still feel the strength in that old body of his – he felt like hard dry biltong, and he still had a twinkle in his very blue eyes. And when he unpacked the big haversack that he had strapped firmly on his hunched back, there to my bemused eyes was his old battered concertina. After swallowing three cups of Five Roses, his favourite tea, he had a wash and felt fresh enough to play a few melodies on it. This was the same concertina that broke up his marriage to Irene! She had to go in the end – for this white man had loved to party, and loved to hunt wildlife just as he hunted women, and the melodies from his music lured and captivated many a damsel's heart. My mother used to tell us that they would throw flowers at him after a party, and then of course he would slip away for the whole night into the unknown, until she just couldn't stand it any longer.

My grandfather had always been a great musician. But in fact my mother could also play a guitar quite well. She had an old battered one at home when we were young. I heard her play her favourite number called 'Red River Valley' one Christmas Day. Mama loved music; she used to hum and sing, and when she did not know the words in English she would just put her own words in. I think though that my father must have bashed my mother's guitar on her head during one of their many fights, because we never saw it again.

We also had a big old gramophone with a loudspeaker and 'His Master's Voice' written near a little white dog. My mother would sharpen the needles for the gramophone on the river stones and put them back on. The sound would be all right for a few seconds and then all of a sudden it would sound like a dying pig!

When my grandpa Nunn came to visit me in Vryheid I was highly honoured and happy; the only snag was I worried my husband might fight with me in front of him. Or would he show some respect?

The children were amazed to see the grand old man, and Rhonda, who couldn't have been nine years old, was a bit shy and whispered to me: 'Mummy, the police will arrest us for keeping a white man in our house!' So I explained to her that he was my mother's father, and he had been a warden at Mkuzi Game Reserve. He told us many wonderful hunting stories, including how he was once nearly eaten up by a lion and stayed in the top of a tree for three days until the lion went away. I am sorry now that I didn't listen to more of those stories. I was just too busy being scared of my husband and not knowing when he might start his nonsense. But Lemmy seemed to have a feeling for the old man and treated him with respect.

Grandfather Nunn spent two weeks with us, but as I was working I hardly had much time with him. Sometimes when I came home he had actually cooked the supper. I loved him so much, I wished he could have stayed longer, but he had to go. He said he had a job to do in Durban, because he was also a builder. After that I heard he was very sick in Addington Hospital, and then he died. God bless his soul. I thank God that at least he came to give me a blessing before he went to rest. He took with him so many love stories and wildlife adventures in Mkuzi Game Reserve.

My children had very few friends and I had little time to play with them. But every Sunday when I hadn't been bashed I had taken them to Sunday school, till my eldest was old enough to walk with the little ones. Sometimes they'd come back black and blue, for they had to pass many white people's homes, and if there were white children on the road they'd be ordered to move from the pavement and walk in the veld. If they couldn't run fast enough the white kids would aim stones at them and hit the little ones who couldn't run quickly. They'd come home crying and upset – but that was part of being black or Coloured. You knew you couldn't do anything about that kind of thing. Even if one of them had died on the road there would probably have been no case; that's why I went with them as often as I could.

Now my children were being taken away from me, through no fault of my own. When the day came for my little girls to go to the Home in Durban, I couldn't stop crying. I felt bitter against my husband. He never even said goodbye to them. It was I who took them to St Monica's Home in Hillary, Durban. Oh, I was scared – I'd never been in a train before.

The girls got busy making padkos for the journey. Rocky came to me with pleading eyes and asked if he could please take his lorries and broken handmade cars with him, and Butch asked if he could take his dog Boxer. My heart was very sore when I had to tell the boys that they could not take these with them, as we were going on a very long journey. Oh, the bewilderment of not knowing where I was taking my children! My heart was very disturbed.

Mrs Swartz was at my home early that afternoon to take us to the station, as the train was leaving at 6 p.m. We had just settled in the train when lo and behold there was Boxer, the dog, in the train. He had run all the way from home to the station. The conductor came by to collect our tickets and with a thunderous voice demanded that we throw the dog off the train. With a heavy heart we let the dog off the train at the next stop. Butch screamed for his dog.

When the train pulled into Stilwater station there was Boxer back in our compartment, to Butch's pleasant surprise. As the conductor did not come for our tickets again until Newcastle, the main junction, Boxer ended up coming to Durban with us. I had to keep him with us all the way. Even when I had to return to Vryheid he was by my side.

When we arrived at Durban station it was a nightmare! I trembled with fright – I'd never seen so many people, and I'd never seen Indians wearing saris. Getting off the train I didn't know what to do. I clutched my children and prayed for someone to come to my rescue. Someone was to meet us at the station.

Just then I heard a loud voice saying: 'Mrs Agnes Lottering, please come to the front entrance – a gentleman dressed in brown wearing horn-rimmed glasses will be waiting for you. Mrs Agnes Lottering, please!'

I looked up startled – I'd never heard someone speak through a microphone before, and I was relieved that someone had come for me. A porter came along with a little wagon and said he would take my luggage.

'No!' I said. 'How dare you take my things!' I started performing and said I would call the police if he dared to take them – and then he made me understand that he merely wanted to help people with their luggage and he charged a little fee for that and was called a porter. I had no idea what was going on. I'd heard people say that in Durban you had to be aware of tsotsis, so I clutched my bag and my babies; but he put the two boys on the wagon and they were enjoying themselves. I was directly behind and half falling in my haste to keep up – frightened the man would go off with my children and my luggage!

I wondered how people could live like this, in a jungle of concrete and clay – buildings like huge castles, hardly any trees, no fresh air. I felt sorry for them and thought about the wilderness. These thoughts only left me when we were right at the school. It was beautiful – there were flowers and trees and birds. I knew my kids would be happy there.

The ride on the train back home was sad. I felt empty and alone, despite the two boys sitting next to me, and my heart was heavy with pain. I tried to console myself by thinking of my children's future. They'd grow up to be ladies; they could become nurses or teachers or even doctors or lawyers, with good husbands who wouldn't bash them. I prayed hard for them not to have the problems that I had had. They would work in Durban in these tall buildings, and dress in smart clothes like film stars. Oh, I just got carried away dreaming of their future ... I couldn't share my thoughts nor my feelings, my pains, my desires – I was just a bundle of nerves.

On the trip my thoughts went back to the time when we used to go to school in an ox-wagon, and how we used to ride on horseback right from Ngome to Ehlanzeni, and by ox-wagon across the Black Umfolozi and the White Umfolozi to catch a railway bus going to Eshowe from Pangode. That was in the early forties. I remembered how once when the Umfolozi was flooded we had to camp on the bank of the river for days on end. My father and his brother's children all used to be transported in this wagon, so we were a large group.

We children used to have such fun, especially when at dusk they would make a campfire, and cook the meals. They would bring live chickens and mealie-meal and flour, and the men would make hard cakes on the coal to have with coffee in the mornings. It was so beautiful to sit around the campfire and listen to the sounds of the wild.

Ndimeni, one of the workers at the farm, had a paraffin tin guitar, and he would strum it vigorously and sing something that sounded like wailing jackals around the campfire. We never knew how to distinguish his wailing from theirs! But my uncles and the younger Zulu boys would join in the wailing, and soon everyone would be roaring with laughter. Ndimeni would then sing something in English which resembled: 'Gentleman Jack, the lady's man, he can make love like nobody can'. But you had to know the song to understand what he meant, as he had his own version. He added his own words and thought he was very impressive; he boasted about working in Johannesburg when he was younger. He wore trousers – he had become a modern. He used to call the others 'bheshu boys' and make fun of their homemade violins.

My uncles and the boys would hunt for rabbits and an occasional buck to roast over the fire. Some nights we could hear the lions roaring down in the valley in the Game Reserve and of course we were scared, but the old people used to build a fire around the wagon for protection.

After we had been camping for almost a week, an attempt was made to cross the river. The water was still deep in some places, and two of the first oxen got washed downstream. Immediately there were shouts for men at the back to help. We children found the huge commotion very funny. We laughed at the men trying to rescue the oxen from drowning. One Zulu man was particularly daring and swam naked to lasso one of the oxen. Following his example, some of the other men tried to save the remaining ox, but their pants were ripped off by the tumbling water and the force of the waves was so strong they couldn't get them back on again.

My father was the youngest of them, and very strong, and he pulled my uncle back by his long johns, but as he pulled the pants were ripped off. They both seemed to be drowning, so all the Zulu boys who came with the wagon jumped in to help. They were quite naked and we children were shrieking with excitement, laughing at all these naked men – little realising that they could all have drowned. But they saved the oxen, and they were saved too, and we were reprimanded severely for laughing at big people.

I always felt at peace with myself when I thought of my childhood days. I thought of Tobile – what would she say if she knew I had been to Durban on a train? Oh my goodness, she'd never stop talking! Was she happily married? Or did her boyfriend marry his other girl? The other was the first girlfriend and Tobile knew all about her, and told me how jealous she was, because when he came from working in Johannesburg in the mines he would visit her first, and he brought her a mirror while Tobile had none.

I remember that Tobile used mud to straighten her hair and make it soft, and she used a certain herb to perfume herself, especially when her boyfriend was due to visit her. Of course he never came anywhere near her home until he had finished paying lobola. She cooked food for him and hid it in the clay pot when she went to fetch water – then she'd slip away to the bush near the spring, to where her boyfriend was hiding, to give him the food.

She took me to see him once. He was all dressed up in his warrior gear. His skin skirt was the finest, big black and white patterns, made from the best ox hide, and his head gear was made of fine eagle's feathers to prove his strength and might. His beadwork was delicately woven by Tobile, as a token of her love. All the love letters were woven together, like a beautiful butterfly with many colours. He was tall and had rippling muscles, and on his arms he wore armbands of many shapes and designs to prove his prowess. Cowering under the thicket he looked like a black leopard with bloodshot eyes. I felt quite scared of him, so I told Tobile I had to fetch water for Mama.

Tobile used to tell me many stories about the Zulus' bedroom manners, but I really didn't understand them for I was still very young. We all knew that the women were not allowed to interrupt when men were talking, but they were also not allowed to move at all during sex – or take any initiative. It must have been difficult to refrain from taking part in the action or showing any pleasure!

I do remember Tobile once telling me about her auntie who married a man with two wives. He was very highly sexed, and he used to tie both her legs up on either side of the hut door. The hut door had two leather thongs to ease in a piece of log to keep the door secured. This man would strap his wife's feet into the thongs so that her legs stayed open. Then he would demonstrate his might and strength by trying to dive straight into her vagina. If he missed, he would try again and again until he struck the target. Of course he would have her pressed right against the hut door, which is woven with wild twine and is very strong, but at the same time it would serve as a back rest, so that she would be quite comfortable. He proved his strength by the time he would take, and she proved that she was a proper woman by how long she could endure this 'love-making'. This is why a Zulu woman was not admired by the ancient Zulu males unless she had huge buttocks.

Sometimes they would end up by breaking the door, and then the man would feel very proud of himself and boast to his personal friends at a beer drink. They never discussed such things in their own kraals, as the other wives might get jealous and start using the many forms of witchcraft, or cast an evil spell on the other woman. Even when the headman did speak about his bedroom achievements, he would never describe it openly; men always spoke in riddles or parables. When they challenged one another for fights, which was quite often, then they would boast about what they had achieved in the bedroom, and say to each other: 'Have you ever broken the hut door? No? Then you are not a man!'

I remember Tobile saying: 'When you marry the umlungu, will you share a bed with him even when you are menstruating? Or will you sleep on the grass mat on the floor? A woman doesn't share a bed with her husband when she's had a baby either – it's bad luck. Your baby will die. You've got to sleep on your own until your baby is a year old.'

I thought of how Tobile had spoken, with round eyes, and with the sincere intention to protect a friend. Every time she disapproved of something she would say that it was bad luck – the ancestors would never approve of that.

Remembering all this, I started giggling and my boys thought I was just enjoying the train ride. I told them I wished it would go on and on – but I willed my thoughts back to Tobile. I thought about her wedding and wondered how my wedding to Pieter would have been. Would I have worn a white dress, one of those beautiful lacy ones? Would I have gone to church? This would have been in Swaziland. Maybe his father would have arrived in time to shoot him while he was standing at the altar!

What had made me think of his father was the ticket examiner who was so big and burly and rude. I fumbled in my bag for our tickets as he said: 'Maak gou, ek het nie die hele nag om hier te staan nie – Hurry up!'

These Boers were so cruel – how could I have loved one? But to me Pieter wasn't a Boer, he was a human being. I know some very cruel people who are Coloured or Zulu or Indian, so it was not just the Boers who were cruel. For instance, Tobile's father who had pushed her mother down a cliff – and my own father who was so often cruel to my mother.

And we did get married, Pieter and I, long ago in the wilderness in Ngome. My ring was plaited grass, my wedding dress of finest green was woven by nature in the form of ferns, my necklace was a garland of wild African violets, my headgear creamy-white wild apple blossoms. We had the crickets shrieking our wedding march, and the bumble bees hummed along. Everyone in the wilderness was our guest – they all watched us getting married, so what more did I want? I'd always stay married to Pieter, I thought.

As we travelled on I felt a wave of anger and despair. The train jerked and halted abruptly, as if to stop me from my thoughts. We were in Glencoe, the main junction where we had to change trains. In no time we were on our way to Vryheid.

I felt almost as if I was going into the unknown. And I felt frightened – I hardly knew where I was going. I tried to piece my thoughts together and think about my shack. Would Layila come back from the farm? She went away at weekends and came back on Mondays to stay with me. When would she grow tired of living with people who fought and shouted almost every day? She was still so young, yet she had seen too much pain in my home. Was it fair to expect her to come back, and if she didn't what would I do alone with the children? How would I work when there was no one to look after them?

I even thought that perhaps over the weekend my husband might have died in an accident, or someone might have killed him so that when I came home he wouldn't be there. Oh God! How can I think such wicked thoughts? Please forgive me – but I just don't know how I am going to go on living with him. Can't this train turn back? It was too late. I was scared of my thoughts, scared for myself and my children.

As I looked through the window at the huts and the wilderness, I noticed with disappointment that there were hardly any grass huts left. There were tin roofs and little windows, and some tin shanties. This was the early sixties and the Zulus were fast becoming urbanised – no more little bheshu boys herding the few cattle that looked so skinny and hungry.

I noticed how sparse the grass was, unlike Ngome. Ngome was a paradise; everything stayed green right through the year. I also noticed with pity the dongas which seemed to have grown wider, and the rivers and springs which were growing narrower. Oh Mother Nature! I wished I could protect her from being hurt, as she had protected me all through my childhood.

The train slowed down. This time a fat, red-faced ticket examiner came to our door. He had beady eyes, like the pigs my father slaughtered every winter, but he was a well-scrubbed pig. His cheeks and nose had fine blue blood-vessels, his stomach protruded and his braces looked as though they couldn't take the strain much longer. I wanted to laugh. I felt hungry thinking of what he must have eaten for breakfast. He glowed with the goodness of life; he must have had a dozen pork chops and half-a-dozen eggs, freshly baked bread thickly laden with farm-fresh butter, and coffee with dollops of fresh cream. Oh my, these Boers could eat like kings.

My stomach was cramping with hunger, and I knew I was going to the shack where I'd probably find dirty mouldy pots and nothing to eat. Anyway I had a few chickens and I reckoned I could slaughter one and make dumplings, so with the few shillings I had left I bought flour at the shop next to the station. When we came home Layila was there, thank God! I was so relieved. My husband was at work, and in no time we had a good lunch ready. I thought of the fat man and wondered what he was eating now.

When my husband came home he was sober: he usually was during the week. He did not greet me but I couldn't have cared less. I dished up his supper, which was chicken and dumplings, and still he didn't say a word. I knew there was a storm brewing. As I passed him to fetch water in a bucket from the tap outside, he slapped me so hard that I went flying, bucket and all, towards the stove which was still red hot as I was going to put bath water on for the children.

'Where have you been? Now you've taken the girls to a Home, do you think you'll take me next? Get out of my house!' – and all the names in the swear-book came tumbling out. 'You've been to Durban – how many men did you meet? Answer me, woman!' Bash, bash, boom, bang … Oh dear God! I screamed and begged him to stop. Layila grabbed the children and ran to hide in the grass. The hot stove left a long mark on my arm. I was badly burned; it blistered for days and today I still have the scar.

We slept in the grass till all was quiet. In the morning when he left for work he locked the house, so we had to break the lock in order to get inside. I was black and blue and swollen, and very sad and lonely. I could not go to work, and cried a lot that morning, as I thought of Pieter and Tobile and the wilderness. I just wanted to go home to Ngome.

Iris Rose (Baby) was born 11 April, 1961, by caesarean at the Vryheid Hospital – I remember being wheeled to the theatre when I got to the hospital because my blood pressure was so high. I was swollen and my head was pounding. Dr Simon was at my side and all the nurses looked so serene in their theatre attire and with all the equipment. This room called theatre looked like a place where I was going to be slaughtered and die! I thought of my Mama, longing just to see her and for her to be there, as I had no idea what was going to take place in this theatre. I had never been in one before.

The next morning I found myself in a ward with lots of pain and wondered what had happened to my baby and what had happened to me. I was in much pain and so, so scared. I felt like running away, but I had to see my baby first. Just then nurse Gusto came in with my bouncing, pink, chubby baby girl! The nurse tucked her in on my side and tried to get her to suckle from me, as I was much too weak from all the pain to do this myself. All the while she sang sweet melodies to my baby and said: 'You so cute, pink and chubby! I think we should call you Iris, like the flowers!'

Auntie Rosie and some other ladies came to visit me. She also commented on how rosy and pinkish my baby was. She took her little fingers, folding them out and saying: 'Rosy.' This is how her name became Iris Rose.

In walked my husband, and not visiting hour yet! Well, he was my husband, you know. He was supposed to be visiting me. Instead he ordered me out of bed, swearing at me, and drunk, of course. This performance was all for me to go home with him.

Nurse Gusto called Security and ordered him out at once. Some of the nurses knew Lemmy Lottering, especially when he was nice and sossed and people were afraid of him.

I cried as I was in such pain and this man, supposed to be my husband, comes and performs as though he was ready for some Hollywood movie, to take part as some very handsome actor.

After a week pus and a little blood started oozing from the stitching of these silver clips, dripping on my linen, nightwear and onto the plank floors. I screamed for a nurse, who came running, shouting: 'Quickly, someone help the lady Aggie! She is to be dying. Someone lun (run), lun, quickly!' And I had to go back into theatre to be redone. This was the most painful moment of my life. I remember vomiting something almost black. It could've been old blood. I was not able to eat anything. Dr Green-Thompson had to be called, and the priest, to give me my last rites to make peace with my Creator. Oh, if only my Mama was with me! I was longing for her and hoping that I would not die before I saw my baby and my mother again.

After one month I was finally discharged and finding things very difficult to do around the house. It was very cold in this little two-roomed tin shanty with the zinc roofing and bits of soot sometimes dropping from the ceiling. I made a fire inside to keep my little home warm for my family. Rhonda, my eldest daughter, had to go to the railway lines with her brothers and sister and Layile to pick up coal that had fallen from the goods trains and to collect some dry wood. It was an adventure for my children and they used to be excited and afraid at the same time, especially of the trains. I would tell them to hide in the bush because the train drivers would pour hot water over them. Rocky would pick up broken pieces of tin and come home to make homemade cars for himself.

Lemmy loved the baby very much. He used to buy sweets and chocolates and chips for her. I used to keep her on my back, tightly strapped up, as I was scared of anything happening to her. She was safe with me, on my back like that.

Iris Rose loved her breast milk. Most times she would come and make me sit and pull them out as she wanted to suck, and I would look into her eyes that looked like pigeon's eyes and would love her even more. She was spoilt by the whole family. We all eventually called her Baby, because at three years old she was still on the breast!

Chapter 9

A child strays off and Agnes gets the blame when he's found again. Thoughts of suicide. The other children also taken to a Home. Agnes's thoughts.

THE DAYS WENT BY and when I felt better I took my boys to church. While walking home my youngest boy picked up a little tin and started playing with it. Deep in thought, I didn't notice that the child was not following us any more. He took the wrong turn and went the wrong way. I ran back and called his name, but he was nowhere to be seen. I walked around in circles calling for almost an hour.

Then a police van screeched to a stop in front of us. I was scared – I thought they would arrest me for losing my child. To my horror my husband and child were in the van. They'd already come from our shack and they were looking for us to tell us they'd found the child. They dropped us on the next corner and we walked home – except that I never walked, for as soon as the police van was out of sight my husband turned into a madman. He kicked me off my feet and swore at me, saying I had lost the child because I was thinking of men in Durban. He had been drinking from the time we left home in the morning. I'll never forget how he dragged me by my legs – my back was bruised right through my pretty Sunday dress. My children ran home to tell Layila, who hadn't gone home that weekend. She then ran to Ou Nooi who called the police again. The van screeched to a halt right in front of us – once again. We hadn't reached our corner yet.

The police picked me up bleeding and bruised – my clothes were all ripped – and took me straight to hospital. They booked him and threw him inside the van. I had a broken jaw. I had to have clips tying my jaw together, but after two days they sent me home and I went back to the shack to find my husband waiting for me! I was happy to see my children, and Layila said Ou Nooi had given them some maas and they were all right.

In those days there were so many things I couldn't understand. Why didn't they lock Lemmy up for good? Why did he do this to me? What kind of a human being was he? But then my father was also cruel, though not as cruel as my husband, for he didn't bash Mama every week and he didn't drink. I was always crying and I didn't know what to do.

I started thinking of killing myself and actually began to plan it. I told Layila. She was so young, but so serious about life. She said: 'Where will your soul go to rest if you kill yourself?'

That sentence carried a lot of wisdom. I pondered it, and that thought never came to my mind again. She made me stronger and I was determined to go on fighting for myself and my children. One day I'd have a house for them and they'd be happy. I realised that I had two of the most loyal friends in Tobile and Layila.

When I thought of Tobile in those days my heart ached out of longing for her. We were born free in spirit and we lived with the wind, with the birds and all of nature. We were sad together and laughed together. I longed for the wild days of freedom, for now I felt caged, like a circus animal that has to be lashed and forced to do things that it doesn't really understand.

The day came when my boys also had to go to the Home, and my little girl too. Baby was going to St Monica's to be with her sisters, but the boys would be by themselves as they knew no one at St Theresa's Home. This time the social worker took me herself by car – I think they felt they couldn't trust me alone with my children, for I was too confused.

The ride to Durban was different from the train journey. I hardly spoke as my thoughts were so muddled. I just wanted to die. I remember thinking about the day I had clutched two shillings in my hand and boarded a bus into the unknown. The feeling I had then was the same feeling as I had now. I was totally baffled as to what life was all about. Why did I grow up? Was this a part of adulthood or was it my punishment for sleeping with a white man? Was God angry with me? I tried to pray, but I couldn't even say the Our Father properly.

The social worker was kind for a white woman. She even gave me a hug and said: 'Alles sal regkom!' I tried to look at the scenery I loved so well, but my mind just couldn't focus properly. I thought of the bush and nature and the springs and Pieter. My love was somewhere, lost between all these things, and I drew strength from thinking about them all. I felt as though I drew my breath from nature and Pieter and my baby, and I wanted to live and learn more about life, because if I lived I might find them again.

And Tobile came to my mind again, and how she always spoke about ancestors; if something happens or doesn't happen then it's because of the fulfilment or non-fulfilment of their desires. Had my ancestors declared doom upon me? I had never seen my firstborn child for the baboons had taken it away; now those that I had seen with my own eyes were also being taken from me. Mama had always said I must stop torturing myself with the past – God had given me more children. But why was he taking them away from me again? Perhaps the ancestors wanted them all living together in the bush with the spirits of nature and with their little sister or brother who was taken by baboons. Perhaps these baboons lived in paradise somewhere in the bush at Ngome? The bush was so dense you never knew, maybe they had a secret hiding place where they kept my child. Oh Tobile, if only you were here to interpret the meaning of all this pain that was happening to me!

My mind had many funny thoughts. Some were quite without any basis. I had to stop myself from thinking ridiculous things. My children were alive, and they were going to school to be looked after the right way. They'd have a proper education and I should be happy and not sad. Anyway, I would see them again next holidays and that would be soon.

So we travelled on and my thoughts travelled along with us.

Chapter 10

*News that Agnes's parents will be forced to leave Ngome.
Agnes considers writing to the government. The move to
Esikwebezi. Agnes's mother is ailing.*

THE FIRST TIME I WENT BACK HOME to the farm, after leaving my
kids at school in Durban, I was very sad. I arrived home at Ngome
to some more sad news. My father greeted me and held me tight, and
I felt there was something strange in that hug. Was it old age? Was he
sick? He seemed aged, depressed. And as if he sensed my thoughts,
he spoke gently and said: 'My child, we have to leave the farm. This
letter came from the Forestry Department last week. We've got to go.
The government wants no farming at Ngome – no people must live
here. It's the laws of the white man. Oh my child! I don't know where
I'm going to live. I am an old man now, heading for senility – where
will I start a new life? Where will I find another paradise like Ngome?'
He stopped and tears rolled down his cheeks.

I felt something clutch at my heart.

I didn't know how to handle this situation, for my father and I had
never really been close, and all of a sudden I felt the impulse to hold
him and tell him no one would make him leave his beloved Ngome.
I choked with tears and my heart bled for him and for my beloved
Mama. And for Ngome, my childhood home – for all its pains and
dreams, for all the laughter I'd shared here with Tobile and my childhood friends, for every blade of grass I had touched, every bird that
sang, and my first love and my virginity that was lost in the wilderness of Ngome.

Surely this just couldn't happen? I ran blinded by tears to look for
Mama. She sat huddled up near the old black coal stove, gazing into
the dying embers with a blank look on her face as if she didn't see me.
Her thin hands were clutched tightly together as if in prayer, her
knuckles almost blue-black, and there were dark rings around her
eyes as though she had not slept well for days. Oh Mama, Mama! I
threw myself at her feet and sobbed hysterically for almost five minutes before I could talk, and Mama just held me. The smaller children
came and put their arms round us, and Mama sobbed bitterly.

At last she whispered: 'When I was younger I wanted to run away
from the farm. But now my life is over – where will I begin again at

my age? My child, where will I start? I wish to die here with your father. We've had our ups and downs but we've lived here half our lives.
Now where will we go? The letter from the government says we must
be gone next year, early in July, just when we've finished reaping our
last crop, and they say we must sell our cattle now and leave just the
oxen to plough with. Your father is going to die! His heart is broken.
Please, my child, write to the government and tell them we want to
stay here until we die.'

I was confused. I had my own problems and I didn't understand
how to write – to which government department? How does one write
to people so high up? I could not explain my confusion to the old
people. They didn't have much schooling, and they thought that just
because we could read and write the government would listen to us.

Who would dare write such a letter? Could you go to jail for it?
My father knew all the laws of the apartheid system, and he believed
that this was a move under the Group Areas Act. He refused to accept this kind of pain.

I was astonished – how could the government drive people away,
like cattle from the grazing lands? These were human beings, not animals. I felt such anger on their behalf. At this moment I hated the
whites. I thought of the nuns and priests and Pieter – they were all
white and they didn't care if we lived or died. I couldn't believe what
I was hearing: I had to read the letter myself.

It was true, though it had nothing to do with Group Areas removals.
Ngome had been declared a State Forest Reserve and in future nobody of any race would be allowed to live or farm there. In July, after the reaping, everyone would have to be gone from Ngome. There
would be big trucks waiting at the police station to move those who
wanted to settle in other parts of the land, but most of them were offered homesteads in Paulpietersburg and Ngotshe, so the trucks
would move them away with only their meagre belongings and no
cattle, as they could not travel with livestock to a different area for
fear of foot-and-mouth disease. No dogs, no cats were to be taken.
Start slaughtering or selling your cattle now!

I was not very well educated, and I wondered if I knew how to
write to the government. I started trying to think in big words, half-
blaming my father for not sending me to school for longer. At least if
I had had Matric I would have known how to write such a letter
properly.

There was nothing we could do. Ngome was to return to the wilderness. It seemed to me then that there was an atmosphere of ill omen in the air; it didn't seem fresh any more. The very birds were sad and the whole forest hung her head in sorrow. The springs were weeping and the skies seemed grey every day. The people passed one another on their way to their different tasks and hardly spoke; that joyous greeting was gone. It was very dull and sad: 'Sawubona, ninjani?', 'Nisaphila na?' 'Yebo, sikhona. Yebo. Sala kahle.'

The girls down by the river had no more girlish giggles; even the herdboys seemed to stop playing their homemade violins. The cattle moved slowly, as if they didn't want to live any more. Everyone was sad: no more talk about new marriages or young girls to lobola. It put me in mind of Paradise when Adam and Eve were chased out of the garden and left all its beauty behind. But these poor people had committed no sins at all.

I stayed a whole week to comfort my parents and to try to make them understand that the land was being conserved as a forest, and that nothing could be done about it.

A new priest came along on Sundays to give my mother Communion, as Father Jacob had retired and returned to Germany. I spoke to him about the old people's sadness, and he prayed with us; but I felt real hurt and resentment even towards him as he was white. I ended up having a heated argument with him and he left feeling very bitter.

My mother was upset because I was angry at the priest. She said: 'My child, it's not his fault.' She knew I had an Irish temper and she said one day it would get me into big trouble, but she admired me because I always spoke my mind. I was brave, having been brought up in a hard way, and I was always the boy at home. I used to be very aggressive at times and of course she understood why I was so upset.

When I went back home to Vryheid to my little house I met many people on the way, preparing for their journeys. Some were leaving immediately, and some were even excited about going to live near towns, where they could buy whatever they needed, and would not have to walk for hours to the store. This was the younger generation. The older ones couldn't accept leaving the place of their birth for ever. Old Vukayibambe and his friend Xijimphi still wore their bheshus with dignified pride. They walked in front of the others as was the custom of the Zulus, where the proud chiefs and indunas lead their people onwards, as though to battle with the white man. They were going to the Forestry Department to ask what would happen to their huts: could the white men load their huts on to the lorries, as they were too old to build new ones? It was easy to uproot a hut, the round grass huts, as they were stuck together with wild twine and sharp sticks pushed into the ground – all you had to do was pull them out and your hut would be unharmed, and like a tent, you could re-erect it.

A Zulu's hut was of great importance to him and there were many customs connected with its building. Huts were not personally owned, and when a new one was to be built the head of the kraal would invite friends and neighbours to come and help build it. Everyone joined in and helped.

The men would cut saplings and collect sticks. The women would cut the special grasses, which they might have to walk long distances to find. Even children played their part. They would search for ant heaps for the fine sand that was used.

The first step was to dig a circular trench. Then the men sharpen the end of a sapling and plant it in the trench to form a framework. The saplings were bent and tied together with ropes of plaited grass. Then a second row of saplings was placed to cross the first at an angle and were bound at the top. Two big posts were erected as pillars to support the roof and there was a strong cross tie, which was used to hang mealies by the husk. There was a doorframe which was used at night and as a windbreak, and it was kept low to put off intruders. They used to bury a peg or bone at the door to ward off witches.

The women thatched the roof with a big piece of wood sharpened like a needle, which they used like a darning needle. One woman would be inside and one outside; they would work as a team to pull the wood through and so 'darn' with the grass. Mats were used to cover the hut and to decorate it. Some people lined the inside of their hut with mats as well.

The fire was made inside in winter, outside in summer. A fireplace was built inside the door, where the roof was high enough not to set the hut afire. The hearth was formed of two stones, with a clay border. Soot from the fire was used as medicine for stomach problems, like charcoal is used. It was also used at funerals or to put on a baby's head, so it had great significance.

The headman's hut was his bedroom and he never visited his wives in their own huts because the children were always there. The only time he would stoop in at the doorway was when he came to invite her to come to his hut that night. It was a respected custom in Zulu homes for a woman never to invite her husband into her hut. The husband had to invite his wives to his, one by one, for sometimes there were as many as six wives, or even ten, and they all took their turn in the bedroom.

We went through the forest into the clearing and another group of people was sitting around a fire looking sad, and even their conversation was subdued. They spoke in hushed tones about the big terrible indaba that had taken place in Ngome.

We carried on towards the next entrance to the forest, where I had made and lost my baby, and there were baboons jumping in and out of the huge trees and causing a scuffle. I immediately stopped and wandered away by myself to the spot where it had happened, to be alone, just to say goodbye. I couldn't cry, I was too depressed and disappointed, and so I picked a bunch of wild ferns and flowers and threw them on the spot which was like a grave to me.

It was at this time that I began to feel such resentment against Pieter. I thought in my heart: he is a white man. Why did he just vanish? Was he really dead? Perhaps he never really loved me. I was older now and I could think like an adult, and I was learning a lot of ugly things about the whites.

I decided that Pieter had just had a good time with me. And I thought of Father Felix and Goatie Boy at school: they were all the same, those with a white skin. They had just one intention – to fool around with anyone who wasn't white. Oh! My mind went round and round, and I was so angry at having had to go through such pain and disgrace all by myself. I had thought I knew Pieter, but now I had my doubts.

In July I had to go to Durban to fetch my children for the holidays, and I had to go to the farm to help my parents move. My father was going to live at Esikwebezi at his brother Walter's place. He refused to go further away from Ngome. The most painful time was that of the move. We loaded the horse cart; the herdboys were gone with their families far and wide, so my brothers helped to drive the cattle. My mother and father were so miserable I didn't think they'd make it across the valley down to Esikwebezi. Shifting took a whole two

weeks. And my children helped as much as they could, carrying little
things and trying to look after their grandmother at the same time.

Esikwebezi is not too far from Ngome; it is below the mountains
of Ngome. But when we arrived at the homestead my mother looked
as though she would not live another day, and frankly none of us
could appreciate this new home. It was forlorn and desolate, and it
was not our home, but we had to be thankful, because it was already
built.

My father's brother had died and left the old homestead to his sons,
who refused to live there or do any farming – they wanted to live in
town or in some place where they could be near their work. My father was grateful for that, because living there he could still see his
beloved Ngome just above the hills. He would stand outside in the
mornings and look up at the hills where Ngome was and weep like a
baby. That was very painful. He couldn't enjoy his early morning cup
of tea as he had done at Ngome when he used to drink it at the crack
of dawn accompanied by the song of the birds. There seemed to be no
birds here: the land was barren. He also complained about the water. There was no spring water, we had to fetch it from the river; and
even though the river flowed from Ngome we had to boil the water
for drinking purposes. We soon collected firewood with the help of local herdboys and a few of the women came to help us settle in. We
were lucky that a few of them had moved to Ezikwebezi from Ngome with us.

Vukayibambe's family all came down with us to Esikwebezi, but
they put up their huts on the other side of the hill. His main hut was
carried there on a sledge instead of on a truck to Paulpietersburg. He
too had refused to move further away from Ngome, so my father still
had a few friends with him from the old place. They spoke a lot about
their loss and wondered if their cattle would live through the dry win-
ters. They spoke about ploughing and the wood to build new cattle
kraals, and things like that.

But Vukayibambe too was so thin and old that I felt sorry for him
and his wife. He had two wives, but the older one had died, and the
second was very much younger than he was. She had two sons, and
he had nine children from the elder wife. This made me understand
why he was so set on shifting his hut; it was sacred to him as he had
conceived so many sons and daughters in that hut and there were
many sweet memories.

The deepest source of my anger at this time was that my mother was getting sick; she couldn't eat. We tried giving her goat's milk but it didn't help. But all the herbs which we knew were good for such ailments had been left in Ngome. I was particularly worried because my brothers were younger than me and they were boys. Juliana had left for Durban a long time ago, and Jessie too was living far away from home. They couldn't stay and help Mama to cook, and I knew that eventually I would have to leave them and go home to Vryheid.

When I did get back my husband was angry that I had stayed away so long. So once again I got bashed up at the weekend, and as usual I was black and blue ...

Chapter 11

Agnes describes her mother's death and remembers the secret shared only with her. Some stories related to the secret.

MY MOTHER DIED AT THE AGE OF SIXTY-ONE, in Addington Hospital. I fetched her from the farm, as she really had no one to look after her. I held her hands, coarse and skinny, and whispered to her: 'Please, Mama, go to rest now. You will rest in Heaven.' I did not shed a tear, not then – not even after we buried her.

Only the following week when I went out to put flowers on her grave and to speak to her, then I felt such deep pain. They were not real flowers that you buy at a flower stall – I just picked some wild grass and little white flowers along the roadside, and put them on her grave. The pain I felt was that of long ago. All of a sudden I noticed the mound of earth and the little wild flowers and the wild grass and I felt shaky and weak in my knees. I knelt down, and a flash like lightning went through my mind.

For my mother had died with my secret. She had left me to deal with it alone. (Oh Mama, Mama, how will I live by myself, with such a secret? How can you leave me?) I cried so loud that the man who tended the graves came up to comfort me. I couldn't stop, I was shaking, my heart felt like it was wrenched right out of my body – a moment of total despair, a loss that I couldn't understand – no, except that I was seeing that little mound of leaves and sand and ferns that was my baby's grave ...

I was so broken and hurting so much inside that my mind seemed to relive the whole scene of what had happened when I was fifteen. I started screaming: 'My baby! My baby! My child, I want my child!' I started digging at the grave with my bare hands. The caretaker came along and told me to stop digging, my mama was dead.

I kept saying: 'No, it's my baby, it's not dead. The baboons took my baby, it's not dead! Take it out please, help me, try to find it before it suffocates and dies!' It was so bad the caretaker took me in his arms and first tried to calm me and then fetched water.

I must have collapsed, because I woke up at home with a doctor and all my children by my side. I was feeling very silly, as I couldn't tell them what had happened. The doctor asked me if I had lost my first-born, and I said no – but I was choking with tears, and I fell off to sleep crying. Of course that night I dreamt again of the baboons taking my baby. It was like a terrible nightmare. I was always so sure that my baby was alive in my dreams. I even dreamt I was suckling it. The baby was always a boy; sometimes he hovered over me like an old doctor, with shaggy eyebrows and hair coming out of his ears; always it was a boy child, but sometimes he looked like a baboon, and I was so afraid in my dream that he would hurt me. But sometimes he was loving and called me Mama.

I would get up after a dream like that and cry silently because my husband always used to say I roused him, and he would get so angry. Sometimes one of my children would hear me and come and comfort me, and at times I would get up and look around the house in the corners to see if the baby was not hiding somewhere. Sometimes I would go outside to listen, and if I heard a baby crying, perhaps from a neighbour's place, I would always drop what I was doing and peek to see who it was. My heart would pound inside me and I would start crying.

For years I lived a lie, with a secret so sad and so beautiful, and yet it was such a shame in those days – I could never tell anyone. I suffered in silence.

When I went to town I was always looking for my son. I almost lost control once and went up to a man who resembled Pieter's father. This man wore a tweed jacket and old-fashioned brown bush shoes, a farmer's hat, and his moustache was trimmed so neatly. Horn-rimmed glasses, grey-blue eyes with a mischievous twinkle, a square jawline, very strong, six foot tall, and he had black hair. This was Pieter – I was sure! How should I speak to him? Where have you been all these years? You are not dead after all! Here you are alive! What happened to our baby?

I followed the man into the lift. He got out before me, but gazed at me in such a puzzled manner, as if to say: What is wrong with you, are you drunk or something?

I was so angry and so hurt. Angry because I didn't speak to him though I felt so sure it was him. My heart was sore, for I knew it could not be him. I said to myself: I know he's dead, but my mind kept saying: How do you know that he really died? Did you see his grave?

A thousand unanswered questions went through my mind as I got more and more angry with myself. I burst into tears and went to cry in a toilet. A lady asked me if I was sick. She comforted me and gave me a hug. I told her that I had just lost my mother and I was depressed because I missed her so much.

Sometimes I used to speak to Pieter out loud, and ask him why he left me alone with a dead baby. He could have let the damned horse run away for all I cared, and then maybe the baboons wouldn't have taken my baby.

And then I would hear my own voice, and get scared, and think I was going crazy.

I used to go to town some days just to look for him. But I never found him again, nor could I find anyone to talk to and ask about his family. Because I knew only their surname, and if I saw such a surname I'd almost go crazy looking in the directory and thinking about phoning to ask where they came from and did they know someone of that name who died in the Drakensberg mountains climbing in 1952? But I could never get as far as dialling the number, even though it was right in front of me. I would just get scared and feel so hurt that I would lock myself up in the toilet and cry silently.

Then there were days I'd tell myself it never happened – I must have dreamed it. Then again the memories would be so vivid and so painful that I'd miss them both as if they had gone away from me just yesterday.

Now I am older and I understand a lot of things in my life. I think that he had just had to stop seeing me because his father would have killed him. It would never have worked out. He was white and I was Coloured, and the laws of apartheid were so severe, so cruel, and yet so real. Nothing could have come of our love for each other – it was doomed before it even started. Maybe it was just as well the baby died ...

When I greeted my father at my mother's funeral, I did not know that this would be the last time that I would see him. He suffered a stroke some time after, and died before I could visit him in hospital. But I made the trip all the way to the farm to greet him in his coffin. I was so sorry that I had not held his hand one last time. As I gazed at his ancient-looking face and his shrivelled body, I felt his presence.

Chapter 12

Agnes and Lemmy move to Durban. Life there. The police-man Tom enters Agnes's life. Lemmy is institutionalized.

NOT LONG AFTER MY MOTHER'S DEATH, my husband was com-mitted by the court to a rehabilitation centre. He spent six months there so I had some peace at last. And the first time he came back much improved. He was doing well at work – he was a good printer – and in fact was due for promotion to a higher grade which wasn't avail-able at the small printing works in Vryheid. Then a letter came from his firm. He had been promoted to work in Durban at John Dickin-son's. We packed up, sold what little we had, and boarded the train for Durban.

We found a little room in the Indian area. I had never lived in such a cramped space before. The room was a cellar, with one little peep-hole for a window, but at least I was near my children, and I tried very hard to find a bigger place.

I had auntie Nettie in Durban, and my sister Juliana was living near us; she had come to Durban long before. When she left me in Vryheid, the time my husband nearly killed her with a chopper, she had headed for the city and got a job nursing at Addington Hospital. She had met up with a few friends that we had been to school with and of course she took me to Auntie Nettie's flat.

This was the saucy auntie who lived right in town in Beatrice Street. Oh my, she was naughty. She just laughed at me and said: 'Are you still with that animal? I'll see to it that I find a job for you and I'll do my best to get you a home!'

And in no time she did. Soon I was working at a hotel, counting linen and sorting out waiters' jackets and tablecloths. Then I got a better job there as a waitress, and we moved to Wentworth. Eventually I got a job in the factory Feltex, where they made shoes and felt and wool slippers.

Meanwhile I had got us one of those big old soldiers' homes they let to Coloured people at Wentworth. It was a bit like a barracks but it was very comfortable, with a bathroom and hot and cold water and a big yard, and of course electricity. The rent was high, for in those days you paid rent according to your husband's earnings. I was excited and happy – at any rate while I was at work. My children were released from the Homes as I now had my own place. We had no furniture except for a few wooden boxes and five little beds that the matron gave me from St Monica's Home, as well as some curtains and bedding. The social workers gave me a big old stove and a little fridge, which I was very proud of and felt really grateful for. I used that stove for fifteen years till it completely broke down!

Of course my problems at home never ended. My husband was now living closer to the shebeens. He worked at Jacobs in a printing press, but the police never stopped coming to my home. The fights seemed to get worse. I always looked forward to work on Mondays – even though I sometimes had a black eye or a swollen jaw, or big cuts on my hands or arms from trying to duck the knives or spades, or – on one occasion – a rake.

One day he almost killed me with a garden fork. A miracle happened that day. I came running from behind the house and would have run head-on into the garden fork Lemmy was holding, but there was a tall policeman standing directly behind Lemmy. He grabbed the fork away in the split second before I would have been impaled upon it.

That policeman saved my life. I fell down and my nose was bleeding, as my husband had earlier on been fisting and kicking me as usual. Oh my God! The policeman grappled with him and they fell down, and at one stage I thought Lemmy was going to overpower him. But another constable came along and together they pulled him into the waiting van and whisked him off to the police station. I was crying with relief – and terrified as the thought hit me that I had very nearly died and left my children on their own.

It was always like a circus at my place at weekends – everyone would be watching from the street and they would feel sorry for me and wonder what kind of a man this was. And they would tell their children not to go near that house as that man was a demon! I was living in isolation again, just as I had done in Vryheid. My children were older now of course – Baby was fifteen. But the fights went on and the police kept coming. Neighbours were always phoning them when our fights began.

One day the same tall policeman came to keep the peace. It was a Friday evening and I was badly hurt. I needed stitches as my thumb was cut and hanging. I bled quite a bit, so the policeman took me in the van to Addington Hospital and brought me back again two hours later. My husband was even more furious when I returned and started fisting me again. I immediately ran up to the police station, as the policeman had told me that if he started hitting me again I should come right up to report him. The police station was only three minutes' walk from my house.

The tall policeman put me in the van, drove like the wind to my house and started dealing with my husband. 'Why do you bash the poor woman like this? What has she done to you? Don't you listen? Now I am going to throw you in jail and she must make a statement. I am going to arrest you!'

As he was talking my husband darted for me and gave me a blow so hard that I fell. The policeman booted him and handcuffed him and threw him into the van. Then he came over to me in the bathroom while I was washing my face because my nose was still bleeding. He held me and helped me to wash. I was scared – a policeman holding me so tight! He was really sorry for me though, and he said: 'Why do you stay with a man who is so violent?'

I blurted out hysterically that he was my husband and he had been doing this ever since I married him and I was so terrified of him I didn't know what to do or where to turn, as he would probably kill me if I left for good – and anyway what about my children because they'd been in Homes and now I'd just got them back again and I'd got a home and I wanted to try to make a good home for them …

The policeman held my face in his big hands and looked me in the eyes and said to me: 'Tell me, do you honestly love this man? You are such a young, good-looking woman, how can you stay with an animal like that?'

It was only when I looked at him properly that I noticed his teeth when he spoke, how big and strong they were, and how tall he was. I realised he was still holding me, and a little pang of guilt ran through my aching body. I thought I felt Pieter at my side – I could almost hear his voice: 'Bruin meisie, ek is so lief vir jou.' His very voice was Pieter's. That coarse police uniform was Pieter's riding coat, an old soldier's coat. I shivered and pulled away from him, quite confused. Since Pieter had died, no one had made me feel that way – and I was afraid of my feelings.

The next week I started enquiring about this policeman. I hardly knew anyone in the section where we lived yet, so it was difficult; but I just couldn't stop thinking about him. Only not really about him – Pieter was the man uppermost in my mind. Why did this man remind me so much of him? I turned it over and over in my mind.

One Friday morning I was running to work as usual – I was always running and always late because I had to see to my children and my husband's lunch, and there was never enough bread, and sometimes I'd get a slap from him before I went off, though fortunately my workplace was not far away from home. I was running to work, as I say, when this car screeched to a stop in front of me and someone said: 'Can I give you a lift?'

I thought the car was speaking because the voice was so big. Then I peeped in and saw my policeman, who was wearing plain clothes. I said: 'Yes, thank you,' because I was late, and got in.

'How are you keeping,' he asked. 'I am Tom.' I was at work in a minute.

I thought about him at work, which made my day happier. The next week I started sewing a new dress and started wearing lipstick and really seeing to my appearance. I used to giggle in those early days and think of Auntie Nettie and her lipstick. Of course, by now she had retired and gone to live with my uncle Walter's eldest son in Eshowe. Auntie Nettie would have been highly amused to hear that I'd met someone who interested me, and would have encouraged me. I'm sure she would have bought me a new dress, and some fashionable shoes, and she would have given me earrings and lipsticks and perfume ... Oh well, she had gone now, but I really wished she was still living in Beatrice Street.

I met Tom again when he came to investigate the next fight at my home, but he didn't say much. I felt disappointed and recoiled back into my empty shell. I began to realise how lonely I felt. This man had stirred up lost memories, and I cried a lot and told myself that I could never be like other women. I was not meant to love or be loved.

I believed I had to go along with whatever life held for me. I should just forget about trying to make myself look attractive for this man, or anyone else. Maybe he was married, or had lots of girlfriends. Why should he bother himself with a married woman? In any case, who wants to get involved with the wife of such a violent man? After all, I thought, he is a policeman, a man of principle, not given to lustful thoughts concerning other people's wives.

Life went on as usual. Two years passed in which I dragged myself to and from work, working even harder at home sewing for my children, mending and trying to keep the peace.

But God knows my husband seemed to become even more violent. He practically lived in the shebeens. I was glad because that meant he was hardly ever there at weekends. I only saw him again on Monday early in the morning when he came home to wash and take his lunch.

But one Saturday morning he came home all tattered and torn, and acting very strange. He was very drunk. Once again I had to report him. This time Welfare sent him to Town Hill in Pietermaritzburg, for observation. On the day the police came to fetch him, oh, my God, all hell broke loose. Lemmy performed and swore in all kinds of horrible languages, all directed at me. He swore that he would sort me out for doing this to him. Neighbours and across the road from the flats people peeped out their windows. Of course some were already out on the pavement to watch this bioscope. Some found this very annoying; some found this very funny.

Six policemen physically escorted Lemmy to the van while I trotted behind carrying his suitcase. In spite of all the abusive language I felt compassion in my heart for him, as he was the father of my children. When the van pulled off I broke down and cried because he was still cursing me and shouting in the back of van. But I was happy, thinking that I would be rid of him for some time and then he would return a normal man.

Lemmy stayed at Town Hill for a year. During that time he sent a parcel for me which contained apricot and peach pits, with instructions how to plant them. He also wrote regularly, using beautiful phrases to express his undying love for me: 'My beautiful wife I still smaak you plenty ...'

He had become quite mad; there was nothing they could do for him, they told me, because he had permanent brain damage from excessive use of alcohol. After some time I divorced him.

Tom came to visit me while my husband was away. I had got to know him well in the two years since we first met, and one day he asked me to go with him to the St Valentine's Ball at the Himalaya Hotel. We were both adults, after all, and he had just got a divorce from his wife. He had two children and he was six years younger than me. He knew everything about me except my body. This body that was so ravaged by the scars of pain and hurt and misery; this body which still had a soul that could feel pain and loneliness, and a heart that was hungry for love.

My girl friends at work were always telling me about their love episodes. This time it was me telling them: 'Hey girls, guess what? I am going to the Valentine's ball on Saturday at the Limies. You're going to be shocked to know who with.'

'Hey Aggie, it's high time you found someone in your life. Get a life for yourself.'

I was flying up and down the steps, humming a tune. Mrs Marion, my supervisor, said: 'Agnes, what's come over you? I've got the reports on my desk at ten o'clock. Sometimes I get them at two o'clock.'

'Aggie's bok. She's got a boyfriend!' Mr Cass chirped like a young boy.

Everybody wanted to get a job at Feltex. We were like a big family. We knew everybody's secrets. The best day in the factory was payday on Friday, and today was Friday. After work I was going to Mohamed's to buy a cheap dress for tomorrow night and some Body Mist. Oh shame, I thought of Lemmy and King Kong. How happy I had been then and what an ending it had.

I was definitely not buying blue. No, my dress was a stunning red Crimplene. Then my shoes, silver high heels. I bought them in a dingy little old shop in Clarewood. They were full of dust, but they fitted well and cost only R3. My dress was R9,99. But for once in my life, I wasn't bothered with the price. I just took my parcel into the bus, got home, and started cooking, happily.

Tom sent a friend of his to give me the tickets lest I change my mind. Oh, I felt so shy. When the car hooted for me, I wasn't quite ready. I never got dressed so fast before. I was trying to walk nicely like a lady to the car with my little daughter, Iris, hugging me and saying: 'Mummy you look pretty. Please come back with sweets for me.'

We walked upstairs in the Himalaya Hotel, which was very famous those years. Tom paid me such lovely compliments. 'Oh Agnes, you look so young. Come on, let's dance.'

He danced well. If I made a mistake he'd just say, don't take notice of it, just carry on like nothing happened.

Oh, that was a beautiful night! After the dance we drove around in circles, finally deciding to go to Isipingo Beach, which Tom said was a beautiful place.

'I know you'll like it there; you love the sea. I know an Indian restaurant that serves lovely curry and roti. You've got to taste their prawn curry, and their crab.'

Tom was trying to introduce me to seafood.

'How can I eat crab? Ah, never. I'll get sick!'

'I am not talking about river crabs. These come from the ocean. There you see, there's the sea, there's Isipingo Beach. Come on, see the sights, enjoy yourself, you are always so sad. Put on a smile, you have such a lovely smile. Listen to the ocean. The echoes of a million seashells. The sound of the sea-gull's distant cry.'

Nothing seemed to dampen Tom's spirit.

'Oh, there's the place now. Aggie, can you smell the aroma of the curry? Now you're going to taste real Indian curry.'

We parked the car and we were hugging like newlyweds. Before we could even sit down he had ordered two crabs, two rotis, kingklip, soup and sambals, fresh carrots, green chillies, and dhania. I didn't know some of these names, but when the waiter came to serve us my mouth was watering.

Tom enjoyed his food, and the way he chewed and smacked his lips made me feel good. There was something old-fashioned about him, a touch of class. He was well bred. Like my father he had table manners; he conversed with such graciousness, respecting me as a lady.

I tried very hard to enjoy the crab. When Tom showed me how to eat it, I relaxed and felt very special.

I loved the way he used his toothpick. I loved the way his big broad mouth showed his perfect set of teeth. Of course he ordered a beer for a wash down. I had dessert and a glass of fresh orange juice.

His laugh was intoxicating, soothing, ironing smooth my creased-up soul. I felt like my crushed heart was springing back to its original position. Slowly I could feel it regaining its strength.

I was scared, because I didn't know how to resist this.

'Come, I want to show you the best place to see spooks,' he said, hugging me right around. He was six foot tall and I just fitted snugly under his armpit. I had no resistance. He drove very slowly and thoughtfully.

'Did you enjoy the crab?'

'Yes, I enjoyed the crab.' I had made sure to rinse my mouth properly in the lady's room afterwards. When I saw my face, it had a new glow. 'I'd like to taste prawns the next time.'

'Oh, sure baby, there will be plenty of next times, but right now I want to show you some exciting spooks.'

'How can you drive into the graveyard? I am scared.'

'How can you be scared? I am with you. Remember, I am a policeman. You're safe, baby.'

It was going for eight o'clock at night. We had been out the whole afternoon. He parked behind a huge tombstone.

'This is where we policemen came to guard the graves sometimes, so the spooks are familiar with us.'

He jumped out and asked me to come to the back seat while he locked the driver's door. I was trembling. I knew what he was going to do.

His mouth was on mine. I had no words. He was kissing me so tenderly. I pulled away. What I felt was scary. My heart was pounding. He whispered hoarsely: 'Relax, baby. Don't be so tense. Just let go, don't hold back.'

He kissed me again while his hand gently opened my bra straps. He was undressing me. 'I've longed to do this to you, you have such a beautiful, tough body. Oh baby, I've wanted you from the day I saw you.'

He kissed my body all over. All that was in my heart was Pieter. He must have heard me calling Pieter but he just carried on kissing me and saying all the fond words.

I felt light-headed, as if my senses had left me. I needed sustenance, I'd been under-nourished for far too long.

We drove home in silence. Then as he stopped by my house he asked me in the most tender way: 'Tell me honestly, Aggie, when last did you have intercourse with your husband? I had a virgin tonight.'

Agnes draws her conclusions

TODAY I'VE BECOME AN INDEPENDENT WOMAN. Not money-wise but in experience, for in my life I've had plenty of it – most of it bad. Love was the best, never mind in what form it came. But I can make it alone today. I'm a strong-minded person; I love people and I can get by with very little. I've never had much in the way of material possessions in this life. I've just had myself, a prized possession, and I love myself. In spite of everything I'm not filled with regrets. I've loved life and I've hated life. I cry with those who are hurt and those who are deprived. I respect those who have earned respect. I laugh with those who have attained joy.

But greatest of all, I've tasted love that I never thought existed, and for that I'm grateful. There are people in this world who have never known love, and some have no love at all to give and share with others. I'm sorry for them. If I had a chance to go back in time, all I'd want is to be loved all over again.

When I compare the love I had for my girlhood sweetheart, Pieter, with the love I had for Tom, my policeman, there is a vast difference. Pieter's love was a dream, a fairy-tale, it seemed to me something as beautiful and fragile and tender as a flower – and like a flower it closed with the dusk. Nothing could have been born of it. Tom's love, on the other hand, which also didn't last was real and solid. He was of my kind and there were no reservations, no boundaries.

Today I still dream of the baboons taking my baby. It's a nightmare, for my baby is always alive in my dreams, and I can't reach it. I know what really happened. I am no schizophrenic, but something inside me likes to believe I really had that baby, and somewhere he is alive today – maybe living with the baboons like Tarzan, maybe rescued by Father Jacob or one of the doctors. I saw a TV film about baboons not long ago, and it brought the whole thing back as if it were yesterday. There is no past. It is within ourselves.

And what about my mother saying to me that she had given me her womb? When I look back over my life there seems a lot of truth in it, and I'm struck by the similarities between my mother's life and mine. Both of us conceived outside marriage, and in one way or another had to suffer for it. Even though my lost first child remained a secret, my despair at losing it and at losing Pieter – and also my feeling of guilt – isolated me. My mother and I each experienced an intense love, and each of us had her share of utter despair. Both of us had husbands who treated us with cruelty. Perhaps it was our different temperaments which enabled me to hold on to my resistant spirit, while my mother could only survive by keeping her love alive while she shrank into herself more and more.

It seems to me that Mother Nature has a secret store within her heart where she spins a yarn of life for each one of her children. She hands out to each of us our special fate. And you have to accept it, because it was spun especially for you. So was my fate prepared for me since the beginning of time? Did I have to accept it?

I was born what I was born – and I reckoned I just had to put up with it. As a so-called Coloured I didn't get a fair chance. With a better chance I could have done many things. I have a great zest for life and I have raised five healthy children all on my own, for I had to be father and mother to them and run all the affairs in my home. If I'd had more education my life would perhaps have been more fulfilling. Who can tell what I might have become? I am the kind of person who simply has to be in control. And I should certainly know how to handle a crisis. My life's been full of them.

Yes! My life has been full of crises, too many to mention. So why couldn't I handle all of them? I wanted to be a strong, young, determined woman – but I failed to control circumstances that surrounded me at the time of my marriage, and as a result I feel angry, cheated, confused, and full of regrets. I allowed a demented maniac to practically destroy my own and my children's lives, in particular my self-esteem. I am still angry at myself! This unfeeling animal had me caged in his zoo, amusing himself with my tantrums and screams. He watched me daily licking my wounds – recovering from Pieter's love and death, from my mother's pain, and from the miseries on the farm. I felt foolish and quite helpless. Oh, but in spite of everything I have learned to love myself. I did not lose my dignity, and my spirit survived. I get on with my life, and look back at my past in a new way.

My mother's particular kind of inner strength, which drew its nourishment from her intense love for my father, helped give me strength to carry on. Although void of love or feelings for my husband, the motherly instincts which I acquired from the wilderness gave me the grace and dignity to protect my offspring, with an almost animal obsession. This quality was nurtured by my mother, who gave birth to me in the wilderness and learned all the tricks from nature – all her resources were given her by nature. Her den was reinforced by a fiery barrier of love – nothing could penetrate the walls of such a love! She held on to the last dying embers until the flicker of flame slowly died down.

There's an insatiable hunger, a plate of food left half-eaten right in the middle of the yard. In my heart, I long to go back to find it. Even in my dreams I hear the echoes. They seem to call me, like my mother, down to the river. Come back! Come back! Taunting, mocking, shrieking voices down the dongas, the ravines, the river – always leaving me perplexed, puzzled, bewildered. I will never really understand the events at Ngome Forest, or what happened to my parents' love.

This book is dedicated above all to them; also to Ngome, my home, my Paradise:

Winnefred & Benjamin Rorke
Mysteriously they lived,
Mysteriously they loved.

≈≈≈

FRONT COVER
Centre: Agnes Lottering and her children at the time they moved to Durban
Top: James Michael Rorke, Agnes's grandfather
Bottom: Aunt Jessica on the farm

BACK COVER
Centre: Benjamin Rorke with his son Stephen; Sibiya's wife and children are standing to the left
Top: Benjamin Rorke on the farm in 1980
Right: Uncle Walter, his wife Rosie and his sister Jessica